ATHLETIC INTRUDERS

ONE WEEK LOAN

SUNY series on Sport, Culture, and Social Relations
CL Cole and Michael A. Messner, Editors

ATHLETIC INTRUDERS

*Ethnographic Research on
Women, Culture, and Exercise*

edited by

ANNE BOLIN
AND
JANE GRANSKOG

STATE UNIVERSITY OF NEW YORK PRESS

Published by
State University of New York Press, Albany

© 2003 State University of New York

For information, address State University of New York Press,
90 State Street, Suite 700, Albany, NY 12207

Production by Marilyn P. Semerad
Marketing by Anne M. Valentine

Library of Congress Cataloging-in-Publication Data

Athletic intruders : Ethnographic research on women, culture, and exercise / Anne Bolin
and Jane Granskog, editors.
    p. cm.—(SUNY series on sport, culture, and social relations)
  Includes bibliographical references and index.
  ISBN 0-7914-5583-1 (hard : alk. paper) — ISBN 0-7914-5584-X (pbk. : alk. paper)
    1. Physical education for women—Social aspects. 2. Sports for women—Social aspects.
3. Body image in women—Social aspects. 4. Feminist theory. I. Bolin, Anne. II.
Granskog, Jane.

GV439 .A84 2003

This book is dedicated to my mother, Vivian Bolin, whom I continue to miss more than I ever imagined.

—Anne Bolin

This book is also dedicated to both my parents, E. Walfred and Dorothy Granskog, whose emphasis on the value of education and being of service to others have provided the fundamental core in my own striving to be the best I can be.

—Jane Granskog

CONTENTS

ACKNOWLEDGMENTS

We owe a great debt to those who have laid the groundwork for the study of the ethnography of sport and exercise. Most notable is Alan Klein, who may be credited with bringing to academic attention the field of sport ethnography through his own exemplary work and through his efforts in supporting scholars such as ourselves who conduct ethnographic studies of sports. Alan has inspired and supported us in countless ways. It was Alan who first brought us into the North American Society for the Sociology of Sport (NASSS), where our ethnographic penchant for sport was nurtured. This edited collection began as a NASSS symposium and we want to extend our appreciation to our colleagues in that organization, especially those who have made it possible for us to do feminist sport ethnography.

We are also grateful to CL Cole and Michael Messner for their editorial expertise and insight in the shaping of this volume. Their acumen and vision played an important role in the direction of this manuscript.

Linda Martindale gave life to this book through her tireless efforts in manuscript preparation, formatting, rereading and editing. In addition, Linda is pure magic in the coordination and attention to detail so important in an edited volume.

We want to also thank our respective departments for providing an encouraging atmosphere in which to work: the Department of Sociology and Anthropology at Elon University and the Department of Sociology and Anthropology at California State University at Bakersfield.

Finally, we would each like to offer a word of personal thanks. Anne Bolin would like to thank her spouse Greg Babcock for supporting and loving her always. Greg suggested that she see *Pumping Iron II: The Women,* a movie about women bodybuilders. This captured her anthropological imagination and brought her into the world of competitive bodybuilding. Great appreciation is owed to her gym rat colleagues and to her training partner and cool younger iron "brother" M., "220 pounds of twisted steel and sex appeal."

Jane Granskog would like to thank Laura A. Lowe, her past student, long-term training partner, coach, and dear "sister in spirit" for introducing her to the world of sport, which served as the critical impetus making all this possible. She would also like to thank her "triathlon family" in Bakersfield and elsewhere for the tremendous camaraderie and support they have provided, especially when times got tough over the past fifteen plus years.

INTRODUCTION

ANNE BOLIN AND JANE GRANSKOG

Athletic Intruders: Ethnographic Research on Women, Culture, and Exercise is an anthology edited by Anne Bolin, Professor of Anthropology at Elon University, and Jane Granskog, Professor of Anthropology at California State University at Bakersfield. The book investigates women's place in sport and exercise from a socio-cultural vantage provided by the fields of the anthropology of sport, the sociology of sport, and feminism. We offer this collection as a contribution to the emerging field of sports ethnography and the study of women and gender relations in the interdisciplinary field of sport/exercise/physical activity and the body—hence the title *Athletic Intruders: Ethnographic Research on Women, Culture, and Exercise.* The title suggests that women's participation in sports and exercise has not come without struggle into the sports arenas marked by male hegemony.

This book evolved from the intersection of our lives as anthropologists, feminists, and athletes. As baby boomers growing up before Title IX, we reaped the benefits of the social revolution of the 1960s, which opened new vistas for women. We pursued our respective careers as anthropologists and feminists. Anne pursued her research on gender by studying the lives of transgendered people while Jane's interest in gender progressed by investigating the adaptive strategies of peasant women in Mexico. It was not until our research shifted into sports and exercise that our lives intersected. Anne began ethnographic research among women bodybuilders while Jane worked with women triathletes. A critical component for instigating such research for each of us lay in the fact that we both first became participants in the sports we

1

chose to investigate. It was, in fact, the impact that such participation has had on our lives overall that led us to explore the impact of such activities, and the embodiment of self that emerged as a result, upon women in general. Through the grapevine of our discipline, which includes numerous mechanisms for like-minded people to find one another, we established our friendship (a process actually aided by the fact that very few anthropologists were doing the kind of research we were engaged in at the time). We remember back to 1988 when the American Anthropological Association meetings were in Phoenix, Arizona. Independently of one another and before we met, we both noted that we were the only two papers during the conference devoted to issues of women and sport. We wanted to meet each other to talk about our research but kept missing each other. As scholars and athletes with training agendas, our schedules didn't seem to mesh. However, after becoming friends, we solved that dilemma by training together whenever the opportunity arose—often at the various conferences that we scheduled to attend together. Finding each other wasn't the only catalyst for our research.

Another very important person intersected our lives and brought us together to meet other scholars working in the area of gender and sport. Alan Klein, whom we later came to regard as the parent of contemporary sport ethnography, brought us into the North American Society for the Study of Sport Sociology (NASSS). It was through the presentation of papers at the annual meetings of NASSS in the early 1990s that the impetus for putting together a book that simultaneously addressed issues of sport ethnography and the participation of women in athletic activities emerged. It was also at these meetings that we first encountered the significant research that was being carried out by other feminist scholars in sport sociology, notably the seminal work of Susan Birrell, Nancy Theberge, Sharon Guthrie, Shirley Castelnuovo, CL Cole, and others. The critical analysis of the role of gender in sport that these scholars provided set the tone for our subsequent work.

We have entitled our book *Athletic Intruders: Ethnographic Research on Women, Culture and Exercise* because, as Susan Birrell (1988:459–502) and Ann Hall (1993:48–68; 1996) so clearly argue in their respective reviews of the literature on women's history in sports and research about women and gender relations in sport/exercise, the view often is one in which women have been invisible, excluded, and marginalized. The following quote vividly illustrates the situation of women/sports relations in societies in which power, prestige, and access to resources is a privilege of men. The following account is offered as a poignant example of this exclusion and taken from the writings of the Greek Pausanias in ca. A.D. 170:

As one goes from Skillos down the road to Olympia, but before one crosses the Alpheios River, there is a mountain high and very steep cliffs. The name of the mountain is Typaion. The Eleans have a law to throw off these cliffs any women who are discovered at the Olympic festival, or even on the Olympia side of the Alpheios on the days which are forbidden to women. They say that no woman has ever been caught except Kallipateira. (Some say that the name of the woman was Pherenike, not Kallipateira.) She had been widowed and, disguised like a male trainer, she took her son to Olympia to compete. When her son Peisirodos won, Kallipateira jumped over the fence with which the trainers were restrained, and exposed herself. She was thus discovered to be a woman, but they released her unpunished out of respect for her father (Diagoras of Rhodes), her brothers and her son all of whom had been victors at Olympia. They passed a law, however, that in the future trainers would have to attend the competition in the nude (Miller 1979:35).

Women's participation in sport/exercise began to grow dramatically by the 1970s as a result of a convergence of factors. This included the impact of feminism in the 1960s, which continued the mid- to late-nineteenth-century trajectories of early feminists involved with health and dress reform (Bolin 1992:84–85). A new feminist agenda also contributed to relaxing the boundaries circumscribing femininity and bodily expression as well as challenging patriarchy on all fronts. These antecedents, along with the passage of Title IX in 1972, collectively enhanced women's place in athletics. Paralleling women's increasing athletic participation was a growing research interest in women and sports. The latter is the intellectual lineage that has inspired and fired *Athletic Intruders*.

Ann Hall states: "Epistemologically, we must accept that there are women's ways of knowing. Therefore, it follows that feminist research practices reflect this plurality and there can be no one feminist method" (1996:74). Relying on Hall's (1996) review of research trends in the study of women and sport/exercise, we have identified three prominent "ways of knowing" or themes embossed in the works of the contributors to this book. Hall has discussed the value of 1) interpretive research with a non-positivist thrust, and 2) situated analysis with regard to the "importance of history." As cultural anthropologists and feminists, we offer a third theme that is emerging in sport studies, born of anthropology but adopted by other disciplines: interpretive analysis based on the qualitative methodology of ethnography, specifically postmodern/reflexive ethnography. Women's physical activity and somatic culture are focused upon with a broad lens that accents the theoretical with an emphasis on the social construction of femininity/masculinity and gender relations through nine ethnographic case studies. The case studies we offer illustrate the critical importance of situating feminist research within the context of women's bodily experiences as manifested in personal, social, and cultural discourses. Herein also lies one of the strengths of this text to feminist research. Following the tradition of reflexive and experiential ethnographic research, each of the ethnographic contributions addresses women's somatic experiences and their consequences for the transformation of women's lives as well as the cultural context within which they are located.

In the first chapter, "Reflexive Ethnography, Women, and Sporting Activities," we present an in-depth examination of reflexive ethnography as well as a discussion of the theoretical continuities among the ethnographic case studies. This chapter is followed by nine ethnographic case studies that exemplify current approaches in reflexive and experiential participant-observation. The ethnographies represent recent reflexive and postmodern trends focusing on issues of identity, embodiment, and meaning as expressed in various sports and exercises including triathlons, aerobics, basketball, bodybuilding, weightlifting, motorcycle riding, softball, casual exercise, and rugby. Multicultural and international issues are specifically attended to in three of the ethnographic studies—Terese Stratta's study of African American women in intercollegiate sports at a predominantly white institution, Dona Davis's research in Newfoundland, and P. David Howe's study of women rugby players in England. *Athletic Intruders* concludes with an Afterword that discusses the theoretical intersections of research on sport, exercise, and the body with feminist studies and linkages with the anthropology and sociology of sport. The examination of these diverse ethnographic accounts within such a theoretical framework allows us to better grasp the significance that the gendering of sport, play, and physicality in its myriad forms has upon our lives as a whole. In a very real sense it is the embodiment of gender that informs our lives and sets the parameters for constructing the reality we currently experience. Only by becoming aware of the constraints that circumscribe our expression of ourselves within the world we have defined will we be able to transcend such perceptions to create a different reality that honors the contributions and role of all members. It is with this objective in mind that we offer the following readings.

REFERENCES

Abu-Lughod, Lila. 1991. "Writing against Culture." In *Recapturing Anthropology: Working in the Present*, ed. Richard G. Fox, 137–620. Santa Fe, NM: School of American Research Press.

Bateson, Mary Catherine. 1990. *Composing a Life: Life as a Work in Progress—The Improvisations of Five Extraordinary Women.* New York, NY: Plume Books.

Behar, Ruth. 1994. "Dare We Say 'I'? Bringing the Personal into Scholarship." *Chronicle of Higher Education* XL (43):B1–B2.

Blanchard, Kendall. 1995. *The Anthropology of Sport.* South Hadley, MA: Bergin and Garvey.

Bolin, Anne. 1992. "Vandalized Vanity: Feminine Physiques Betrayed and Portrayed." In *Tattoo, Torture, Adornment and Disfigurement: The Denaturalization of the Body in Culture and Text,* ed. Francis Mascia-Lees and Patricia Sharpe, 79–99. Albany, NY: State University of New York Press.

Clifford, James. 1986 "Introduction: Partial Truths." In *Writing Culture: The Poetics and Politics of Ethnography,* ed. James Clifford and George E. Marcus, 1–26. Berkeley, CA: University of California Press.

Clifford, James, and George E. Marcus, eds. 1986. *Writing Culture: The Poetics and Politics of Ethnography.* Berkeley, CA: University of California Press.

Cohen, Eugene N., and Edwin Eames. 1982. *Cultural Anthropology.* Boston, MA: Little, Brown and Company.

Connell, Robert W. 1987. *Gender and Power.* Stanford, CA: Stanford University Press.

Huizinga, Johan. 1944. *Homo Ludens: A Study of Play Elements in Culture.* Boston, MA: Beacon Press.

Kimmel, Michael S., and Michael A. Messner. 1992. "Introduction." In *Men's Lives,* ed. Michael S. Kimmel and Michael A Messner, 1–11. New York, NY: Macmillan Publishing Co.

Klein, Alan M. 1993. *Little Big Men: Bodybuilding Subculture and Gender Construction.* Albany, NY: State University of New York Press.

Loy, John W. 1968. "The Nature of Sport: A Definitional Effort." *Quest* 10:1–5.

MacNeill, Margaret. 1988. "Active Women, Media Representations, Ideology." In *Not Just a Game,* ed. Jean Harvey and H. Cantelon, 195–212. Atona, Ottowa, Canada: University of Ottowa Press.

Marcus, George, and Michael M. J. Fischer. 1986. *Anthropology as Cultural Critique: An Experimental Moment in the Human Sciences.* Chicago, IL: University of Chicago Press.

Messner, Michael. 1992. "Boyhood, Organized Sports, and the Construction of Masculinities." In *Men's Lives,* ed. Michael S. Kimmel and Michael A. Messner, 161–76. New York, NY: Macmillan Publishing Co.

Miller, Stephen G. 1979. *Arete: Ancient Writers, Papyri, and Inscriptions on the History and Ideals of Greek Athletics and Games.* Chicago, IL: Ares Publishers.

Skomal, Susan. 1994. "Lessons for the Field: Ethics in Fieldwork." *Anthropology Newsletter* 35:1,4.

Theberge, Nancy. 1987. "Sport and Women's Empowerment." *Women's Studies International* Forum 10:387–93.

CHAPTER ONE

Reflexive Ethnography, Women, and Sporting Activities

ANNE BOLIN AND JANE GRANSKOG

INTRODUCTION

The ethnographic studies of sports and exercise presented herein articulate the interrelationships of physical activity and issues of gender relations, asymmetrical ideologies of gender, and embodiment through a feminist and interpretive lens. They also illustrate the critical importance of mooring feminist research within the context of women's bodily experiences in exercise and sports, with attention given to issues of identity. Experiential and reflexive ethnographic methods demonstrate the power of conjoining qualitative methods and feminist interpretive approaches to create a conceptual synergism through: teasing out systems of meaning, locating the points of cultural fracture/fissioning and containment, and addressing culture as dynamic, processual, and negotiable. Collectively, these articles represent the cutting edge of research emerging in feminist studies of women's physical activity: interpretive analysis based on the qualitative methodology of ethnography, specifically a postmodern and reflexive ethnography. It is an approach that crosses both disciplines and perspectives.

THE ETHNOGRAPHY OF SPORT: HISTORICAL CONTEXT

Athletic Intruders: Ethnographic Research on Women, Culture, and Exercise is devoted to the ethnography of sporting and exercising women. All of the authors share an original perspective and approach to the ethnographic enterprise. For some of our readers who may be unfamiliar with the ethnographic method, an explanation of traditional ethnography seems appropriate before launching into more advanced issues of the "new" or reflexive ethnography.

Ethnography is a method as well as an account of peoples' lifeways based on participant-observation. Among the "tribe" calling themselves anthropologists, this type of study is known more simply as fieldwork. Fieldwork involves various degrees of immersion in the field of research with the goal of understanding cultural forms from the perspective of the "native." Ethnography developed as the emblem of cultural anthropology in the late nineteenth and early twentieth centuries and is unique among the social sciences for several reasons. Ethnography is a time- and labor-intensive method that requires the ethnographer not only to observe, but also to become a participant, in her or his field situation. Anthropologists typically spend a minimum of nine months living among their collaborators (the people with whom they are conducting ethnography). Anthropological fieldwork is also unprecedented among research methods in that the ethnographer is the research instrument. "The assumption underlying this approach is that the only way to record another culture is to live it, learn it, and understand it" (Cohen and Eames 1982:30).

In the early days anthropologists were involved in a cultural salvage operation, recording anything and everything about the cultures of indigenous peoples before their cultures were completely transformed by contact and colonialism. As information was collected by anthropologists on the world's peoples, ethnography moved into problem-centered approaches, for example, testing theories in the field and studying culture change and development (Cohen and Eames 1982:21). As the mandate to record information on the world's cultures was fulfilled, anthropologists started to focus more on ethnic groups in Euro-American societies as well as on North American and European cultures. This is the setting in which the ethnography of sport was born.

Sport and exercise ethnography of today is still in its infancy, offering frontier territory for anthropologists and others with training in fieldwork methods and a culturally relativistic stance. Sport ethnography has gained visibility through the work of a number of anthropologists. While Kendall Blanchard and Alyce Cheska (1985) may be credited with public recognition of the field by officially titling their book with that name *(The Anthropology of Sport),* the anthropological study of sport has a long history under the appellation of games. In fact, the anthropological study of sport emerged coterminous with the development of the discipline itself in the work of E. B. Tylor, who is often distinguished as the parent of this topical specialty, in his 1879 paper "On the History of Games" (Blanchard 1995:9–23; Sands 1999:19–29).

Although sports and exercise were included in the traditional womb-to-tomb ethnographic studies since all aspects of cultural life were described, it was not until recently that sports and exercise carved out its own territory as a specialty field of anthropology. It should be noted that the anthropology of sport includes a variety of other research methods germane to anthropology such as ethnohistory, the ethnological methods of cross-cultural correlational studies, and controlled comparisons. However, ethnography remains the signature method for the majority of cultural anthropologists no matter what the endeavor. The anthropology of sport comprised itself in the 1970s and has continued to grow as ethnographic research has moved from the descriptive to the theoretical and problem-centered approaches. Blanchard records the year 1974 as the actual emergence of the anthropology of sport with the formation of the Association for the Anthropological Study of Play. However, much work remains to be done, even in the purely descriptive arena of sports and exercise ethnography, both cross-culturally and intraculturally on North American sports and exercise (Blanchard 1995:83). Adding gender to the equation and incorporating feminist perspectives makes for an even more intellectually lucrative field for the ethnography of sport as it continues the dual task of descriptive and conceptual development.

The editors credit Alan M. Klein with bringing the ethnographic study of sport into prominence and inserting it into an already established interdisciplinary field of sport study dominated by psychology, sociology, and kinesthesics. Alan Klein has long been an advocate and proponent of the value of the ethnography of sport. His efforts are numerous and include a long and active involvement in the North American Association for the Study of Sport Sociology (NASSS)—most recently as president; substantial ethnographic research on sport (in 1991, 1993, and 1997); and the mentoring and encouragement of anthropologists and others interested in working within the framework of ethnographic studies of sport and exercise.

REFLEXIVE ETHNOGRAPHY

There is a small but growing body of ethnographic research on sport. As befitting a discipline whose soul is "cultural relativism," this research in "sport" has a broad lens not just limiting itself to formal sports defined as ". . . gamelike activity having rules, a competitive element, and requiring some form of physical exertion" (Blanchard 1995:9) but expanded to include a diverse array of physical activities, exercise, and movement in addition to the traditional games orientation. Our ethnographic selections therefore include examples of traditionally defined sports and exercise such as P. David Howe's study of women rugby players as well as the nontraditional elements found in Barbara Joans's ethnography of women motorcycle riders. The contributors have been selected as examples of reflexive ethnographies that include feminist postmodern theoretical perspectives on exercise and sporting activities. These ethnographies share a common perspective of the culture concept that incorporates an emphasis on the individual and agency in the production and negotiation of culture and includes both the ethnographer and the research collaborators in the process of cultural creation. The ethnographies are reflexive in that the researchers reflect upon their relations with those studied and integrate discussion of the researcher's place in interactions. The studies also portray the subcultures under study as "an open ended, creative dialogue of subcultures, of insiders and outsiders, and of diverse factions" (Clifford 1983:137).

Whereas anthropologists in the past discussed "informants" and research populations, the up-and-coming reflexive and dialogical anthropology takes a new turn. Informants have become "consultants" in an effort to divest anthropology of the inequalities inherent in researcher and subject relations. According to Lughod (1991:142), this was in part spawned by the work of indigenous anthropologists, ethnic, and feminist anthropologists "not just because they position themselves with reference to two communities but because when they present the Other they are presenting themselves, [and consequently] they speak with a complex awareness of and investment in reception."

Therefore, one important trend in reflexive ethnographic research is the positioning of the anthropologist and her or his status as insider/outsider or as in-between. Many of the researchers involved in the ethnography of physical activity are full participants in their sport/exercise research. Anthropologists may indeed "be" or even "become" whom they study in terms of self-identification as a member of a sport subculture, although this is certainly not a prerequisite. However, such a "becoming" or "being" ushers in a provocative new dimension for the study of women, culture, and exercise/sports for those involved as ethnographers and participants. Such an approach is only one strand in the broader genre of the "new ethnography" and takes some anthropologists into a dimension of research we conceptualize as "extreme ethnography" in which one is "being" or "becoming" whom one studies or, in the anthropological argot, "going native."

New approaches in anthropology have surfaced to challenge "emic" and "etic" as a conceptual dichotomy. By reconceiving the emic/etic distinction as a continuum, "insider" and "outsider" become dialogical, destabilized, and contextual. This is amalgamated with the contemporary reframing of informants and research populations as collaborators with ethnographers in creating an understanding of phenomenon (Skomal 1994:4). As a consequence, no longer is "going native" (what we are calling "extreme ethnography") an anthropological bane and a detriment to one's career. It now may be considered a legitimate part of the reflexive ethnography, as indigenous/ethnic and feminist anthropologists have shown us (cf. Clifford 1986, Clifford and Marcus 1986, Abu-Lughod 1991, Marcus and Fischer 1986). Insider and outsider, researcher and researched, rather than oppositional, are sliding into contexualized categories of distance and closeness (cf. Behar 1994:B1–B2). What are the challenges of the experiential ethnographer who chooses extreme ethnography and who already identifies with or becomes one with whom they study/collaborate? This positioning offers unique opportunities that provide a general bracketing of reflexive ethnography that recognizes the researcher as being in a shifting situation with those she or he studies.

The contributors' articles are in the genre of an experiential reflexive ethnography. Experiential ethnography requires that the anthropologist fully participate in the lives of her or his collaborators (see Turner and Bruner 1986). For ethnographers of physical activity, this requires involvement in the lives of exercisers and athletes at multiple levels. Sands states: "Instead of looking at participation as being a line of research that one crosses or enters into a compromising or contaminating position, it is suggested becoming one of the 'team' acts to open 'doors' of experience that is [sic] needed to know the life of the athlete" (1999:37). This kind of entrenchment implies a long-term and labor-intensive commitment. As mentioned earlier, ethnography does require a substantial time investment because human involvement in groups includes cycles and levels of commitment. Subcultures involve learners and novices just as they may involve elites. The ethnographer often enters at ground level, and, in the process of becoming an ethnographer and anthropologist, experiences her or his own socialization in the lives of the athletes in a sporting subculture. It is through the process of learning the exercise subculture and the levels of participation that the ethnographer can begin to forge an analysis that facilitates her or him seeing "the experience itself and the interpretative framework within which the experience has meaning" (Goulet 1994:32–33).

We would argue that being a bodybuilder, triathlete, aerobicizer, runner, walker, or whatever form of physical exercise a person engages in as part of a group with a social identity necessarily involves a process. Anthropologist Marie Francoise Guedon discovered in her ethnographic research among the Alaskan *Dene tha* that "[b]eing a woman was not a state of being or even a biological fact. It was a process, an act of participation" (1994:43). We would argue that the worldview of the *Dene tha* is equally applicable to researchers who undertake sport ethnography. In this regard, as Guedon notes: "Participant-observation as a methodology became a personal maturation of the ethnographer in the Dene culture, a process carefully supervised and supported by the Dene themselves" (1994:43). Her comment has clear resonance for ethnographers of sport whose own sport and exercise research involves them in a rite of passage as they progress in knowledge of the athletic endeavor through the accumulation of time and experience.

Victor Turner has argued that ". . . lived experience in anthropology is primary, thought is its interpreter" (Turner 1994:73). Again, inspiration can be gathered from Guedon's experiential ethnography whose work has direct application for an experiential ethnography of sport in her statement:

> I found it increasingly difficult to speak of belief—a term with strong intellectual and cognitive connotations—for most of the content of the "belief" I was taught was physical and kinesthetic. Through many similar experiences, experiences embedded in a definite progression in the stories and information given to me, and with the help of Dene friends over many years, I came to realize that perception of process is the key to the Dene way of life as well as to an understanding of their notions of community, technology, family, religion and knowledge (1994:43).

For an ethnography of sport, for a postmodern and truly reflexive ethnography in which the ethnographer is co-collaborator, an experiential approach is a valuable tool. By "experiential" we mean what ethnographer Laurence de Garis (1999:65–74) asserts: the totality of an experience that does not just privilege the visual, the observed, and the verbal, but the kinesthetic and the somatic bodily experience of the activity as well. As the process of fieldwork unfolds, the experiential ethnographer is prepared for analytical contextualization on multiple levels and through layers of knowledge. As we become increasingly subject and object, as we participate on an experiential level with those whom we study, we come to share the position that is neither above nor below but a part of the studied group (Lughod 1991:142; de Garis 1999:67). Because we are part of the group—as co-participants in exercise and sport subcultures—and because we have been involved in the process of developing knowledge through participation that includes time-depth and kinetic/somatic experience in our activity regardless of our actual skill in the physical activity or our particular role, we as researchers grow into our reflexivity and include in our repertoire of research tools an embodied knowledge.

The involvement of the ethnographic contributors in the articles that follow spans a variety of statuses and roles as participant-observers in sporting subcultures. It includes that of the "exteme ethnographer," which we have defined as being or becoming whom one studies in the ethnographies of: Jane Granskog—triathlete, Pirkko Markula—aerobicizer, Anne Bolin—bodybuilder, Barbara Joans—biker in a motorcycle subculture, Shari Dworkin—fitness enthusiast, and Faye Linda Wachs—softball player. Under no circumstances are we arguing that ethnographers must become whom they study or that one must "go native" to conduct sound ethnography. Nor do we think such positioning grants greater authority. Rather, it discourages the anthropological voice as privileged by weaving in that of the anthropologist as co-participant. Such extreme and reflexive ethnography facilitates a particular way of knowing and dialogue. There are, however, certain difficulties embedded in the role of the extreme ethnographer that must be overcome. For example, the problem of familiarization requires that the extreme ethnographer become especially attentive to the process "defamilarization." The critical distancing necessary for reflective analysis is therefore especially crucial lest one risk becoming "stale" (Alan Klein personal communication). Being whom one studies creates a dynamic tension in which the ethnographer slides in and out of being his or her own collaborator, both as participant and observer.

Among the contributors are those whose experiential ethnography is along the lines of the more traditional ethnography. These include Terese M. Peretto Stratta, Dona Davis, and P. David Howe, whose work shares the theme of multicultural and cross-cultural emphasis. These three ethnographers each became embedded in a community as insiders. In all three cases their own athletic involvement provided them access to their respective research community in unique ways. In addition to competing as a NCAA Division I scholarship athlete, Terese M. Peretto Stratta's understanding of cultures, as both an Italian-American woman ethnographer and a native of Chicago, influenced African American female athletes' receptiveness to her. Dona Davis inadvertently became an intrinsic element in the development of diet and exercise fads in Grey Rock Harbour, Newfoundland. Through her own running, she started a jogging fad and contributed to the emergence and cultural recognition of exercise as a demanding but effective method of weight reduction. P. David Howe's research on women's rugby in Wales was inspired through his ethnographic research on elite men's rugby as a distinctive sporting community. By living in a shared house with three women rugby players, Howe was provided with access to a women's rugby club and the distinctive habitus embodied by women rugby players.

Before presenting an overview and theoretical highlights of the ethnographic contributions, we offer the following discussion of the relations of postmodernism and ethnography as background linking theory and method.

POSTMODERNISM AND ETHNOGRAPHY

Reflexive ethnography is imbued with a particular perspective on the culture concept—a perspective that regards culture as dynamic, evolving, contestatory, and heterogeneous, or, in short, postmodern. A *caveat* and an aside are in order here. Before we become too self-congratulatory about the new ethnography and the leaps and conceptual bounds made by postmodern thinking, we would like to remember our anthropological ancestors. Early in the development of the discipline of anthropology, some of our lineage elders proffered a culture concept spawned by the ethnographic method that sounds surprisingly contemporary. In an excellent review of the culture concept, Brightman (1995:509–46) has described challenges and changes in the culture concept since the 1980s. Disciplinary "dis-ease," with the culture concept, contains a number of themes of discontent that are, according to Brightman, generated by ". . . convergent influences from political-economy, modernist and postmodernist anthropologies, varieties of feminist writing, cultural studies, and diverse other sources" (1995:511). It must be reiterated that the ascribed flaws of the culture concept are regarded as derivative of and articulated with the ethnographic method. For a complete discussion of the postmodern critique of the culture concept, see Brightman (1995); however, reiterating a few points should suffice for our purposes (see also Borofsky 1994).

The traditional ethnographic literature and the culture concept used by anthropologists has been critiqued to include the following litany of ethnocentrisms and errors: cultures are presented as homogenous, coherent, holistic, timeless, and superorganic (outside behavior). Peoples are presented as engaging in blind and uncritical "role enactments of cultural rules." Permeating traditional ethnographies are a subtext of difference and hierarchy (1995:511–26).

While the "new and reflexive ethnography" is seen as offering a counter-revolution to these shortcomings, Brightman reminds us of our "disciplinary amnesia" regarding ethnography as method and cultural text. He argues that the recent and postmodern critique of the culture concept embedded in ethnographic writing ignores that culture has not been a uniform concept for anthropologists and that there have been a diversity of voices, both anthropological and indigenous. From the early days in the field, ethnographic texts exist that embrace a concept of culture that is dynamic, inclusive of individuals and events, and that contains contradiction and negotiation as well as historicity. For example, Malinowski in 1926 (p. 12) stated: "Human cultural reality is not a consistent, local scheme, but rather a seething mixture of conflicting principles." Pluralism and historicity were addressed by Radin in 1933 (pp. 184–85): "We are dealing with specific, not generalized, men and women, and with specific, not generalized, events. . . . It is this particularity that is the essence of all history and it is precisely this that ethnology has hitherto balked at doing." According to Sapir (1949:104), culture is ". . . not a static structure defined by tradition, it is . . . a highly intricate network of partial or incomplete understandings between members. . . . It is only apparently a static sum of social institutions; actually it is being reanimated or creatively reaffirmed from day to day by particular acts of a communicative nature which obtain among individuals participating in it" (in Brightman 1995:534–38). These voices from anthropology's past reiterate dominant themes of individual improvisation, social consensus, and agency. We would agree with Brightman (1995:539) that the culture concept is indeed a "labile" one; that it has had many manifestations in its anthropological history; that it is not moribund but rather alive and vigorous. We propose that an experiential ethnography is particularly salient in the contemporary reiteration and reconfiguration of the culture concept in all its complexity. It is especially useful for a contemporary ethnography of sport.

The theoretical milieu of postmodernism conjoined with feminism, and perhaps influenced by more generalized questioning of scientific objectivity brought about by broader trends in the sciences, has led ethnographers to challenge whether an objective otherness is possible or even desirable given the constraints of questions designed to yield results in quantitative terms. In the conventional ethnological paradigm, one acquired an emic or insider's view as a result of fieldwork. To make sense of the emic from a Western scientific or etic perspective required that one separate oneself analytically from one's insider position. The subjective was therefore translated into the empirical objective. However, ethnography as a qualitative method has always contained the seeds of its own transformation since its inception. Qualitative methods and interpretive, symbolic analytical tools asked questions and offered insights beyond the pale of the strictly statistical.

Does this conception of culture mean we must throw out our empirical bathwater with our interpretive babies? We would caution that concern with the individual and agency in ethnography does not necessarily imply that we must give up on the task of discovering the patterning of culture through systematic fieldwork. Just as we may reject notions of culture as homogenized and recognize the complexity of choices and outcomes, we see value in interpretive and humanistic perspectives that dialogue with some forms of analytical distancing. In this regard:

> It is less clear, however, that anthropology attentive to 'lived experience' can dispense with generalization. At what level of generality does generalization become objectionable? What about the locals' own generalizations, both implicit and articulated, in whose terms they necessarily interpret and act upon their experiences? Are we to focus only on the particulars and neglect the regularities? How then can the two be differentiated? Generalization is unavoidable even when it engages heterogeneity . . . it is questionable whether disciplinary attention to the particular can proceed independently of generalizations about cultural form (Brightman 1995:534–35).

We have used the terminology "feminism," "postmodernism," and "interpretation" as inclusionary theoretical stances whose approaches may be incorporative and overlapping rather than exclusionary. Nor do we regard efforts at empiricism and science as antithetical to reflexive and postmodern ethnographic analysis as is suggested by some (cf. Rabinow 1986). Rather, we regard qualitative research methods as engaging the empirical and integral to "good" ethnography. Thus, we have selected ethnographies that seek balance and weave distance and closeness into their analysis. As such, the contributing authors may be regarded as writing in the tradition of feminist anthropology. According to Crapo, feminist anthropologists are ". . . unique in their ability to bridge the gulf between humanist and scientist that more clearly separates practitioners of other approaches in anthropology" (1993:48).

Each of the ethnographies presented contain a common foci on gender relations as experienced and expressed within a culture using a dialogical approach and often contestatory framework for analysis. Gender is also contextualized among the contributors as discursive, accenting themes of femininity/masculinity and the body, and integrating these within the broader perspectives of the structure of power relations and differential access to prestige, resources, and privilege. The following provides discussion of key points and accents the ethnographic contributions of each of the authors.

ETHNOGRAPHIC OVERVIEW

Jane Granskog, chapter 2.
Just "Tri" and "Du" It: The Variable Impact of Female
Involvement in the Triathlon/Duathlon Sport Culture

Jane Granskog is an exemplary ethnographer who bases her research on fifteen years of participant-observation in the multi-sport subcultures of triathletes and duathletes. Taking the case study approach, she analyzes the life histories of four women and focuses on the variable impact that sport participation has had in their lives in terms of their identity as women and athletes. Granskog speaks to participation in sport as a creative force in the development of identity and provides a view of identity as dynamic, a growing and active part of one's life. Thus multi-sport participation becomes woven into the lives of the participants, who are never the same as a result. This is an invigorating exploration that targets the shared parameters of sports culture but also addresses how it is part of an individual's life story. The ethnography successfully addresses the culture concept yet integrates the importance of diversity and different voices in the analysis. Granskog investigates how sports participation, and its variable impact on participants, can be understood as the interaction of three factors: the degree and type of involvement in the sport culture specifically as measured by the number and type of races one enters and completes; the nature and strength of one's athletic support network; and the life stage one is in and the impact this has on one's self-definition as an athlete.

Pirkko Markula, chapter 3.
Postmodern Aerobics: Contradiction and Resistance

Markula offers an analysis of the meaning of aerobics in the lives of women. An avid aerobicizer herself, Markula challenges prevalent sociocultural research on aerobic fitness that has proposed that fitness classes, media representations and video workouts are only about enhancing sexuality and patriarchal notions of femininity, thereby reinforcing the oppression of women (cf. Theberge 1987; MacNeill, among others). Markula's approach to aerobics is as a lived endeavor whose deconstruction must be understood beyond media images of women, just as Bolin argues in chapter 5 for a public/private split in understanding conventional patriarchal images of notions of femininity and the private experience of efficacy and empowerment. Markula's participant-observation reveals hidden agendas in aerobics not readily accessible to the nonparticipant. In the genre of Mary Catherine Bateson's *Composing a*

Life (1989), Markula finds women composing autonomy through what may appear as patriarchal subordination on the surface. She focuses on the cultural creativity in living an aerobics lifestyle and how it expands and surrounds the participants in proactive ways while subverting what others have argued is an ideology of masculinity. This is a postmodern ethnography that locates aerobics within its boundaries and investigates it as contradiction and resistance.

Terese "Terry" M. Peretto Stratta, chapter 4.
Cultural Expressions of African American
Female Athletes in Intercollegiate Sport

Stratta addresses the subject of ethnicity in African American women's intercollegiate sport experiences in a predominantly white institution. Stratta, as an Italian-American ethnographer, has proven herself to be an intrepid participant-observer who successfully gained insider status in the black college sport culture. The central theme of this study is the delineation of African American cultural expression from the broader context of college sport culture in general. Stratta asks the question: "Does college sport allow for African American female athletes to express their culture?" To conduct her investigation, Stratta collected data in the university setting of a NCAA Division IA intercollegiate program through the eyes of an ethnographer steeped in interpretive anthropology. As in the other ethnographies, the meaning of culture is located in the "lived" experiences of the participants. As a result, Stratta has provided a rare insight into the context of African American women's sport culture. She identifies diverse domains that influence the expression of African American women's sport culture, which include team and sport contexts as well as the coach's awareness and sensitivity to ethnic cultural expressions. Stratta concludes that when African American representation is low or moderate (for example, a team that is predominantly white), African American female athletes "are predisposed to feeling like 'athletic intruders.'" Apart from special situations of predominantly black sport participation in which the cultivation of black culture is celebrated, African American women athletes are placed in a situation where they must mask their African American culture in order to conform.

Anne Bolin, chapter 5.
Beauty or the Beast: The Subversive Soma

Bolin's study is a result of nine years of participant-observation in competitive bodybuilding. As a competitive bodybuilder herself, Bolin brings to us an insider's perspective unique in the study of women's bodybuilding. Her research is focused on the lives of women and men who are not professional athletes, but who compete at the local, regional, and national levels as amateurs. In her study Bolin's focus is on the apparently contradictory cultural expression of femininity that is embodied by competitive women bodybuilders and conceptualized in the dichotomy of "beauty and the beast." The "beast" in women's bodybuilding is a bodily contestation of the cultural manifestation of femininity that presents women as the weaker sex. Women's muscular *somas* defy the traditional images of femininity. Bolin then posits that, despite displays of traditional sartorial femininity embodied by the cultural mandate for "beauty," women's muscular physiques are critical, rebellious, and reforming. Competitive women's bodybuilding publicly portrays elements of the culture of beauty while privately betraying and challenging the culture of beauty. Bolin argues that this occurs through a public and private splitting in which the public somatic text (or frontstage displayed in bodybuilding magazines, television shows, and contests) is presented through a lens of traditional femininity while the private somatic text (or backstage that is experienced in the gym through rigorous training) is a subversive script.

Shari L. Dworkin, chapter 6.
A Woman's Place Is in the . . . Cardiovascular Room??
Gender Relations, the Body, and the Gym

Dworkin's ethnography of a local gym is an excellent follow-up piece linking to the previous study by Anne Bolin. Instead of focusing on those women at the extreme, as in Bolin's (1997) research on competitive bodybuilders who challenge the conventional embodiment of beauty as slender and toned, Dworkin's ethnography focuses on bodily management of women who work out to fulfill the conventional embodiment. This study explores why and how women in a local gym structure their "choice" and duration of workouts the way they do. In keeping with the toned, lean, and "not too muscular" embodiment of late-twentieth-century America, Dworkin found an emphasis on long cardiovascular workouts while avoiding the weight room. An upward limit on acceptable strength levels for women was normalized in the gym so it was appropriate to be athletic and muscular as long as women did not lift too much weight and become too muscular. Using Bob Connell's (1987) concept of "emphasized femininity" and Bolin's argument that masculine elements of sport are neutralized through a culture of beauty, Dworkin found that few women engaged in weight training to build muscle and strength. She concludes that while fitness as a muscular form offers an empowering conception of womanhood through strength, male power and privilege are simultaneously reasserted by defining maximum limits on muscular strength and through cultural conceptions of heterosexual feminine attractiveness. Although many women can be said to accommodate the limits, there is indeed a possible backlash for those who threaten men's stronghold on superior physical strength. Women are aware that they may receive possible rejection from men on the heterosexual dating scene and/or may be tagged with a lesbian stigma. The struggle for meaning surrounding female athletes and their bodies continues to be a site of contestation, challenge, and change.

Barbara Joans, chapter 7.
Women Who Ride: The Bitch in the Back Is Dead

Joans, an ethnographer enmeshed in the world of motorcycling, provides gripping insight into gender relations among bikers. The editors have included motorcycling in this book on women, culture, and sport/exercise because biking has elements of sport and requires athletic abilities to participate. Motorcycling is unique in the trajectory of sports, with women's participation actually decreasing through time as motorcycling assumed a mantle of male dominance. Women were transformed from biking women to the biker's woman, in argot "the bitch on the back," by the 1940s. Joans's insider status as a biker allows her to document the cultural dynamics offered by women who contest the conventional Western paradigm of femininity and dare to ride the wind but not as "the bitch on the back." She provides a panorama of gender change existing in the subculture of biking. Until relatively recently, the "bitch on the back" symbolized women's position in a male-dominated biker's world as submissive to the man who was, actually and metaphorically, in the driver's seat. Today, women have created a new place for themselves in motorcycling through numerous groups, clubs, organizations, and chapters designed for the riding women, which are growing in number. As a biking woman, Joans offers insight into the backstage arena where women contest male dominance and traditional femininity among bikers and where not only are gender relations challenged but the symbolic web of the subculture of biking is contested, examined, and redefined. According to Joans, the women bikers of today, including herself, "have rewritten the rules," as they must since women bikers hold anomalous positions in a dangerous and predominantly male world. In the biker's world the language, rituals, and rites of passage have been male-defined, and all women bikers ride the roads at risk.

Faye Linda Wachs, chapter 8.
"I Was There . . .": Gender, Power,
and Discourse in the World of Co-ed Softball

Co-ed softball is the site for Wachs's ethnography research. Wachs's eight years of co-ed softball experience serve as the backdrop and stimulus for her research with five recreational co-ed softball leagues in the greater Los Angeles area. Her methods include playing and observing in four of the leagues while only observing in the fifth for comparison purposes. This study focuses on an understanding of how gendered ideology, bodies, and practices reproduce gendered relations, yet coterminously provide a refractive lens through which those gendered relations are contested and renegotiated. Wachs offers a keen analysis that blends a feminist interpretive perspective with empiricism. She documents specific ideologies of gender difference, such as "the expectation that men are better hitters," as this gendered belief is actually practiced in strategies employed in the game. These beliefs include: 1) men should not try to walk; 2) women should try to walk; and 3) men do not strike out. Despite ideologies and strategic processes that reinforce asymmetrical gender relations, many women and men issue challenges verbally and through their physical performances in a variety of domains. For example, women challenge conceptions of male physical superiority through their performance in male-defined positions and in batting, where they demonstrated resistance through "runs." Wachs suggests that competing ideologies of gender relations are framed as reproduction and contestation and result in an ongoing and dynamic process of negotiation and renegotiation. True to a feminist perspective, attention is given to the gendered body and bodily practice (cf. Hall 1996:49–67).

Dona Davis, chapter 9.
Changing Body Aesthetics: Diet and Exercise Fads
in a Newfoundland Outport Community

Davis is an ethnographer whose own interest in continuing a vigorous exercise regimen during fieldwork inadvertently played into an analysis of exercise fads, body image, and weight loss among Newfoundland women. Davis situates exercise fads along with diet pills in the changing cultural milieu of Grey Rock Harbour, a homogenous community with a population of 766. Although traditional community values persisted, culture change in regard to ideal weight was occurring as a result of exposure to more middle-class weight norms through television and the greater opportunities for community members to travel. The introduction of medical services into the community also provided medical models of ideal weight. Until this began to occur, Grey Rock Harbour was a community in which weight loss was not a burning issue. Davis is on hand to analyze the process of culture change by focusing on the advent of the 1970s exercise fads as these occurred on the heels of a diet pill fad. Davis traces the processes of the development and decline of fads by contextualizing them within the culture of the community and situating them ethnohistorically. She provides a detailed ethnographic analysis of these fads and their participants while addressing several specific questions, including: How do diet fads as collective behavior relate to modernization and acculturation in this Newfoundland community? What is the significance of the female body image and how and why are ideals or body aesthetics changing among Harbour women? What perspectives can anthropologists bring to the issue that others have ignored? And finally, what is the applied relevance of this research to health planning? Davis answers these questions with an ethnographic elegance that integrates the themes of gender, culture, and exercise in a cultural and ethnohistorical context of culture change in a small-scale community that finds itself in the infancy of much larger changes brought about by modernity.

P. David Howe, chapter 10.
Kicking Stereotypes into Touch:
An Ethnographic Account of Women's Rugby

Howe's ethnographic research incorporates several feminist themes. Through his attention to historicity and difference, Howe contextualizes women's rugby within the cultural evolution of the earlier and prior game of men's rugby. His analysis displays an historically situated understanding of rugby as it developed a unique Welsh configuration in contrast to English rugby (cf. Hall 1996:37–40). Howe's ethnography also displays a central concern with "sensitivity to difference" (cf. Hall 1996:40–44) as he locates and unpacks the socio-cultural barriers faced by women who choose to participate in a high-contact sport. By offering an ethnographic account of the distinctive habitus of women who participate in rugby at the very highest amateur level, Howe's study of Welsh women rugby players is in the tradition of the new ethnography with a postmodern thrust on interpretation and meaning generated within a women's sport subculture that includes the issue of bodily representation and gender. For Howe, the sporting body is personal as well as political. He provides an elegant ethnographic description that embeds the study of the body within the Western gender paradigm of femininity and masculinity as well as the role of consumerism in reproducing bodily ideals of buff and beautiful for women. When articulated within the lived community of rugby players, embodiment is a multilayered phenomenon in which bodily discipline reflects a dynamic interplay of actor, agency, and culture. Howe examines through the ethnographic lens the gender-disparate ramifications of an ethic of increasing professionalism for the sport and the consequences this has for women's rugby in particular in comparison to the men's sport. He attends to issues of hegemony and oppression through discussion of the homonegativism attached to the women's sport of rugby.

Each of these ethnographic accounts provides us with a new lens with which to view the significance and meaning of participation in sporting activities and other modes of physicality for women. It is indeed such participation and the myriad forms of "embodied knowledge" gained therein that allows us to form a new definition of self. This definition gives us the courage to redefine the reality that has been constructed for us as women from the hegemonic masculine perspective to one that more accurately reflects the strength and beauty women truly manifest. Only when sufficient numbers of both women and men move to this transformed status, recognizing the worth of all human beings as equals, will we be able to state that we, as women, are no longer athletic intruders but instead an athletic presence to be recognized and honored. Each of the following chapters will take another step in this direction by providing a window for exploring the ways through which we are making our athletic presence known today.

REFERENCES

Abu-Lughod. Lila 1991. "Writing against Culture." In *Recapturing Anthropology: Working in the Present,* ed. R. Fox, 137–62. Santa Fe, NM: School of American Research Press.

Bateson, Mary Catherine. 1990. *Composing a Life: Life as a Work in Progress— The Improvisations of Five Extraordinary Women.* New York, NY: Plume Books.

Behar, Ruth. 1994. "Dare We Say 'I?' Bringing the Personal into Scholarship." *Chronicle of Higher Education* XL (43): B1–B2.

Blanchard, Kendall. 1995. *The Anthropology of Sport.* Westport, CT: Bergin and Garvey.

———, and Alyce Cheska. 1985. *The Anthropology of Sport.* Westport, CT: Bergin and Garvey.

Bolin, Anne. 1992. "Vandalized Vanity: Feminine Physiques Betrayed and Portrayed." In *Tattoo, Torture, Adornment and Disfigurement: The Denaturalization of the Body in Culture and Text,* ed. Francis Mascia-Lees and Patricia Sharpe, 79–99. Albany, NY: State University of New York Press.

———. 1997. "Flex Appeal, Food and Fat: Competitive Bodybuilding, Gender and the Diet." In *Building Bodies,* ed. Pamela S. Moore, 184–208. New Brunswick, NJ: Rutgers University Press (originally published 1992).

Brightman, Robert. 1995. "Forget Culture: Replacement, Transcendence, Reflexification." *Cultural Anthropology* 10 (4):509–46.

Borofsky, Robert, ed. 1994. "Introduction." In *Assessing Cultural Anthropology,* ed. Robert Borofsky, 1–21. New York, NY: McGraw-Hill.

———, ed. 1994. *Assessing Cultural Anthropology.* New York, NY: McGraw-Hill.

Clifford, James. 1983. "On Ethnographic Authority." *Representations* 1 (Spring):118–46.

———. 1986. "Introduction: Partial Truths." In *Writing Culture: The Poetics and Politics of Ethnography,* ed. James Clifford and George E. Marcus, 1–26. Berkeley, CA: University of California Press.

———, and George E. Marcus, eds. 1986. *Writing Culture: The Poetics and Politics of Ethnography.* Berkeley, CA: University of California Press.

Cohen, Eugene N., and Edwin Eames. 1982. *Cultural Anthropology.* Boston, MA: Little, Brown and Company.

Connell, Robert W. 1987. *Gender and Power.* Stanford, CA: Stanford University Press.

De Garis, Laurence. 1999. "Experiments in Pro Wrestling: Toward a Performative and Sensuous Sport Ethnography." *Sociology of Sport Journal* 16:65–74.

Fabian, J. 1990. *Power and Performance: Ethnographic Explorations through Proverbial Wisdom and Theater in Shaba, Zaire.* Madison, WI: University of Wisconsin Press.

Guedon, Marie Francoise. 1994. "*Dene* Ways and the Ethnographer's Culture." In *Being Changed by Cross-Cultural Encounters: the Anthropology of Extraordinary Experience,* ed. David E. Young and Jean-Guy Goulet, 39–70. Orchard Park, NY: Broadview Press.

Hall, M. Ann. 1996. *Feminism and Sporting Bodies: Essays on Theory and Practice.* Champaign, IL: Human Kinetics.

Huizinga, Johan. 1944. *Homo Ludens: A Study of Play Elements in Culture.* Boston, MA: Beacon Press.

Kimmel, Michael S., and Michael A. Messner. 1992. "Introduction." In *Men's Lives,* ed. Michael S. Kimmel and Michael A. Messner, 1–11. New York, NY: Macmillan Publishing Co.

Klein, Allan M. 1991. *Sugarball: The American Game, The Dominican Dream.* New Haven, CT: Yale University Press.

———. 1993. *Little Big Men: Bodybuilding Subculture and Gender Construction.* Albany, NY: State University of New York Press.

———. 1997. *Baseball on the Border: A Tale of Two Laredos.* Princeton, NJ: Princeton University Press.

Loy, John W. 1968. "The Nature of Sport: A Definitional Effort." *Quest* 10:1–5.

MacNeill, Margaret. 1988. "Active Women, Media Representations, Ideology." In *Not Just a Game,* ed. Jean Harvey and H. Cantelon, 195–212. Atona, Ottowa, Canada: University of Ottowa Press.

Marcus, George, and Michael M. J. Fischer. 1986. *Anthropology as Cultural Critique: An Experimental Moment in the Human Sciences.* Chicago, IL: University of Chicago Press.

Messner, Michael. 1992. "Boyhood, Organized Sports, and the Construction of Masculinities." In *Men's Lives,* ed. Michael S. Kimmel and Michael A. Messner, 161–76. New York, NY: Macmillan Publishing Co.

Rabinow, Paul. 1986. "Representations Are Social Facts: Modernity and Post-Modernity in Anthropology." In *Writing Culture,* ed. James Clifford and George E. Marcus, 234–61. Berkeley, CA: University of California Press.

Salzman, Philip C. 1999. *The Anthropology of Real Life.* Prospect Heights, IL: Waveland Press.

Sands, Robert R. 1999. *Sport and Culture, At Play in the Fields of Anthropology.* Needham Heights, MA: Simon and Schuster Custom Publishing.

Scupin, Raymond, and Christopher R. DeCorse. 1998. *Anthropology: A Global Perspective.* Upper Saddle River, NJ: Prentice Hall.

Skomal, Susan. 1994. "Lessons for the Field: Ethics in Fieldwork." *Anthropology Newsletter* 35:1,4.

Theberge, Nancy. 1987. "Sport and Women's Empowerment." *Women's Studies International Forum* 10:387–93.

Turner, Edith. 1994. "A Visible Spirit Form in Zambia." In *Being Changed by Cross-Cultural Encounters: The Anthropology of Extraordinary Experience,* ed. David E. Young and Jean-Guy Goulet, 71–95. Orchard Park, NY: Broadview Press.

Turner, Victor, and Edward Bruner, eds. 1986. *The Anthropology of Experience.* Urbana, IL: University of Illinois Press.

Young, David E. 1994. "Visitors in the Night: A Creative Energy Model of Spontaneous Visions." In *Being Changed by Cross-Cultural Encounters: The Anthropology of Extraordinary Experience,* ed. David E. Young and Jean-Guy Goulet, 166–208. Orchard Park, NY: Broadview Press.

CHAPTER TWO

Just "Tri" and "Du" It:
The Variable Impact of
Female Involvement in the
Triathlon/Duathlon Sport Culture

JANE GRANSKOG

INTRODUCTION

Since the late 1970s there has been a significant increase in the number
of women participating in athletic activities. The focus of this chapter is
on the process by which women become involved in fitness activities,
specifically multi-sport participation in triathlons (swim/bike/run events)
and duathlons (run/bike events) and the correspondent variable impact
that said involvement has upon their lives. While there are a number of
common patterns in both the process by which women begin engaging in
athletic pursuits and the impact that doing so has on their lives, there are
also noteworthy differences in the level, extent, and impact of such participation. In the past I have explored aspects of the socialization process
for becoming a triathlete (Granskog 1991) as well as the impact of participation on the lives of selected older women who completed the
Hawaiian ultra-distance triathlon (Granskog 1992). The focus of this
research was on the commonalities of the athletic experience for such

women, with particular attention being placed upon the personal empowerment they attained as a result of their participation.

Now I shall focus on the *variable* nature of this participation and its impact based on an examination of the lives of four selected women who vary in age (from their late twenties to their early fifties at the starting point of this investigation), triathlon experience and capability, and correspondent involvement in the sport culture. Each case will be examined in terms of how each woman has dealt with key issues in her life over an eight-year span (1988 to 1996) and how participation in the triathlete lifestyle has impacted the manner in which those issues were handled. It is argued that the variable nature of participation can be defined in terms of three interactive factors: the degree and type of involvement in the sport culture, specifically as measured by the number and type of races one enters and completes; the nature and strength of one's athletic support network as reflected in the characteristics of one's training partners and familial response to participation; and the life stage one is in (twenties, thirties, forties, and beyond) and the impact that this, along with the other factors, has upon one's definition of self—and, more specifically, on one's gender role identity and the salience of one's sport identity. Within the context of these three factors, the degree of involvement and impact of participation also depends on the ebb and flow of one's life—one's ongoing assessment of current and future priorities, which, in turn, involves the dynamics of interaction with significant others and perceptions of one's physical and emotional state of well being at a given point in time.

In a number of respects the narratives of the four individuals presented herein are unique. They do not represent the average story of women who decide to incorporate an exercise regimen into their lives and then do so. While they vary in terms of their age, personal background, age at the onset of their athletic participation, and level of competitive performance, they also share a number of characteristics. They all began participating in triathlons between 1983 and 1985. They all come from, and are currently members of, the middle class. Most importantly, they have all taken their level of participation in the multi-sport culture of triathlons to the ultimate level—they have all participated in ultra-distance endurance triathlons and have qualified for and completed the Hawaiian Ironman World Championship Triathlon. They all share a common identity as Ironwomen triathletes.

The description and analysis presented herein are based upon my participation and involvement in triathlon and duathlon activities since 1984. As a result of my participation, I have been able to conduct a number of informal interviews with participants at varying levels—from first-timers to professionals—as well as with race directors, organizers, and volunteers in different parts of the country. Although most of the events I have participated in have been in California, I have raced in ten other states in the Midwest, Southwest, and West from Illinois to Hawaii as well. I have also gathered field notes based on my observations and informal discussions with members of the triathlon community with whom I train and interact on a regular basis. Each of the case studies presented here were based upon several in-depth interviews conducted at various times between 1988 and 1994 with a final follow-up in 1996; the content of the interviews was also discussed and reviewed with each participant. Thus, because I share my research observations and analysis with my fellow triathletes, my insights into the character of this lifestyle and its impact upon individuals are not solely mine. This is, for the most part, a collaborative effort—an analysis of experiences and perceptions shared by and with fellow multi-sport enthusiasts.

The research methodology employed herein thus has two key interactive components. First, it is based on traditional anthropological participant-observation fieldwork with a focus on descriptive life histories as the major data resource. In this regard it can be defined as a qualitative, interpretative approach within the framework delineated by Langness and Frank (1981), Watson and Watson-Franke (1985), and others. Second, and more importantly, it is "insider" research carried out from a feminist perspective. As Abu Lughod (1991) and other feminist researchers (Moore 1988; Hall 1996; Birrell 1988) have argued, the relationship between the researcher and researched as well as the cultural and historical context within which the research is conducted have a significant impact on the kind of research questions addressed and the interpretations reached. This is particularly critical when we wish to examine the nature of the dialectic interaction between gender and sport as it impacts the lives of individuals.

The importance of clarifying the context within which research is conducted, as well as the assumptions on which the research is based, is a dominant theme in current feminist research, regardless of the particular issues being addressed. In her summary overview of feminist methodology, Harding (1987) delineates three distinctive features of recent feminist research that are relevant in this regard. First is the emphasis on viewing the issues addressed "from the perspective of women's experiences" and using "these experiences as a significant indicator of the 'reality' against which hypotheses are tested" (p. 7). An important part of this emphasis is on the diversity of women's experiences based on their differential ethnic, racial, class, and cultural background—there is no singular category that all women necessarily share. Furthermore, not only do our experiences vary across cultural lines, but they also may conflict within a given individual's experience over time.

A second focus is on designing research for women that provides explanations of phenomena that women want and need rather than male-defined interests that typically have been the focus of much traditional social research. A third emphasis is upon the importance of studying ourselves, or as Harding puts it, insisting that "the inquirer her/himself be placed in the same critical plane as the overt subject matter, thereby recovering the entire research process for scrutiny in the results of research. That is, the class, race, culture, and gender assumptions, beliefs, and behaviors of the researcher her/himself must be placed within the frame of the picture that she/he attempts to paint" (p. 9).

I would argue that this effort to make manifest and reflect upon the nature of the relationship between researcher and researched, with an emphasis on exploring the particulars of women's experiences that Harding discusses, illustrates both the opportunities and advantages as well as the limitations of conducting "insider" research. One of the commonly mentioned limitations of doing insider research lies precisely in one of its major strengths (that, as an insider, one is too close to the subject matter) and may for that reason overlook key dimensions (particularly perceived negative aspects or characteristics of said activities) that may be more apparent to someone who is not as involved in the activity or subject matter being investigated. Historically, in the development of scientific inquiry, we have given precedence to the value of objectivity. There is a correspondent underlying uneasiness with employing a subjective approach in that it is often perceived as reflecting a bias that taints the conclusions or value of one's interpretations. If we are to get at the underlying meaning of a phenomenon, if we are to seek to decode the significance of the key symbols present in that which is being investigated, we necessarily have to consider the impact of the ideas, theoretical constructs, values, and everything else that we bring to the investigation.

This is precisely the point of much of the methodological debate that is currently going on regarding the processes involved in doing participant-observation fieldwork. Fieldwork is inherently intersubjective, a product of what we see to be the case based upon our background and awareness interwoven with that which is perceived by our informants (including their reaction to and interpretation of that which we are doing). Moreover, the strategies we develop to carry out research and the impact that they have on who we are and how we perceive our relationships with others are not static. They change and evolve depending on the ongoing discourse we maintain with others in a variety of contexts within the academic community and the larger public arena as well as within the fieldwork setting. In a very real sense, it is the communities within which we immerse ourselves that are critical in these emergent and potentially transforming definitions of self and other. The purpose of this study, within a larger framework, therefore, is to elucidate this process by including myself as one of the four case studies presented. By examining the discourse that I have maintained over the years with fellow triathletes, as well as with colleagues within the academic community, the broader context within which these arguments are set may be clarified.

THE SIGNIFICANCE OF STAGES IN ADULT DEVELOPMENT

The primary focus of this paper as noted above is in delineating the variable involvement of women in the triathlon/duathlon sport culture as well as the variable impact that such participation has on their sense of identity as women and athletes. There are two primary arenas in which this variability is expressed: in the process of becoming socialized into the sport culture and the correspondent establishment of the triathlete identity; and in the variable participation that occurs once one has an established triathlete identity within the community, based in part on the ebb and flow of one's life. In both instances a key component of this variability lies in the life stage one is in when one initiates participation. In other words, I am arguing that the process of attaining a triathlete identity, as well as the way and significance with which it is expressed, will not be the same for a single woman who begins in her twenties as it may be for a married woman with a family who begins participation in her late thirties or early forties.

Research over the past two decades on adult development (cf. Gould 1978; Lerner and Busch-Rossnagel 1981; Rossi 1985; Fiske and Chiriboga 1990) shows that there are significant differences in the issues that women and men face in terms of their definition of self, their definition of goals and priorities, and the way they respond to their life situation depending on their location in the different stages of the life cycle and the correspondent stressors with which they must deal. As Ryff (1985:98–99) has noted in her summary analysis of life-span research, the majority of the earlier literature on adult development comes out of psychology and is based on the life stage theories offered by Erik Erikson, Carl Jung, and others. The primary focus is on the psychosocial, personality changes that the individual goes through from birth to old age, with specific attention being given to the changes that occur during adulthood itself; the struggle with issues of identity and interpersonal intimacy during young adulthood; generativity (productivity and creativity) vs. stagnation during middle age; and issues of integrity (emotional integration and acceptance of the self) vs. despair during old age.

Gould (1978) is a good example of this approach. Based on clinical studies of American men and women, he addresses four central false assumptions that he argues predominate at different stages of adult life (pp. 40–41). The first assumption, "I'll always belong to my parents and believe in their world," is challenged between ages sixteen and twenty-two, when we leave our parent's world and seek to establish our own independence and identity as adults. The second assumption, "doing it their way, with will power and perseverance, will bring results" but if I am "unable to cope, they will step in and show me the right way," is challenged in one's twenties (between ages twenty-two and twenty-eight). During this time, our independence is established and we must make major decisions regarding work, marriage, and family. In learning to take responsibility for those choices, we develop strength and competence in our ability to deal with the external world. The third assumption, "life is simple and controllable," is challenged in our late twenties to early thirties (ages twenty-eight to thirty-four) "when most of the simple rules and supposed-to-be's about life prove ineffectual in the complicated real world." This is when we question the stable worldview of our twenties and begin to open up to a more realistic appraisal of our inner strengths and weaknesses. We begin to address the dynamics of our inner, emotionally defined world. The fourth assumption, "there is no evil or death in the world," "the sinister has been destroyed," is addressed in the mid-life decade from the late thirties into the forties, when we become more aware of the finality of life and our own vulnerability. It is also at this time that intergenerational issues of conflict and control emerge. We simultaneously are required to accept the reality of aging parents, who may be increasingly dependent on us in their old age, along with the demands of young adult children to reject parental control and go their own way. Only if we have been able to deal effectively with each of these challenges will we be able to achieve the final stage, beyond mid-life concerns with status and power, when attention is turned inward toward the integration and acceptance of all facets of ourselves.

According to Ryff, criticisms of Gould and other similar life stage theories center around the fact that they use a male-defined model of development that relies primarily upon male experiences that emphasize "chronological age as a key variable and continuous, uninterrupted series of events in family and occupational realms" and is, therefore, not as applicable to women's development (1985:100). Women's experiences involve a much greater variety of role patterns and sequences that are not so closely tied to chronological age. The timing of their transitions from one stage to another may thus vary significantly. Women's gender role identities are also much more likely to be defined by the relationships that they maintain with others—children, spouses, parents, friends, and co-workers. Such relationships are often central to their definition of self and must be considered, along with their location, within a given life stage. Other criticisms focus on the failure of such theories to assess adequately the significance of the cultural and historical context within which these transformations may take place as well as idiosyncratic stressors that impact the direction of one's life. For instance, the variety of role models and career options open to women as well as cultural attitudes toward variant choices made by women have changed significantly over the past forty years. Nonetheless, more recent research (Rossi 1985; Fiske and Chiriboga 1990) indicates that the primary issues confronting individuals at different stages of life, as delineated by Gould and others, still hold true even though much more research on specific cohorts needs to be done.

One important factor that is overlooked in much of the life-span research, however, is the underlying gender differences inherent in an individual's perception of the relationship between mind, body, and spirit and the correspondent impact this has upon one's personal identity at different points in the life cycle. The cultural dictates of American society stress the importance of youthfulness above all. We all, and women in particular, should strive to at least maintain the image of youthfulness for as long as possible. However, men become more distinguished and respected as they age; women just get old and gray. As Brown and Kerns (1985:5) note in their cross-cultural analysis of middle aged women, this perception of middle-age is characteristic of women in industrial societies. It is not, however, generally true of women in more traditional societies wherein women may gain significant power and status with middle age.

Women in our society also receive a constant barrage of media images that ties their sense of personal identity to the image that they project toward others, particularly males. Despite the significant increase in the number of working women and the changing realities of their lives, what women actually do and how they perceive themselves is still not as important as their appearance. Their bodies are objects to be constantly manipulated in order to achieve an unattainable ideal of youthful beauty. Once they turn thirty, the process of maintaining this youthful facade becomes increasingly difficult to carry out.

There is no doubt in my mind that for American women, body image, perception of femininity, and sense of personal identity are closely correlated with one another. For many, this also poses an impossible dilemma because our culture promotes a disembodiment and disparagement of the female self at the same time that it promotes an unattainable ideal body type as the only meaningful source of identity.

Beautiful women are less likely to be taken seriously or valued for their intellectual and other capabilities. Yet, at the same time, a primary means of attaining status and value, as a woman, is in terms of one's physical attributes. Moreover, it is this script, equating body image with self-worth, that is most often followed.

The significance of this perception is illustrated by the fact that every woman over thirty (including myself and most of the younger women as well) that I have interviewed cited the desire to lose weight and thereby improve one's body image as *the* major reason for starting an exercise program. One may hopefully thereby postpone the aging process and the loss of self-worth a bit longer. The crisis that women face as they move into middle age—from their thirties into their forties and beyond—is also compounded by the fact that the traditional feminine script defining their role as women via the care and nurturance of children also becomes less significant. Children grow up and move out. The lessening of their traditional responsibilities towards others coupled with the inevitable loss of a youthful image, in sum, can lead to an erosion of personal identity and self-concept.

Even though women may begin an exercise program to improve their image and forestall the inevitable, the consequences of doing so are much more far-reaching than most initially realize. Once one is "hooked" into an athletic lifestyle, one can never go back to what one was before. Aerobic exercise provides a vehicle for becoming tuned into oneself—in an emotional as well as a physical sense. There is a sense of strength and power from within that one attains through exercise that is not easily attained by other means. One becomes reconnected to one's body; with embodiment comes empowerment. Exercise thus becomes a major strategy for coping with the stresses and strains of daily life—a mechanism to facilitate the transition from one life stage to the next.

In this analysis the major transitions defined by Gould will be used as the basis for presenting the four cases discussed herein. Because of the length of time being covered for each case study, however, the ways in which each of these women have used their athletic endeavors to help them successfully move from one stage into the next will also be addressed. The four case studies representing four primary stages of adult development are as follows:

1. *From the Twenties into the Thirties: Defining the Self.* One of the key issues women in their twenties face is in establishing their identity and determining the life path they wish to follow. As noted above, according to societal dictates, the major life options a woman has to choose from remain the caretaker role of wife, mother, and nurturer or some combination of career and

wife/mother. Often, the latter is phrased as a choice between the role of career first, nurturer deferred, or vice versa. Women are still defined, to a large extent, in terms of their relationships to others and in their role as nurturers. For women who do not choose to follow this traditional path, the issue of defining the self becomes even more critical. Laura, my first case study, fits in this category. She began participating in triathlons and duathlons at age twenty-three; she has been a competitive runner since she was fourteen. However, the primary issue for her in her late twenties was in deciding what career to follow; the caretaker role of mother was never a seriously considered option. It should also be noted that participation in athletics for women at this stage, as well as the emphasis upon having a career, is not as critical or controversial for one's sense of identity as it may be for older women given the increased opportunities for sport participation since 1972 with the passage of Title IX and the significant increase of women in the workforce.

2. *Balancing the Demands of Family and Self—A Mother in Her Thirties.* For many women in their early thirties who chose marriage in their early twenties, the key issue revolves around balancing the demands of the family with their own needs, however nebulously those needs may be defined. Donna, the second case study, fits this category. Married at nineteen, she began triathloning in her late twenties when her first two children were still young. Although her triathlon activities have become an important part of defining her sense of self, the critical component of her identity remains her role as mother.

3. *The Midlife Crisis and the Redefining of Self.* As Gould and others have noted, a critical juncture in the life cycle usually begins in the mid- to late-thirties into one's forties. This is a time for a reassessment of who one is, what one's priorities are, and where one wants to be in the future. This may also be a time when women come into their own. Since I started triathloning when I was thirty-eight and am now past fifty, I will use my own experiences as a basis for discussing the issues of this stage.

4. *Bringing it All Together—Achieving Integration.* If one is successful in dealing with the midlife transition of the forties, this is the final stage wherein one may seek to achieve a sense of harmony and balance in one's life—to become more attuned to the inner spiritual dynamics of self. It is also a time when one begins to explore the meaning of menopause and how that impacts the sense of self and one's relationships with others. Betty is a woman in her fifties who

successfully used athletic participation and triathloning to negotiate that midlife transition and is now experiencing the joy of entering "cronehood." She will be the case study for this stage.

THE CULTURAL CONTEXT

Prior to discussing each of the case studies it is necessary to describe the cultural context that has served to define and shape the nature of our involvement in multi-sports. Bakersfield is a mid-sized city located in the southern portion of the Central Valley of California (a state long touted as the mecca for triathletes). We have had strong running and cycling clubs in the area since the 1970s and an active triathlon club since the mid-1980s. We also have one of the most active, dedicated local parks and recreation districts in the country—the North Bakersfield Recreation and Parks District (NBRPD)—which works with the local clubs and promotes sporting activities in the region.

There are two triathlon events that the NBRPD has put on that have played a key role in the socialization process for triathletes. First, from 1982 to 1992, the NBRPD conducted a winter and summer series of time trial triathlons. (These were discontinued after 1992 primarily because of budget cuts, a change in the management of NBRPD and also because interest had tapered off.) Each series consisted of six time trials held two to three weeks apart. Each time trial had three separate events—a 10-mile time trial bike race followed by a 3.1 mi. (5K) run and a 600-yard pool swim in the winter (400 yards in the summer). Individuals would do as many of the events as they wished. The emphasis of these time trials was to help individuals, especially those with little experience, prepare for participating in a triathlon. In most cases they were used as a means of preparation for the Bakersfield Bud Light Triathlon (BBLT)—the major event of the year—that has been held on the outskirts of the city since May 1981. From 1983 to 1989, the BBLT consisted of a two-kilometer swim, a forty-kilometer bike, and a fifteen-kilometer cross-country run and was one of six regional qualifying races for the prestigious Ironman World Championship Triathlon in Hawaii (an ultradistance event consisting of a 2.4-mile ocean swim followed by a 112-mile bike ride and a 26.2-mile run). In 1990, in order to retain its status as one of three regional qualifying races for the Hawaiian Ironman, the bike event was lengthened to eighty kilometers. In 1991, however, due in part to decreased participation and an effort to increase local participation, the course was shortened again to a 1.5K swim, 40K bike, and 10K run. As a result, it gave up its Ironman qualifier status. The BBLT has also gained a national reputation for being one of the best-run events in the country as well as one of the toughest races in the region (because of the heat and nature of the hilly run course). It is considered by local triathletes to be one of the most important, if not *the* most important, race of the year. Participating in this race marks one's confirmation as a "real" triathlete and a bona fide member of the triathlon community.

All of us began our participation in triathlons with the time trials. The BBLT was also the first triathlon in which each of us participated. The BBLT also illustrates a number of the key attributes of the triathlete lifestyle—the socializing and camaraderie that take place beforehand, during registration and race packet pick-up, and after the event. In races of this distance there is little conversing during the event itself though one often gives encouragement to friends one sees out on the course. A major time for socializing and reviewing the day's performances is after the race is over, at the barbecue afterwards and during awards presentations.

The day following the BBLT is also important for marking the sense of family and socialization of the next generation of triathletes, for this is when the TRI FOR KIDS event takes place at the nearby California State University, Bakersfield campus. This is a mini-tri for seven to ten and eleven to fourteen year olds. The seven to ten year olds do a 100-yard swim, 3.1-mi. bike, and .6-mi. run; the eleven to fourteen year olds do double that distance. The local triathletes who do the BBLT serve as volunteers and organizers of the kids' event.

With this brief overview of the cultural context, I would now like to turn to each of the case studies.

CASE STUDY I: DEFINING THE SELF—THE STRUGGLING PROFESSIONAL

Laura is currently in her late thirties and has never been married. She has been active in athletics since the age of twelve and had particular success as a runner on the cross-country team both in high school in Des Moines, Iowa, and later in college in California. She and I began training in the three events in the fall of 1984, when she was twenty-three. The Bakersfield Bud Light Triathlon (BBLT) in May 1985 was her first triathlon, and the most difficult part of that for her was getting through the swim—having aggressive males swimming over the top of her was an overwhelming and frightening experience, one she had difficulty dealing with until she completed the Hawaiian Ironman World Championship Triathlon for the first time in 1989. Having to battle the waves with 1,400 other competitors for 2.4 miles made her aware that she could indeed swim over them and fight back if necessary.

Her primary focus throughout her childhood and into her twenties was on establishing her sense of self as an individual and aggressive achiever—as a student in the academic arena as well as in athletics. Defining her sense of self in terms of others and the traditional feminine role was never an issue. As a tomboy at age ten, she decided she did not want to marry; as a teenager, her dream was to compete in the Olympics. Defining herself in terms of her athletic pursuits has always been critical to her sense of identity. Running was also the major strategy she used to cope with the stresses of life. It became an important way to deal with the authoritarian structure of the Catholic schools she attended from elementary school through high school. As she puts it as "a painfully shy high school sophomore, who desperately wanted to shine as a star," the way to popularity was by becoming "the BEST runner on the cross-country team." She did so and continued to do so as a student in college. In 1985 she received the Outstanding Scholar-Athlete Award and the President's Award for the Outstanding Student of the graduating class at California State University, Bakersfield. After finishing her M.A. in Sport Psychology in 1987, she decided to take a break in her academic studies and pursue a career as a professional biathlete/duathlete. From 1988 to 1991, she consistently ranked among the top ten duathletes in the United States. She placed in the top twenty women overall at the Hawaiian Ironman Triathlon World Championship in both 1989 and 1990. In 1991 she set a new course record and was the first overall woman at the Vineman Ironman Triathlon. Her primary focus in life, as she noted in a letter to her sponsors late in 1990, was "to represent the sports of triathlon and biathlon, as well as my sponsors, in the most professional manner I know. Because, as it is so often said, you create your own reality, so you might as well create the best one possible. And that's exactly what I intend to do!" Needless to say, that has been her attitude toward everything in life, regardless of the professional paths that she has chosen.

Laura's desire to continue as a professional athlete, however, was hampered by the limited opportunities and awards for her efforts that were available. Furthermore, she was not taken seriously as a professional athlete. As she noted, "people would ask me what I did for a living and when I told them I was a professional duathlete, they would then ask me what my 'real' job was." Her sense of identity as an athlete conflicted with the need to obtain a career through which she could adequately support herself and obtain a sense of legitimacy in her chosen career. The purse at various biathlons/duathlons also decreased from 1989 to 1990 and 1991 while the number of contenders for those awards increased. By March 1991 Laura had moved to Arizona and began teaching part-time at a community college while continuing to race as a professional duathlete and amateur triathlete. After completing her first Hawaiian Ironman Triathlon in 1989, she also realized that being an Ironwoman (and amateur triathlete moreso than a professional duathlete) was pivotal to her sense of identity. For her, it was the mark of true self-actualization and empowerment. As she noted:

> The significance of '89 was the fact that I could actually go out and compete for ten hours and twenty-seven minutes or ten and a half hours and the fact that I had the strength from within to do so. I mean, [it's a] transformative experience—I have not been the same person since. It was a spiritual quest, as I tell my students, when I go out to Hawaii, or any triathlon for that matter, but particularly Hawaii, I'm out there self-actualizing on the fields.

Even though she had begun her academic career by 1991, her core identity remained as an athlete. She describes it as being an "academic athlete" rather than an "athletic academic."

The strain of holding down several jobs, teaching a heavy schedule, and continuing to "push the envelope" with extensive training, however, took its toll. Early in 1993 she became very ill, first with a virus and then with periodic bouts of chronic fatigue. It was the strength of the Ironman experience, the ability to persevere under the most difficult of circumstances, that she used to get through that difficult period. It was also during this time that she began to pay more attention to the interaction between her mental and physical states—to look within and assess the significance of the impact of her emotional state on all areas of her life. This had been brought home earlier with particular clarity during the 1991 Hawaiian Ironman. During the 112-mile bike ride she refrained from urinating while riding because she didn't want to get her new race bike dirty or lose any time. By mile eighty-five her urethra went into spasm, she could not urinate even though she tried, and she spent the next almost thirty miles in "complete and utter agony"; it took everything she had within herself just to finish the bike segment. After almost forty-five minutes in the medical tent in the transition area, she was able to relieve herself. And although the medical personnel wanted her to drop out of the race, she insisted on finishing the event. As she noted, "they thought I was crazy, but I ran one of my best times for the marathon." Reflecting on this experience later on, she said "I paid too much attention to the external aspects, I mean, I looked at my body as an object, something I could control and I found out that you just can't do that. When your body tells you something, you better listen; it's telling you something about yourself. The interconnections between the mind and the body are incredible."

In an interview in late 1991, while she was still a part-time instructor in Arizona, I asked Laura if she could describe the critical struggle that she had to face during this period in terms of her sense of identity. She summed it up as follows:

Well, the critical sense was the identity itself. It was trying to validate my existence and my definition of who and what I was as an adult, OK? Erik Erikson talks about it. I know I'm being totally psychological here, but that's my context, my window, if you will, my lookout to the world. Erik Erikson talks about the eight stages of humans . . . in terms of psychosocial development. One stage he talks about in particular is the "ego identity" versus "role confusion" stage, which most adolescents encounter at the time of pubescence or high school or whatnot. And basically what he says is that either an adolescent, a person, develops a strong sense of who one is and what one stands for along with accepting adulthood and the developing adult sense of self along with the occupational roles and duties that go along with that . . . or they do not, and then they find themselves—or one finds him or herself—in role confusion. That is to say, a lack of ego identity, a non-acceptance of the adult responsibilities. And . . . I saw very much a part of myself, up until this year, in that stage. I've been fixated in that stage for the last twelve years. I've never truly resolved that crisis that Erikson talks about—ego identity versus role confusion. I have never truly felt that I had an adult role or a valid self, or a valid sense of who or what I was and unfortunately . . . in our society we define ourselves as an adult by making money . . . or choosing the role, for females, choosing the traditional roles of housewifedom and motherhood. . . . Because I didn't choose that I felt an . . . angst, a true identity crisis. I mean, that's what Erikson talks about, that if one doesn't develop an ego identity, then, one will therefore fall into role confusion, which, in turn, results in identity crisis, OK? We talk about identity crisis occurring in middle adulthood, but it can also occur during the stages of a lack of accepting adult responsibilities. And I really do believe that was exactly what I was doing . . . that's the way I felt. I felt like an adolescent still in angst, not having yet found my true role in life too well. . . . And/or if you don't choose the traditional role of motherhood . . . you still have to make a choice in terms of making your own way as a career. . . . Identity is defined in terms of what you do. What is your occupation? So what do you do for a living? You know? I mean, how many times have I been asked that prior to this year, and I have felt so much at a loss, I mean, so embarrassed and humiliated, if you will.

But I just know for myself, psychologically speaking, that the only way in which I could feel as though I were validating myself was to establish a "career identity," an adult occupational role, if you will, OK? I really feel that I have been suffering. . . . I mean, yes, professional biathlon has brought me a tremendous sense of celebrity, a tremendous sense of physical fitness, but it never fulfilled me completely, OK? I'm not saying that my career now fulfills me completely either. It's so new to me at this point in time, and the fact that I've never made more than the amount of money that I'm making now, and it is a paltry amount of money that I'm making—less than a thousand a month—but because I've never made that much money before, I feel validated, I feel psychologically secure. I have a job. I mean, I'm looked upon, even though I don't see myself as a professor, that's what people call me, Professor. I'm an instructor at a community college. I mean, that is a valid role to have.

Because there was very little chance of obtaining a full-time teaching position in Arizona, she returned to Bakersfield in the fall of 1993, and shortly thereafter obtained a teaching position at the local community college. By 1996 she was teaching full-time at the community college in addition to training for ultradistance triathlon events. In October of 1994 she participated in the inaugural ultradistance Maui Ironteam and Individual Triathlon Championship in Hawaii (a 2.4-mile swim, 112-mile bike, and 26.2-mile run) and came in as the first woman overall (eleventh overall including the men). In 1995 she competed in three Iron distance events within the space of ten weeks: she set a new course record for women at the Vineman Ironman Triathlon in July, came in first woman overall at the Maui Triathlon in early September and completed the Hawaiian Ironman in October. Although her athletic identity is no longer the means by which she makes a living, it remains critical to how she views herself and the world around her as well as her primary mechanism for coping with the politics of a male-defined workplace. It is also integrated within her professional life as a health/sport psychologist and community college instructor.

CASE STUDY II: BALANCING FAMILY AND SELF— THE NURTURANT MOTHER

By our last interview in 1996 Donna had just turned forty-two and was married, with four children—a twenty-one-year-old daughter, and three sons, ages seventeen, five, and four. She grew up in the San Diego area and married at age nineteen after her first year in college. Sports were what her brothers did well, but as she noted:

> . . . being the oldest and being a girl I never did. And there was nothing to help me develop that, there was more of a sense that I would not have to ever go to work . . . and there was the feeling, the attitude that if you go to church every Sunday that's really all you really need to know. . . . Your education is not important, your sports are not important, go to church every Sunday and you will learn everything you need to know for life. Be a good mother and a good wife. So then, you'll be taken care of all your life.

Being a good wife and mother has been critical to Donna's sense of identity. She started running in about 1982 while in her mid-twenties because a friend with whom she played racketball thought it would be a good idea. (She began to play racketball primarily because the facility where she played provided childcare services.) Another friend that she met had gone over to Hawaii and watched several triathletes from Bakersfield complete the Ironman; she had also watched friends complete the local BBLT. Both decided that they wanted to do the BBLT and proceeded to do the local triathlon time trials in preparation. Both also had small children who rode around with them on their bicycles. When they proceeded to do the ten-mile bike time trial, they received considerable teasing—especially from male cyclists—about leaving the baby baskets on their bikes. Donna borrowed a bicycle from a local bike shop in order to do the BBLT that year (1983) and was just happy to finish. In 1988, using a much more sophisticated racing bike, she came in second in her age group at the BBLT and qualified for and later completed the Hawaiian Ironman. In 1989 she described the impact of her participation in triathlon activities not just in terms of herself but in terms of the impact that it has had upon her family as well. As she put it:

> Running and triathloning is very tangible. My kids can see how tangible it is. . . . My daughter knows that she cannot run four miles without being totally exhausted . . . five miles, ten miles, she sees [me running] that and it gives her a respect for my strength and my determination and the fact that I can set goals and stick with them. . . . And the same thing with my son, I mean, he might be rough and tough and try to be the big guy on the playground . . . but he also sees me, that I have a sense of commitment too and I think when your kids see you having a sense of commitment, that is a good example that you can set for them, as a wonderful example. How many people have the opportunity to set that kind of example for their kids? Most parents go to work and kids don't know what their parents do. They have some kind of job that someone is paying them for what's going on in their mind but in the physical sense others can see . . . others can relate . . . it's tangible . . . running and triathloning to other people is something tangible that they can see . . .
>
> I've always told [my husband] I wouldn't be in this position that I am without you so I really think that my successes are your successes. And I think that it makes me understand. He was carrying me along with his successes of CPA and I didn't understand that I was a part of his success and now I understand that . . . me making a stable environment and family for him, I was a part of his success just as I think that he is a part of my successes because he has allowed me the time . . . to be myself and to go out and pursue this and to make me the best person that I can possibly be. And I feel that . . . all that running has done for me selfishly I feel that I have given back to the community, back to my family, back to everyone, because

I'm just a better person and I think that I advocate for good health and well being just in who I am and what I do. And I used to have to run at 5 A.M. in the morning because I thought I had to be as productive with my day as any working individual had to be with their day. And I could not allow myself the leisure to run during daytime working hours . . . that the only time I could run was I had to get up early and do it just like the men had to do it because I could not let it interfere with my life. This was not a stipulation my husband put on me, this is one that I put on myself. That if I was going to recreate I could not recreate during working hours. I had to clean my house during working hours and I could recreate [only after hours] . . .

That . . . changed, with my training for the Ironman . . . my husband was the first one who ever told me "I want you to take care of yourself. We are all going to make sure that you take care of yourself and you be good to yourself." After the Ironman, I realized that I do give a lot and there is time for me in my day to enjoy pastimes, to enjoy recreating, to enjoy my running and to do it in the day and to continue to get my eight hours of sleep. I don't need to live on five hours of sleep just so that I can run. . . . The one thing that I think that a lot of women fall into the trap of, if they have the luxury of training, or I don't know if a lot of women do, but I fell into the trap that here I had the luxury and the time to train but . . . I felt I needed to commit that time to other things and that my recreating, my pastime, my hobby which was running, I would have to do that after hours. And now I realize . . . and . . . [my husband] affords me the opportunity, my kids afford me the opportunity, and I mostly allow myself the opportunity . . . that's the bottom, that's the biggest change, I allow myself the opportunity now to train when I want to train. I'm still efficient with my time when I'm not training . . . we used to think that we had to be super everything and I think that I am moving away from the idea that I have to be super everything. We're all just human and we all make mistakes and we all do the best that we can and you know sometimes you have to say no to certain things, you can't say yes to everything.

To sum it up:

Training for the Ironman gave me the opportunity to be good to myself; it taught me how to pace myself in life, how to be more patient with myself and with others, how to manage my life better. Before, I had low self-esteem and sought to define myself in terms of my husband and children. I never felt that I was good enough as a mother or as a wife. Now I have learned how to balance my own priorities (what's good for me) with those of significant others more. Learning how to put myself first is still my greatest weakness but now I know who I am—I am strong and I can do anything that I set my mind to do.

Even after completing the Hawaiian Ironman for the first time in 1988, Donna did not feel that she deserved all the attention she had received for completing this event. She decided to try to qualify for it again and did so at another ultradistance event (the World's Toughest Triathlon at Lake Tahoe) in August 1989. Doing so allowed her to accept her athletic accomplishments as legitimate. She had also decided to go back to school (at California State University, Bakersfield) at the same time. In part because of the personal changes she went through as a result of her athletic achievements, her school activities, and the cost in time and money that it would take to return to do the Hawaiian Ironman, she decided not to do it after all. During this time she also went through a re-evaluation of her marriage.

Critical to her finding a new sense of identity as an individual in her own right—during this transitional period—in addition to her role as mother, was the acknowledgement that if she could do the Ironman, she could handle any difficulty that came her way. She also wanted to share in the development of others by becoming an elementary school teacher and, to this end, continued her college education. When asked what were the significant markers that stood out in this period, she put it this way:

> Yes, '89 to '90 was . . . total fear but just knowing . . . just using the same discipline that I had used for . . . triathloning, and training for and doing the Ironman; just the idea that you take it one step at a time. . . . You just stay consistent and persistent and you just plod along and you cannot, you can't move things any faster then they're meant to move, you can't make things happen that aren't meant to happen, you have to be able to work with your environment. . . . There is a certain growth process. . . . And I can say that during that year that I was on my own, I used that time not to focus on what [my husband] needed to do but what I needed to do to make myself a better person, a more whole person . . . school, taking care of myself and my kids and . . . I don't know but a lot of things have happened since then too. Probably Ironman experience moves into all the other areas of my life since that time. Especially when it comes to taking on new challenges, and conquering fears and that there's a certain exhilaration that comes along with conquering fears when you look at something like . . . on the bike ride where you're going up the hill or coming down the hill. As you're going up the hill you're not quite sure what you're going to find on the other side but . . . sometimes going down the hill can be fearful but you just . . . allow yourself to go with it. . . . You just don't resist. You move with your environment, you move in sync with your environment.
>
> . . . And I have been a different mother, a different person . . . I think I was a good mother and a good person before . . . I think it's on a different level or . . . on a different plane now, so to speak.
>
> . . . [We have to] learn to love ourselves . . . because you have to go through that dark side of yourself to go and to do Ironman because you're putting yourself on the line, what if you don't finish, what are you going to

do, you know? Or if your body breaks down, or you fall apart, you have to deal with those . . . all of those fears, those things. But you know it's been interesting to me because not too many people will go through a separation as lengthy and at a time where the person who has asked for the separation is just really in a self absorbed state where they know that they just need to grow more. [Jane: And that's what you were in?] Oh absolutely. A personal growth. I just had to do it and it had to be something where I had to see if I could do it. I do not know how to explain it. I had to . . . and then coming back as a more whole person, having been able to accomplish that what you set out to accomplish and to come back.

After a period of separation from her husband, they were able to work out their differences and reunited. The nature of their relationship, however, was significantly different; both placed more attention on the importance of maintaining quality family time. Shortly after reuniting with her husband, she became pregnant with a third child, and then about a year later, pregnant with a fourth. Her husband played an important nurturant role for both infants; a role he had not carried out for the first two children. As she noted, "I may have been the mother but . . . we equally shared the mother responsibility. . . . That's *very* much how our family operated and I did not feel any less of a person to have [my husband] move in, in some of the nurturing, mothering capacities and I felt pretty strong in other areas."

While Donna has put her athletic activities on the back burner for the present, she still continues to exercise and plans on continuing her triathloning when her youngest children are older. Her athletic activities remain an important part of her identity but they are incorporated into her roles as a wife, mother, and soon-to-be teacher, which are equally important. When asked to summarize the important features of this stage of her life in an interview in late 1994, she noted the following:

First I wanted to say that I'm in control but you know, that's not the word that I want to use. It's like my life is in balance, there's a balance. OK? . . . There's things around that can happen and there's highs and lows and whatever but . . . I'm able to work with elements and the challenges and not try to overcome them or push them, but work with them. It's like juggling some balls. And sometimes a ball will fall, you know, but hey, you just pick it back up and you just keep juggling. And it just works. And also, . . . moving in a forward direction . . . I used to feel stagnant and stuck. And [now] I feel like I'm moving, I feel like . . . there's this journey, I'm enjoying the journey.

[And it's] just the idea that you can make it, you made it through other tough times. . . . It's almost as if you're plugging along in the run [of the Ironman] and you're not saying, "I've got to get to the finish now," there's a sense that . . . you're going to get there. There's a faith, a hope there, too, that things are going to work out. And I felt that the whole time I did Iron-man. There was this . . . incredible sense of knowing and not trying to get anywhere before you were supposed to be there, but take it with the pace that it is supposed to be taken at, at the pace that it is given to you, and at the pace that you know. . . . It's like the idea that "Gee, am I . . . darn it, I gotta poop, am I going to stop at the bathroom or just going to [keep on running]? Well, you know, at a certain point you better stop because you're not going to be able to run with a loaded pair of pants! You know? You can only fight it so much. You just have to go with the flow.

CASE STUDY III: THE MIDLIFE CRISES AND THE FINDING OF SELF

My story is similar to the others in terms of the process of becoming a triathlete. However, the impact of participation upon how I define myself is different because I began participation during that critical period of transition between the ages of thirty-five and forty-five. I learned how to swim in college and used my bicycle as my only means of transportation while in graduate school. There were no opportunities for women to participate in organized athletics in the Upper Peninsula of Michigan where I grew up, although I did do a considerable amount of farmwork as a youngster. In addition to having a farm, my father was also the vocational agricultural teacher at the local high school. My mother started out as an elementary school teacher and then later went back to school to obtain a Masters degree and, at the age of fifty-four, a Ph.D. Although I knew I was going to be a scientist by the time I was in the eighth grade, I did not decide to major in anthropology until my freshman year in college. I have never looked back. I chose a career in anthropology over marriage and children.

Immediately after finishing my B.S. degree, I enrolled in the graduate program at the University of Texas at Austin. My research for my Ph.D. dissertation entailed spending two years in the more remote areas of Mexico. Throughout my twenties and into my thirties, therefore, my major source of identity was as an anthropologist. After graduate school, I obtained a teaching position at California State College, Bakersfield. After teaching for about ten years, at age thirty-seven, I was disenchanted with my life, with where and what I was doing. I had initiated a number of research projects during that time period but none really held my interest.

I began to swim and bike again on a regular basis—for the first time since graduate school—in the spring and summer of 1984. I did so primarily to lose some weight and get back into shape before my twenty-year high school reunion. I also took a class to Oaxaca, Mexico, that summer and one of the students was the cross-country runner, Laura, who insisted on running every day. Since I did not want her to run alone, I agreed to run with her every morning to the best of my ability at the time. Within several weeks after our return to the states, she encouraged me to enter my first 10K (6.2 mile) race. Later that fall, when out riding my bike with several friends, we saw an announcement for a triathlon and decided that, since we were already doing all three activities, we might as well try to do one.

My first triathlon was the local BBLT in May 1985. I came in third in my age group at that race and have never looked back. That first year, I completed three more triathlons and two duathlons in addition to participating in the local time trials. I also became fascinated with the way participation affected my sense of self. Each year after that I competed in more and more races. In 1986 I backed off in terms of the amount of racing I did but continued my training activities. In 1987 I completed over fifteen triathlons and biathlons and qualified for and completed the Hawaiian Ironman for the first time in addition to three marathons. I also took two quarters of sabbatical leave in order to study the social networks of female triathletes. In 1988 and 1989 I competed much more than I had done before—a total of more than forty-five races each year, including time trials and local running events as well as Ironman and other triathlons and duathlons. In 1990 and 1991 I did fewer races but more long events, including two Ironman distance events each year. In the 1990 Hawaiian Ironman, under brutal conditions, I was blown over by a wind gust of more than forty-five mph halfway through the bike leg but got back on and finished the race. The high point during this period was finishing third in the forty-five to forty-nine age group at the Hawaiian Ironman World Championship Triathlon in 1991. The same year I was ranked among the top ten women in my age group as a *Triathlon Today* All-American.

I cannot imagine not participating in this lifestyle. It has totally transformed my view of myself and of the world around me. It is a major focus of my ongoing research. I know I can achieve anything I put my mind to. Completing the Hawaiian Ironman in 1987, 1988, 1989, 1990, 1991, and again in 1995 has just reinforced that feeling. There is a wholeness to my life, a sense of self-actualization, that I did not have before. Nonetheless, I, too, have learned that there is an ebb and flow to everyone's life and that one cannot continue at the same breakneck pace forever. In 1992, while seeking to qualify for my sixth Hawaiian Ironman (and eighth ultradistance triathlon), I sustained an injury (achilles tendinitis) and was unable to train for over six weeks. Then, during the summer of 1993, after qualifying for the Hawaiian Ironman in May, I became increasingly allergic to chlorinated pool water (with sinus problems compounded by skin rashes after even short periods in the water) and was forced to withdraw from the Ironman event. Since then I have had a number of recurrent injuries that have affected my participation.

The most important fact that I have learned from the ebb and flow of my participation in this lifestyle is in terms of its effect on my core identity. It was only when I became injured that I began to explore exactly what participation really meant to me on an emotional, internal level. It has been the impact of participation on my body that has forced me to reflect on and reevaluate the broader meaning of my participation in the sport itself. I have since learned to strive for a more balanced perspective on all that I do—most importantly, to listen to my body. Training and participating in the triathlon lifestyle, and particularly in ultra-distance events, is an engrained part of my identity. I also completed the Maui Ironteam and Individual Triathlon Championship in October of 1994, as well as the three Iron distance events in 1995, with Laura, as noted above. Now my definition of self has three critical components. I am a woman, an Ironwoman triathlete, and an anthropologist. And in every respect it is the validation and support I receive from significant others in my life, friends and family, that re-affirms and makes each of those definitions of self meaningful. I will continue to participate in this lifestyle for the rest of my life, maybe not at the same level or intensity, but I will be out there "tri-ing and du-ing" to the best of my ability. Moreover, it is the embodiment of these experiences that continues to inform my research. It is the embodiment of these experiences that lies at the root of the sense of empowerment I feel that defines who I am.

CASE STUDY IV: ACHIEVING BALANCE AND INTEGRATION

Betty's story is similar to mine in terms of the process of establishing her triathlete identity. Her level of involvement as measured by the number of races she competes in, however, is significantly different. In 1996 she was fifty-nine, with three grown children ranging in age from twenty-eight to thirty-four, and had been married for thirty-six years. She had come out to California from Georgia to teach after receiving her B.A., met her husband in her first year, got married, and continued to teach one more year before stopping to raise her children. At age thirty-six, by her own admission, she was overweight, smoked too much, and did not know what to do with herself. On a visit back East she noticed the new health and vitality of her sister, who had taken up jogging. With the encouragement and support of her sister, Betty, too, started to run. She had never participated in any athletic activities while growing up. Her husband also began running about the same time. In 1984, after ten years of running (including a number of marathons), she watched her husband complete the Bakersfield Bud Light Triathlon (BBLT) for the first time and saw how much he enjoyed it. Several days after the event, while on a training run together, he suggested that she might like to do the event. That encouragement gave her the incentive to do the same. She immediately went out and purchased a bathing suit (with considerable trepidation) and enrolled in a swimming class at the University so she could learn to swim. The next year (1985) she did the BBLT as her first triathlon. Her primary goal (as with all of us in our first race) was simply to finish. Two years later, when her good friend Susan qualified for the Ironman at the BBLT, she too decided to try to do the same and did so a month later at a half Ironman race in Monterey Bay (a 1.2-mile swim, 56-mile bike, and 13.1-mile run). She completed the Hawaiian Ironman for the second time in 1989. When asked whether participation in this lifestyle changed her life in terms of her sense of self, as well as her relationships with others, her response was an emphatic yes. As she noted:

> It has been revolutionary. It has brought such a sense of joy and empowerment to my life, . . . one that simply intensified after finishing the Ironman. Participating in this lifestyle has given me the courage to do some inner homework, to change inside. I see the major benefit of participation in the whole person development—mental, physical, emotional, and spiritual—that I have achieved. I continue to grow more every day. It's simply wonderful.

Needless to say, when asked (in 1989) if she could ever give up triathloning, her response was "Heavens no! I want to be one of the first to start a new age group category when I'm ninety." Yet Betty also noted a change in her approach to her triathloning activities. "When I was in my forties and started doing tri's I felt more competitive . . . how well I did in races against my competitors was important. . . . Now, I don't feel so strongly about doing so . . . helping . . . [my friend (a novice triathlete in her fifties)] prepare for the BBLT has been more rewarding. I feel like I have achieved a balance in my life . . . inner strength . . . that's what is important now." Nonetheless, her caretaker, nurturant role is still important—as a role model and teacher for others in the triathlon community, or as she refers to it, "our triathlon family."

In 1990, in an effort to encourage more participation in triathlons, she initiated a program called "Each One Coach One" wherein experienced triathletes (members of the Kern County Triathlon Club [KCTC]) would work one-on-one with inexperienced novices with the goal of completing their first triathlon. In October 1991 she reinstated and organized the "Hugs and Kisses Triathlon," a local sprint triathlon put on by the KCTC for club members. There was a $15 entry fee for newcomers, which included a one-year membership in the club; current members did not have to pay for entering. Everyone, upon completion of the event, was greeted with "hugs and kisses." At the informal get-together and awards ceremony afterwards, there was plenty of food and the opportunity to share one's experience with others. In both of these instances, as in her training with her friend, Betty's focus and intent has been to share the growth and self-development that she has experienced through triathloning with others.

More recently, in part because of injuries she sustained in the early 1990s, she has reevaluated whether she would take on the training required to complete the Hawaiian Ironman again. She also saw herself as approaching a new period in her life and used that opportunity to do much more "innerwork" on who she was and where she wanted to be. One of the consequences of spending a great deal of time in training activities (for both herself and her husband) was that less quality time was available for herself with her husband. His work also took him away much of the time. By mid-1993, shortly after the marriage of her only daughter, through the beginning of 1994, she began to seriously reevaluate her relationship with her husband. What was critical to her was the difference between what was apparent on the surface, her representation of self to the outside world, and what was going on underneath, in particular the lack of an open communication with her spouse. She felt that she was growing in a new direction that her husband could not follow. She also felt that she had no right to ask him to do so. After much soul searching, she, too, separated from her husband. But, as she noted in an interview in August 1994, considering "the travail I have been through this last year with him [her husband] it is wonderful that we [Betty and myself] can sit here, looking ahead, each toward our own lives and feeling good. That's really a consequence of some of the things that we have chosen to believe in and do and experience and have as a major part of our lives. For both of us, each in our own individual ways, the inner and spiritual way of living out the outer life is what is essential. During this period of separation, what kept her going was the same strength and perseverance that she used to finish the Hawaiian Ironman. As she put it, "I've been doing an Ironman every day," in order to deal with these issues. By September 1994 she and her husband were able to work things through and reunite. For Betty, it was the Hawaiian Ironman experience that gave her the strength to be able to do so.

SUMMARY

Perhaps the main point to make here is that while all four of us are established members of the triathlon community—we have all completed the Hawaiian Ironman and have played an important role within the triathlon community—we do it differently. Although we all participate in a shared culture, we simultaneously express that culture in our own unique way, which reflect, in part, the different stages of the life cycle in which we have been located. Nonetheless, at the same time there are several common patterns to the process in which each one of us has engaged. As women, we have all been socialized to define ourselves in terms of our relationship to others and in terms of our role as potential mothers/caretakers. We all also have had to make choices in our lives as to whether we would pursue a career in addition to, or instead of, our potential role as wives and mothers. If we chose to do both, we had to determine how we would balance our public/career and domestic roles. As triathletes, we have also been engaged in the process of self-actualization. Participation in athletic activities has provided us with the opportunity to find ourselves, to become more integrated, whole, and empowered as individuals. Embodiment, realizing the physical strength and centeredness of our bodies, has meant empowerment in an emotional as well as physical and mental sense of well-being.

Laura and I both chose to follow a career path. And although we began at different points in our lives, our identity as Ironwomen forms a critical component of our identity as individuals—how we express ourselves and look at the world in general. At the same time, the career path we both chose—teaching at the college/university level—is also, though in a perhaps more indirect fashion, a nurturant role, one in which a central concern is the development and empowerment of others. Donna and Betty, on the other hand, both have placed primary emphasis upon their domestic nurturant role as wives and mothers. In similar fashion, their participation in athletics has provided an important balance and centering force in their lives. They are able to define themselves as strong, empowered women in their own right. Their domestic role, while still a critical component of their identity, does not subsume their identity as individuals. In the final analysis, regardless of the stage in the life cycle in which we find ourselves, participation in the triathlon lifestyle has been the primary mechanism for the ongoing transformation in our perception of self and the way in which we interact with others that we continue to experience.

REFERENCES

Abu-Lughod, Lila. 1991. "Writing against Culture." In *Recapturing Anthropology: Working in the Present*, ed. R. Fox, 137–62. Santa Fe, NM: School of American Research Press.

Brown, Judith, and Virginia Kerns, eds. 1985. *In Her Prime: A New View of Middle-Aged Women*. Urbana, IL: University of Illinois Press.

Fiske, Marjorie, and David Chiriboga. 1990. *Change and Continuity in Adult Life*. San Francisco, CA: Jossey-Bass Publishers.

Gould, Roger. 1978. *Transformations, Growth and Change in Adult Life*. New York, NY: Simon and Schuster.

Granskog, Jane. 1991. "Tri-ing for Life: The Emergence of the Triathlon Sport Sub-Culture and its Impact upon Changing Gender Roles in American Society." In *Sport . . . The Third Millenium, Proceedings of the Quebec City International Symposium,* ed. Fernand Landry, Marc Landry, and Magdeleine Yerles. Quebec City, Canada: Presses de L' Universite Laval.

———. 1992. "The Impact of Tri-ing Later in Life: Female Empowerment and the Masters Triathlete." The Annual Meetings of the North American Society for the Sociology of Sport, November 4–7, Toledo, Ohio.

Hall, M. Ann. 1996. *Feminism and Sporting Bodies, Essays on Theory and Practice*. Champaign, IL: Human Kinetics.

Harding, Sandra, ed. 1987. *Feminism and Methodology*. Bloomington, IN: Indiana University Press.

Langness, L. L., and Gelya Frank. 1981. *Lives, An Anthropological Approach to Biography*. Novato, CA: Chandler and Sharp Publishers.

Lerner, Richard, and Nancy Busch-Rossnagel, eds. 1981. *Individuals as Producers of Their Development, A Life-Span Perspective*. New York, NY: Academic Press.

Moore, Henrietta. 1988. *Feminism and Anthropology*. Minneapolis, MN: University of Minnesota Press.

Rossi, Alice, ed. 1985. *Gender and the Life Course*. New York, NY: Aldine Publishing Co.

Ryff, Carol. 1985. "The Subjective Experience of Life-Span Transitions." In *Gender and the Life Course,* ed. Alice Rossi. New York, NY: Aldine Publishing Co.

Watson, Laurence, and Maria Watson-Franke. 1985. *Interpreting Life Histories, An Anthropological Inquiry*. New Brunswick, NJ: Rutgers University Press.

CHAPTER THREE

Postmodern Aerobics:
Contradiction and Resistance

PIRKKO MARKULA

INTRODUCTION

I was first introduced to aerobics in 1987 when I arrived in the United States. My initial assignment as a University graduate assistant was to teach aerobics classes in the undergraduate physical activities program. Soon, I became an avid aerobicizer myself. Being interested in the latest knowledge about this exercise form, I paid attention to different sources of information about the most current trends of fitness.

For example, women's magazines seemed to offer a variety of "workouts" aimed at helping women with their fitness pursuits. These workouts, however, were geared around weight loss and restructuring the body. I was guaranteed to downsize my body through "no-fail diet/fitness programs." Or, I was promised to get in the "best shape ever" through toning programs that built sexy, firm muscles fast or honed those troublesome hips into a sleeker form. The exercise videos seemed to work on a similar premise. A myriad of video instructors advised me how to obtain "buns of steel" or "sculpt" my abs, hips, and thighs through "Fat Burning Workouts." If magazine articles and video-tapes advocated fitness for better body, what did the research say about the meaning of the women's fitness movement?

Much of the research within my own area of interest, the socio-cultural study of physical activity, centered on women's sport. Many scholars demonstrated that sport could be a site of resistance for women in an otherwise masculine society and that women transformed sport to correspond to their own needs and values (Birrell and Richter 1987; Birrell and Theberge 1994; Boutilier and SanGiovanni 1983; Varpalotai 1987; Wheatley 1988). In the late 1980s only a few studies, however, examined the role aerobics played in women's lives. Some researchers were interested in the ways aerobics was represented through media. Nancy Theberge (1987) and Margaret MacNeill (1988) analyzed how television constructed the image of aerobics.

Theberge (1987) argued that the women's fitness movement was a sexualizing rather than an empowering experience for women. The goal of women's fitness classes, according to Theberge, was not to develop physical strength or even fitness, but to increase women's sexual attractiveness and appeal. Theberge (1987:195) concluded that such activities as dancercise, jazzersize, and the television fitness program *20 Minute Workout*, "are developing women's potential in the sexual marketplace, not in athletics: the suggestive poses assumed by activity leaders, and breathy voices exhorting participants, convey images of dominance and submission." Thus, Theberge asserted that, in many ways, the fitness movement perpetuated women's continued oppression by the dominant ideology of masculinity.

Similarly, MacNeill (1988) reaffirmed that *20 Minute Workout*, a popular televised fitness program at the time, was penetrated with influences of dominant ideology of masculinity. She claimed that although this program symbolized women's increased opportunities to be physically active, it also reproduced patterns that subjugated women:

> Physical activity, yes, but on a form that stresses preoccupation with beauty, glamour, and sex appeal as status symbols. . . . Thus, women move back into positions of inferiority . . . by participating in aerobics less for reasons of fitness and personal freedom and more for reasons that reaffirm the patriarchal notions of femininity (i.e. to lose weight, to improve sex appeal). (1988:205–6)

MacNeill, like Theberge, pointed out that *20 Minute Workout* emphasized sexuality rather than the proper and safe exercise forms. This objectifies, according to MacNeill (1988:208), the image of the active female body into the sexually active female body and "tends to fabricate pornographic and erotic myths about how activity is to be experienced and what an active women should look like" (206). She concluded that such a presentation of the female body in motion reinforced the patriarchal subordination of women.

This research verified my own observations: the popular media advocated aerobics as a means to improve one's appearance. Because of this emphasis on body shape, the researchers added, aerobics sexualized and degraded women and promoted patriarchal hegemony through its practice. This view of aerobics as a "body shaper," did not, however, correspond completely with my experience in aerobics.

Regardless of the numerous hours I have spent with my women friends complaining about my body shape, and despite my occasional urges to perform reversed push-ups in vague hopes to tone some of that flab under my upper arms, I attended aerobics classes for reasons other than to rebuild my body. For instance, I felt true pleasure while moving through a clever new combination of steps. I also improved my physical fitness through aerobics. Consequently, I disagreed with the idea that aerobics only contributed to the dominance of patriarchy. Yet I, operating within the aerobics, could have been unaware how thoroughly patriarchal hegemony dictated the everyday practices in aerobics classes. Perhaps I was the only one in the class interested in other aspects of fitness than an improved body shape? Through my own confusion, I became interested in discovering whether other aerobicizers' views reflected the societal discourse of women's exercise.

When I searched through research on aerobics at the time, I came across only one study that examined the participants' views regarding aerobics. In addition to participating in aerobics classes, Regina Kenen (1987) had interviewed aerobicizers for her study. She classified aerobicizers in four "psycho-social orientations": the committed, the trendy, the medicinians, and the enjoyers.

The committed attended classes year after year, whether it was fashionable or not. The trendy, however, were likely to pick an exercise form which was socially "in" at the time and tend to wear the latest aerobics fashion. The medicinians exercised because it was good for their health. They viewed participation as "a chore and an obligation much the same as those who regularly take vitamins or medicine" (Kenen 1987:75). The enjoyers purely enjoyed the physical activity and obtained pleasures from the effects of the exercise.

Kenen did not explain why some participants meticulously attended the same classes or why some aerobicizers found exercise a chore while others really enjoyed it. I, in contrast, was interested in examining the meaning of aerobics in women's everyday experience. I assumed that aerobicizers kept going to aerobics sessions because exercising was somehow meaningful to them. To achieve this aim, I embarked in an ethnographic study on aerobics from 1990 to 1992. To gain more in-depth understanding of the meanings aerobics held for its participants, I interviewed thirty-three female aerobicizers. All of the interviewees assumed anonymity, and I refer to them here by their pseudonyms. The exercisers in my study were mostly students, but also secretaries, staff members, and researchers. This research, therefore, was based on the experiences of a select group. The typical aerobicizer in my study was a white, well-educated, eighteen to forty-five year-old female who—according to nationwide surveys—also characterized an average aerobics exerciser around the United States (Rothlein 1987).

In this chapter I plan to discuss some of the meanings aerobicizers attach to their exercise practices based on the findings from my fieldwork. I will focus specifically on their understanding of aerobics as an exercise mode—what aspects of aerobics make it a meaningful exercise form for its participants. As the aerobicizers often reflect their understanding of aerobics against the widely circulated media images of aerobics and aerobicizers, I have included discussions of magazine and exercise video representations of aerobics. To locate aerobicizers' meanings within a larger cultural context, I will begin with a definition of the postmodern cultural condition. This chapter concludes with a reflection on the meaning of my ethnographic work for present-day research on aerobics.

AEROBICS IN POSTMODERN CULTURE: CHANGING DEFINITIONS

In the early 1990s I was fascinated by the postmodern theorists whose thoughts had just started to penetrate the field of anthropology. Although there is no agreement upon an exact definition of postmodern culture, I found aspects of this theory particularly illuminating for my study of aerobics. First, several scholars found constant and irregular change, instead of steady and linear progression, which characterized the postmodern cultural mode (Clifford 1986; Jameson 1983; Taussig 1980). For example, Michael Taussig (1980:443–44) described the outstanding qualities of culture as follows: "its irregularly stopping and starting, its fragment interruptedness, its sudden swerves and changes in pace and the peculiar way by which it is not only a massive dominating force but is open to interruption by anyone and anything." Postmodern theorists capture the idea of culture as an ongoing, changing process in such terms as "pastiche" (Jameson 1983), "surrealism" (Clifford 1988), or "montage" (Taussig 1980). In essence, these words signify that human cultures are neither necessarily coherent nor homogeneous. I believe that aerobics mirror this postmodern cultural context. New ideas and trends regarding aerobics come in an invariable succession, yet in rather irregular tempo, stirring aerobics to constant change. Aerobics was by no means a homogeneous or coherent phenomenon. For example, during my fieldwork in aerobics classes, I was keeping my eye on magazines to learn more about aerobics in the United States. At first I did not seem to come across much information about aerobics, which surprised me as I considered aerobics to be very popular among women. Soon I realized that for the magazines, aerobics was an umbrella term for many types of women's fitness activities, not one coherent, clearly defined exercise form. One journalist painted a postmodern montage of aerobics for me: "aerobics isn't just dance exercise any more—it's a lifestyle . . . instruction has expanded to include sport specific training, age specific training, and 'fringe' classes, like aqua aerobics and programs for the obese and disabled" (Davis in Madsen 1989:22). This statement was definitely true. Magazine articles constantly introduced either new innovative forms of aerobics exercise or new equipment for more effective toning workouts.

Second, postmodern theory provides a justification for my, at the time, unusual topic on a popular cultural form of physical activity. The definitions of many cultural phenomena are expanded in postmodernism. This often results in the collapse of the hierarchical distinctions between high culture and mass culture, between intellectual culture and popular culture, between society and everyday life (e.g., Dunn 1991; Featherstone 1988). For example, many popular phenomena (such as TV, music videos, romance novels, or soap operas) have previously been considered too trivial for serious consideration by social scientists but are now found to be particularly fruitful topics to understand culture (Dunn 1991; Featherstone 1988; Johnston 1989; MacRobbie 1984; Rosaldo 1988). Similarly, as I studied women's fitness—an everyday experience for many women in society—I found some might consider aerobics a trivial activity in comparison to the more culturally refined and developed movement (like ballet or sport). However, as my research evolved, I noticed a developing relationship between sport and aerobics in the magazine pages. Instead of prescribing exercise for a better body shape, fitness articles referred to the sport-like qualities of aerobics. Was this a sign of a postmodern cultural condition where hierarchical distinction between aerobics and sport is demolished?

AEROBICS IS SERIOUS SPORT: MAGAZINE READINGS

In the early 1990s magazines introduced several new forms of aerobic exercise, and they were geared around sport themes. Examples included slide, step aerobics, interval circuit training or plyometrics, and such combo classes as boxerzise, karaerobics, or cardio-combat, which mixed aerobics with other sport disciplines. These variations stripped aerobics of its dance-type elements. For example, the use of space became more restricted; movement combinations included more sport moves and less coordinated dance moves, or aerobic dance routines were removed entirely as in interval circuit training. To further illustrate this sport trend, the arm position vocabulary of step aerobics was borrowed directly from the weight training vocabulary. Aerobics was switched from using coordination moves to moves requiring more strength.

Such developments seem to blur the boundaries between sport and aerobics. One could argue that "sport movements" effectively increase the fitness benefits of aerobics and inspire the participants to reach for new spheres of physical condition. It could also be interpreted as a sign when aerobics studios attempted to respond to the needs of the more advanced women who want more challenging, demanding exercise classes. Furthermore, the magazines claim that such a sport connection provides a better public image of aerobics. Consider the following vivid quotations from three of the magazines:

> Aerobic dance had undergone an amazing metamorphosis. Though some once considered it a candy-coated activity, characterized by splashy leotards, prancing feet, whoops and shrieks, these days aerobics is regarded as a serious sport. (Malanka 1990:59)

> It wasn't so long ago that the word "aerobics" conjured up visions of fad-following devotees more interested in fashion than fitness . . . aerobics has earned an honored spot on the world of sport and fitness. (Madsen 1989:22)

> Finally—aerobics for athletes. (Veit 1992:49)

These writers imply that previously aerobics was more of a women's weight-loss method than effective physical training (see also Markula 1993). The connection with athleticism is directed to redefine aerobics as a serious enterprise. The mindset of aerobics, magazine articles proclaimed, now has changed from "hoot and holler and look good" to a new athletic realm. Aerobics, in this realm, is not entertainment, fun, or play, but rather is hard work that pays off with real results like muscle growth. Aerobicizers are expected to push themselves harder; the instructor is seen more as a coach who has made sure that the performance is correct. This is a far cry from the "traditional" aerobics instructor who with smiles attempted to energize the participants to follow her or him (Veit 1992). This "sport spirited" aerobics emphasizes serious physical performance and hard work. In the 1990s the newly developed aerobics competitions, such as annual World Aerobics Championships, further aligned aerobics with sports. In addition, aerobics shoe advertisers quickly latched onto this new athletic image.

One issue of *Shape* magazine (May 1994) serves as a good example of aerobics-sport connection in advertising. Three major women's aerobics shoe manufacturers (Avia, Nike, and Reebok) featured their products prominently. All three advertising lines, directly or indirectly, were aimed to convince us that aerobics is a sport. For instance, one advertisement promised: "Reebok believes in the athlete" and added, as if to especially include the previously unthinkable aerobicizers, *"In all of us."* The Avia shoe advertisement constructed aerobics class as a sporting event:

> This is a sport? Where are the trophies, and the medals, and the instant replays? How do you know who wins without the instant replays? Easy, just look around you. Can't you see the sweat and muscle? Can't you feel the commitment and determination? Don't you get it? On this floor, everybody's a winner. And you don't need a score board to tell you that. (32–33)

Nike's advertisement asked aerobics instructor Alison Low to name the SPORTS in which she participates and whether Nike aerobics shoes meet the requirements of her SPORTS. Naturally, Alison found Nikes the "coolest" footwear for her beloved step aerobics, hi-lo aerobics, circuit-training, and weight training.

Whether elevating aerobics into the more respected sport realm changed its image is debatable. Although the text in the shoe advertisements emphatically emphasizes that aerobics (and buying their shoes) made one feel strong, liberated, and free, they still pictured the ideal "feminine" women: hair perfectly groomed, impeccably make-up, thin, and toned. Purchasing innovative, supportive, and versatile aerobics shoes is the first step on the way to a better, more beautiful body. Cheryl Cole and Amy Hribar (1995) labeled women's empowerment that continues to be embedded in bodily maintenance as "commodity feminism." They demonstrate that Nike's advertising for women, while presenting itself as pro-women, progressive, and socially responsible, is actually designed to seduce women to consume Nike products. Nike's rhetoric of empowering athleticism is based on the logic of the individual's responsibility for her health and on her freedom to consume. The Nike images, Cole and Hribar (1995:35) argue, "disseminated by promotional culture routinely and repetitiously solicit the hard body, the deep self, and free will (which aroused the desire to work on the body and consume commodities in order to maintain the body and stabilize identity)." Following Cole's and Hribar's examples, I could argue that the aerobic shoe advertisements connect empowerment with being a sports woman who is free to choose to "just do it." In actuality, the female aerobics athlete's liberation is based on building and maintaining the traditional good looks.

If, in a shoe advertisement, aerobics remained merely a means for a beautiful body, *Shape*'s publisher, Joe Wieder (1992:14), gives aerobics the status of another kind of "a means":

> More than an end in itself, we see aerobics as a means to an end, a way to achieve a level of fitness that can open the door to activities you never dreamed you could do—rock climbing, long distance cycling, mountain biking, even triathlons. Like Danskin, *Shape* encourages women to venture beyond the aerobics studio to a world with no walls or full-length mirrors, one that reflects not just what we look like but who we are.

Therefore, aerobics could serve as a means for different ends: the better body or, at best, "real" athletic endeavors. Despite all this effort to convince the public that aerobics is as tough and serious as sport, it remains inferior to sport. Moreover, I am intrigued that in order to be taken seriously as a physical activity in our society, aerobics need to approximate sport—to be hard work and involve competition rather than being identified as an exercise that emphasizes fun and playfulness. Such values as strength, discipline, hard work, and competition are emphasized, and popular new forms of aerobics were created on the basis of these qualities.

While I observe aerobics transforming from women's exercise into a serious sport in the public discourse of aerobics, I wonder whether my fellow participants long to be athletes rather than exercisers. As I mentioned earlier, I suspect that the meanings aerobicizers give to their exercise experiences might significantly differ from the dominant, public-cultural discourses. I also believe that these private voices could influence or originate the process of cultural change.

WOMEN'S VOICES IN POSTMODERN CULTURE

Within my recently discovered postmodern theory, dominant practices in society are not viewed as closed systems uninfluenced by the voices of individual people living in society (Lyotard 1986). At the time of my research, following Michail Bakhtin (1986), I viewed postmodern culture as communication among different voices. These voices, some more dominant than others, struggle over each other to give meaning to cultural phenomena. Therefore, the cultural meaning of aerobics is a result of many voices, some of which contradict each other or work to replace each other. Furthermore, I assumed that dominant practices, although determining our lives up to certain point, created space for individual resistance. In this way, dominance could be challenged and cultural change would take place.

In my ethnographic field aerobics are primarily a women's activity. To specify the cultural dynamics surrounding women's everyday experience, I must employ feminist theory in addition to postmodern theory. I assume that women actively created their own meanings based on their own reality. However, these meanings are not created in a vacuum. Women live and think in a society, and their actions and thoughts are shaped partly by the dominant practices of that society (e.g., Gottlieb 1989; Ortner 1984; Strathern 1987). In Western societies this dominance is largely gendered. In our patriarchal society men dominate women. Women could, and did, shape the societal power systems through resistant practices (Martin 1988; Radway 1986; Spitzack 1990). This means that women actively make sense out of their social world and construct different meanings in different social contexts.

Because I assumed that women were actively speaking about their reality, I defined my research as a dialogue between me—the researcher—and the aerobicizers. In this process they partly constructed my understanding of the meanings of aerobics and I, in turn, influenced their visions by asking certain questions. Together we negotiated a shared understanding of aerobics as a cultural phenomenon. I must also acknowledge that my work was based on my subjective interpretation of some aerobicizers' meanings, and its readings could not be generalized to other aerobicizers throughout the United States.

AEROBICIZERS' READINGS: "IT WAS DANCING ALL THE TIME"

Although the media links aerobics frequently with sport, aerobicizers often referred to the dance-like qualities of aerobics during the interviews. For most of the participants, aerobics is clearly distinctive from dance movements. The defining difference is the emphasis on the result in aerobics. This outcome orientation is voiced by Daedra: "(In aerobics) you are focusing on trying to get your heart rate up, trying to get thinner . . . in dance you are focusing exactly on movement and how well you are doing and how you feel about what you are doing"; and by Eileen: "In aerobics, you are working out, it's not entertaining, when you dance you exercise, but they are not focused to improving parts of your body."

Aerobics, however, is enriched with qualities comparable to dance. Ann found her low-impact aerobics corresponding to her earlier dance experience:

> In low-impact you are basically using your whole body instead of just letting your legs move you . . . and I found that that was much more integral

to what I studied as a dancer . . . you are taught to use your whole body whenever you move . . . it just seemed to be more natural to me. I thought: "Well, if I feel good, the other people must feel the same way" and it's true, I think most people don't like to jump up and down . . . it hurts.

Ann's description of low-impact routines resonates with images of dance routines: one is "constantly moving in crisscross patterns." Also, other participants have recognized how dance steps are incorporated into routines: "Lots of the moves that are more like dance, are [a] lot more fun . . . it's flowing back and forth" (Molly) or "moving around" brings dance flair to aerobics: "There are some steps that kind of make you just feel like flying through the air, make me feel more like I was dancing, not just running in place" (Lucia). These adjustments add variety and fun to the exercise.

I have argued elsewhere (Markula 1993) that aerobics was originally created as an interesting and fun alternative to jogging. The boredom of running is killed by adding music and dance-type moves. Yet, in a simplified version, this does not scare off the women who have no dance experience. The exercisers seemed to enjoy the feeling of dance as long as the moves did not get too complicated. The "dancy" feeling comes from small additions such as hip and shoulder movements, snapping and clapping, which make the exercise movements flow more gracefully.

These exercisers seem to enjoy the aspects that the new "serious" sport aerobics is dismissing. They do not connect the degrading "hollering" image of aerobics to the dance movements. On the contrary, these movements are the best part of aerobics. Therefore, turning aerobics into sport, these aerobicizers feel, does not liberate aerobics from its burden as "a candy-coated activity." On the contrary, Colleen finds "dance" aerobics a more liberating experience than sport:

> I feel like that's the right place for competition. . . . It's not like a team sport, where you are competing against another team or racing against another person. . . . It's not like being in a ballet class where the teacher has a stick in her hand saying everyone has to be the same.

Colleen's statement introduced an aerobics class in which the individual-participant could change the movements according to one's own fitness level, interest, mood, or purpose. This finding stands in sharp contrast with the research of Elizabeth Kagan and Margaret Morse (1988), who found aerobics lacking any potential for individual choice or adaptability. It also challenges the results of studies (MacNeill 1988; Theberge 1987) that see aerobics as only promoting women's oppression through its single focus on appearance.

In everyday situations participants "modify" the movements when they adapt the class to meet their individual preferences. The women I spoke with have learned to adjust the moves to meet their own personal needs and correspond to their limitations. It seems that the participants listen to their own inner feelings about their body to choose the suitable exercise procedure. As Colleen stated: "Sometimes I would do it because I would have pain—not a pain that would make me stop. But I would get sore ankles or shins, because my ankles and shins are probably ten or fifteen years older than everyone else in the class. And I just feel like I know when to tune things down and not to jump up and down." Evidently, aerobicizers follow their individual exercise preferences, and no one can make them (neither did the instructors intend) to follow uniform instructions.

Because they prefer to modify their moves, many aerobicizers, like Colleen, consider competition inappropriate for an exercise class. However, Helen Lenskyj (1986) believes that competition exists in aerobics classes when, for example, the exercisers compare their physical abilities and body types. Lenskyj (1986:129–30) speculates that such spirit makes aerobics an uncomfortable, instead of liberating, experience for participants:

> It (aerobics) was developed for women, offered at convenient times and locales, in predominantly or exclusively female environments that promised to be supportive and non-threatening, especially to women new to physical activity. But many women felt pressured to lose weight, to work on specific body parts (thighs, hips, breasts) that fitness experts had diagnosed as a "problem," and to keep up with the instructor and the class, both in appearance and performance, regardless of individual goals, body type, or fitness level.

In the classes I observed, many of the exercisers found themselves comparing their bodies and abilities to those of other participants: "I think it (comparing) isn't so overt, but it's there, a lot of comparison goes on" (Melissa); "I think it's inherent in women (to compare) and they do it no matter what. I think they compare themselves to anybody" (Lucia); "Yeah, I compare, but a lot of girls do" (Daedra). For Stacy, such comparison seems to be more conscious in terms of her body: she compares her body build to others, but does not care how others perceives her condition level or other movement abilities:

> STACY: Not really [do I compare myself to others], tonight I did, because I was really apathetic tonight, like: "Oh, everyone else is doing it," but not usually.
>
> PIRKKO: Do you compare your body to others?
>
> STACY: Sure.

Such comparisons in terms of body, but not skill or fitness levels, reflects the societal emphasis on the female body that Susan Bordo (1990), Kim Chernin (1981), and Carole Spitzack (1990) have pointed out. Women are accustomed to constant attention directed on their bodies. Their value in society is strongly connected to their attractiveness instead of their performance or achievements. Consequently, women have internalized checking out their bodies in aerobics rather than contrasting physical skills.

Even if they compare their bodies, the aerobicizers simultaneously recognize natural differences in body types and do not strive to achieve something utterly impossible to them:

SARAH: I think everyone compares.

HELEN: But the thing is that everyone is built up so differently.

COLLEEN: I looked at her and I thought it would be nice to have that kind of muscle definition . . . but the comparison to the fact that I have to attain that . . . I know what my limitations are, I know how hard I would have to work to keep it like that and I don't think I can give it that much time right now. It's not really that important either.

Mirrors in the aerobics studios may facilitate the comparison. As one woman notes: "Not necessarily [do I compare], I do more so when I'm in a spot with a mirror in front of me, when I can see myself. I always compare myself to everyone else. When I can't see myself, like over at Gym, I don't compare myself, how I look or how I do it to them" (Jane).

Others feel that comparison with other women is not completely negative. Exercisers become motivated when they notice someone else who looks as they want to appear someday. Cari ponders her reasons to look at others in the class: "I think I sit and watch the others to motivate myself because a lot of them are in better shape: . . . gosh, she looks so nice, she is so much in shape, she keeps it up so well." Colleen (who is thirty-seven) feels that comparisons might have something to do with age—younger people seem to be more apt to compare themselves to others: "I don't feel like I have to compete with anyone else in the class. . . . It's me and that might be just because of the difference in age between other people and me. Maybe they feel more competitive than I do, but I just don't feel like that's the right place for competition." Instead of feeling pressured by comparisons in the group setting, a majority of the aerobicizers find that exercising in a class is motivating and makes the workout more fun: "Exercising with people, people will push you . . . yeah. If everyone else is going, it really does help" (Anna). "It's boring by yourself; but here you are, in a whole group, and they are all doing it" (Cari). "I like aerobics in that, when you do it with other people, it makes you do it. You go. You are more committed to it . . . that gives you the encouragement to do it and I think that helps" (Lisa).

Many exercisers do not support the serious sport spirit promoted by magazines. In my research I discovered parallel voices to aerobicizers merging through the media. Aerobics classes such as non-impact aerobics or funk aerobics emphasize softer, more mentally inspiring, and enjoyable classes. Malanka (1990:65), like the exercisers, believes that "despite the new emphasis on athletic, sporty moves, and classes that rely on machines and weights, a good percentage of aerobic exercisers still want to dance." In the public world of aerobics, dance forms are accepted and tolerated alongside the "athletic aerobicizing."

In addition to urging us to adopt a new "athletic spirit" toward aerobics, magazines and videotapes help us to reshape our bodies. Various body sculpting programs and articles also introduce the model body that we are to achieve if we follow their advice. This focus is exactly what the sport-spirited aerobics is supposed to battle for: the extreme emphasis on women's bodies. Here the media discourse contradicts itself. I define this contradiction as a battle between different voices in the media field of aerobics. Should the "appearance orientation" (exercise to reshape one's body) or the serious athleticism be the dominant meaning of aerobics exercise? Historically, aerobics has a strong stigma as a means to a better body (Markula 1993). How did all this start? I see the roots of the appearance-orientation coming from the image culture surrounding aerobics.

THE POSTMODERN AEROBICS: IMAGES ON VIDEOTAPES

Jane Fonda has provided a widely distributed aerobics image through her 1981 *Workout Book* and the exercise videotape that followed publication of her book. Fonda's emphasis is clearly on an improved appearance through exercise. The outcome makes the exercise worthwhile: "When you make yourself exercise and afterwards feel that tingle through your body, the sense of exhilaration and your own pleasure in your discipline, you'll agree it was worth it" (Fonda 1981:56).

A similar image of aerobics is conveyed through the film *Perfect*, in which Jamie Lee Curtis portrays an aerobics instructor in a health club where she leads her class through sets of bouncing, fast-paced exercises while standing in front of the class. Images of hard working, sweating, exhausted, and serious aerobicizers flash to the audience during the movie. I find this mode of aerobics (Fonda, *Perfect*) reflecting the notions of the so-called consumer culture as sketched by Mike Featherstone (1983). The aerobicizers do not exercise purely for the sake of being physically active, but for the outcome of it: for a better body, for physical fitness, or for other health benefits. In addition, this kind of aerobics workout requires a tremendous amount of hard work and discipline to bear the fruit of a change in appearance. The emphasis of the exercise program shifts from fun to stress the importance of appearance and the "look."

The researchers of postmodern culture emphasize the visibility of images as found in the aerobics body. The culture surrounding us, they observe, is filled with images that we encounter every day (Slowikowski and Newell 1990). Researchers also discuss the meaning and production of aerobics images.

Jean Baudrillard (1983) argues that in the postmodern culture the image world becomes more real than the original world. In this "image" world the boundaries of the real and unreal blur. Baudrillard (1983:146) specifies: "The real is not only what can be reproduced, but that which is always already reproduced, the hyperreal." For example, a person who has never attended an aerobics class could have a set idea of these workouts because s/he has watched exercise videotapes or read through magazine workouts. These media images of aerobics clearly precede one's "real" experience in an aerobics class. In other words, the simulation model of aerobics could constitute and count as "the real" in our hyperreal society. Barry Glassner (1989) examines further how exercise videos and women's magazines have provided a context for image construction of aerobics.

Glassner (1989:184) names the exercise video "a quintessential postmodern object." Two factors have contributed, according to Glassner, to this label. First, the exercise image, rather than being a copy of "the real," has become the model that "real exercisers" strive to obtain. Consequently, the "real" has become a copy of the image. Second, there are no originals for exercise videos. Although for the viewer it is a continuous lesson, the tape is actually constructed of separate "shoots" filmed over a long period of time. I propose that in this cultural era of images, our understanding about aerobics is strongly influenced by these media images. This image world could even become our world of aerobics. The fashionably dressed, thin, and toned aerobicizers who we meet while flipping through women's magazines or viewing an exercise video shape our understanding of aerobics and, in general, women's exercise in this society. However, participating in a "real" aerobics class would be quite a different experience from exercising alone with a videotape.

Kagan and Morse (1988) in their research have analyzed images on a particular aerobics videotape and investigated the potential empowering elements in Jane Fonda's *New Workout Video* (1986). While they acknowledge that aerobics provide women with strength and powerful femininity to some extent, the potential power has been channeled by the requirement of shaping the body to the commercially supported ideas of femininity. Aerobics is, thus, ripped off of its positive elements. It does not, the researchers argue, change women's present condition in life or provide access to women's self-empowerment. Although they recognize that many instructors did transcend the limitations of an exercise videotape, Kagan and Morse (1988) conclude their study with quite a negative impression of aerobics. Nevertheless, these researchers have structured their view of aerobics based on the hyperreality of the exercise videotape. This image world of aerobics has become more real than the "real," with the researchers not reaching out to seek the aerobicizers' subjective meanings of aerobics.

I want to transcend from the hyperreality of the media image world to interpret other realities of aerobics. I must ask the question of how the aerobicizers view the images depicted in exercise videotapes, magazines articles, and television workout programs.

"IT'S VERY MADE UP": EXERCISERS' VIEWS OF AEROBICS IMAGES

Exercisers' impressions of video aerobics vary from liking them (Shannon and Anna) to irritation with them. For example, Christy asks: "Have you ever seen [the] Jane Fonda aerobics tapes? These really bug me because they do things like 'OK, feel the burn and BURN IT!' And you are going WHOOAAA! That really bugs me." Generally, aerobicizers do not use exercise videotapes unless they cannot attend class. Ann feels that videos can create a feeling of incompetence. Rosi summarizes: "I liked the tape but I think [that] when I had to follow them, I wasn't doing what I should have been doing. I spent more time watching the beautiful women on this tape."

Anna describes a perfect example of an exercising woman on a videotape: "She is fit, because you can tell, she's got an incredible body. She is completely tight; she has no fat on the body. She's totally muscular . . . she is real tall." This image puzzles many of the women in the aerobics classes. The "perfectness" of the media exercisers appears somehow unreal, even irritating. Anna and Eileen find such a presentation of exercising women ridiculous:

EILEEN: There are two girls there and they are like all sexy.

ANNA: And those girls are all hyper.

EILEEN : Ding, dong, yeah!

ANNA : It's funny.

EILEEN : They were weird!

Such a portrayal of women makes the exercisers cast doubts on the expertise of the demonstrators: they suspect that these models are there because of the way they look and not because of their exercise knowledge: "[They are] usually the instructor type, looks fine in a leotard since they are just photos. They don't have to be necessarily fit, they could just be someone who looks good in a leotard and say put your body in this position" (Christy). Daedra expresses a similar frustration with the model demonstrators, but adds, interestingly, that such a portrayal of women is all she expects from the media: "I expect that anyone demonstrating any exercise in any magazine is going to have close to that ideal body, I don't think I expect anything but that."

Exercising with such ideal people also intimidates the ordinary aerobicizers: "They had perfect bodies and it was intimidating, we are jiggling and wiggling but they are just fine" (Sarah). Rosi feels almost paralyzed when confronted with such ideals as those on her videotape: "Most of them were so slim that I was just watching them." Neither do they believe that the perfect media exercisers work out for real: "It doesn't seem like they are really realistic, because they are made up and they are all there in matching outfits . . . it's in the studio . . . there are no other people around . . . it's very made up" (April). Contrary to some other exercisers, Kathy feels that "actually it kind of makes you work a little bit harder, when you see the perfect bodies." Stacy would like to have achieved such a goal, but "can't see it happening."

Rather than perfect bodies, the participants desire to see "normal people" or an expert who knows what s/he is doing: "I think it's important to show demonstrators who really work out, you can see that this person maybe has muscular legs or when lifting weights, they have muscular arms" (Colleen). Some exercise videos have included different types of people in their model classes. Daedra finds these tapes more motivating, although with an exception to the rule: "It's geared toward people who haven't exercised [in] a while, it has some with great bodies . . . a couple of people there who are overweight in comparison, but it's neat because they are working out and that can give some inspiration to people who are trying to lose weight . . . but that's in that one particular one, I never seen any others." According to Anna's experience, the videos are more realistic in their portrayals of people than TV and, perhaps, videos give a more professional impression: "They are better, they know what they are doing . . . not like TV. TV is more flashy. . . . In Kathy Smith they are like normal people and what she does, she has the group behind her and then she has the TV screen: the beginners, intermediate, and advanced, who are doing different level of the exercise." Thus the interviewees seem to find the thin and toned media ideal incomplete. They long to see "normal" women exercising besides the "pencil thin fashion models."

Anna points out that exercise videos are self-defeating and she would never recommend them to anyone. She is concerned that a person trying to follow the video aerobicizers might be doing the exercises incorrectly. Rather than buying videotapes, Anna urges people to move their bodies from the front of the TV to the class, where it is possible to get individual feedback from the instructor and support from the group. Daedra has found some of the videotapes so potentially harmful that she now prefers to have an expert check the safety of the exercises.

If the aerobicizers are skeptical about the videotapes, they are also quite critical of magazine presentations about exercise. They feel tired of reading advice concerning different exercises that will reshape their bodies. Maria and Molly characterize the magazine fitness information as follows: "Most of it is just sport exercises, trim your thighs kind of stuff . . . they have those all the time." Many of the participants in this study are suspect of the quality of the actual exercises as well as whether they "really, really work." Anna and Eileen have discussed the validity of the magazine exercises:

> ANNA: Like *Cosmopolitan* and *Vogue;* how to stay in shape; how to get in shape for summer, bikini weather. They always have articles like that and you read them. I have set my own ways about what to do and I don't follow that stuff. I used to, but I don't any more, because I know my own how to do things now.
>
> EILEEN: Some of them are fad. Like the articles that say like flat stomach in two weeks. There is no way you can isolate one muscle and burn fat.
>
> ANNA : Plus they have like fifteen stretches to a better body . . . that's not going to help you, stretches!

Christy has stopped paying attention to such exercise columns and, like Anna, does her "own stuff now." It is interesting that the women trusted their own exercise knowledge more than the information found in the magazines. Colleen is so frustrated that she has stopped buying magazines after finding the exercise information geared towards improving the same body spots.

Aerobicizers consider the media's aerobics image unrealistic. The perfect media aerobicizers do not exist in the world they have experienced but are a creation of media technology. Therefore, women are well aware of the hyperreality of the images in postmodern society. Many exercisers criticize this image precisely because it is a construction that does not represent their experiences of aerobics. Their critique is also directed to correctness or safety of the media exercises. Some suspect that the potential ability of the workouts are to aid in sculpting their bodies. For example, Anna feels that stretches will not help one to reshape the body; Colleen wants to find new exercises to tone different body parts. This is a curious contradiction: aerobicizers defined the media image as unrealistic; however, they still want to tone their bodies and lose weight by exercising. By doing this they attempt to imitate the very same image that they have judged as degrading, unrealistic, and misleading. What has made them question and at the same complement this image?

POSTMODERN AEROBICS: CONTRADICTION AND RESISTANCE

Despite privately questioning the media images, the aerobicizers do not really expect these images to change nor do they completely reject them. However, if the women are unhappy with the public image of aerobics, if the feminist research has found them degrading, and the sport aerobics is promoted to discard it, why does it still persist?

At the time of this study, the feminist argument centers on the dominant masculine ideology that has shaped the images of aerobics to serve its own purposes: aerobics had been feminized to perpetuate the patriarchal, oppressing notions of femininity. This practice deepens the power of masculine hegemony over women (Kagan and Morse 1988; MacNeill 1988; Theberge 1987).

Simultaneously, other scholars explained that the image was so powerful because it was maintained by both patriarchal and capitalist powers that dominate our society. In this society, also characterized as "consumer culture," the desired body was youthful, slim, and healthy, and we were all persuaded to strive for it (Featherstone 1983; Hargreaves 1987). I agreed that the magazines promoted new fashionable forms of aerobics to make us spend more money for new classes, for new equipment, for new aerobics gear, and for a new body.

Still pondering the possibilities of masculine hegemony or consumer culture to explain my contradictory findings, I discovered Carol Spitzack's (1990) work on women's dieting practices. Spitzack did not connect the image production with any particular power source in our society. She, following Michel Foucault, believes that this dominance has an unidentifiable source. This ubiquitous power controls us through discursive practices that are a combination of the political, economical, and historical forces in society. For example, the aerobics image was, then, created within the discourses of femininity, medicine and health, which attempted to explain why we all should exercise. Spitzack (1990) claims that dieting is connected with health to make us believe that being thin means also being healthy. In a similar manner, I argue, women connect exercise with thinness and ultimately with health. Aerobicizers had internalized their responsibility to stay in shape like they had accepted the responsibility to take care of the other aspects of their health. The healthy look, Spitzack (1990) continues, also equals beautiful in this society. Consequently, aerobicizers in my study worked hard to change their body shapes to obtain that beautiful, healthy body. In addition, Spitzack argues that the dominant practices did not use openly suppressive power mechanisms to keep us disciplined. Rather, they persuade us to accept their control through an invisible gaze. I believe that aerobicizers' endless quest for better bodies follows this logic. Exercisers keep sculpting their bodies toward "healthy" tone and slimness because unhealthy people are stared at and judged to be disgusting and ugly. In other words, fat or loose body appears undisciplined, out-of-control, and unacceptable for the invisible societal gaze.

However, at the same time, women question the perfect media image. They are annoyed with it and want to see more "normal" women like themselves exercising in the media. Therefore, they do not blindly accept the body image. These aerobicizers actively resist the discursive power. For example, they have stopped buying magazines because the exercise articles in them are repetitive and futile. Women do not exercise with videotapes because they find the tapes dangerous and unprofessional. I believe, like Spitzack (1990), that individual women's resistant voices have had the potential to change the oppressive practices in society.

Women's aerobics practices, I conclude, embed numerous contradictions. The live aerobics class provides women with a positive sense of femininity, although the exercisers agree with the research that the media images of aerobics are degrading to and sexualizing of women. They resist the image, but concomitantly desire to look like the model exercisers no matter how unrealistic that goal is. A similar contradiction emerges within the public narrative of aerobics. Aerobics is simultaneously connected to serious sport and to body sculpting. The aerobicizers, thus, live in constant contradiction as they aim to find a balance between following the dominant discourses and resisting the suffocating, irrational, oppressive exercise practices.

CONCLUSION

Ten years later, I now reflect on my ethnographic work on aerobics with mixed feelings. I can still vividly remember my discussions with the aerobicizers, how helpful and enthusiastic they were about my study and how much I learned from their stories. I am still very grateful to all the participants in my research. But a lot has changed in ten years.

In the early 1990s, when I was conducting my study, hardly any research existed on women's fitness practices. I could only find three media studies regarding aerobics and one study examining the actual aerobics classes through interviews. Since then, research on aerobics and fitness has become more visible. We now have media readings on fitness advertisements (Cole and Hribar 1995; White and Gillett 1994), fitness videos (McNeill 1998), and fitness magazines (Duncan 1994; Eskes, Duncan, and Miller 1998). There are theoretical readings of women's fitness (Cole 1998; Lloyd 1996; McDermott 1996) and several studies analyzing aerobicizers' experiences (Haravon 1995; Loland 2000; Maguire and Mansfield 1996; Markula 1995; McDermott 2000; Poole 1999). These studies aim to understand fitness and aerobics from multiple theoretical perspectives. When I now read my earlier interpretation of aerobics, I am impressed with the richness of my "data" but can see how my theoretical approach reflected the general development of feminist sport studies. Feminist sport studies had come to a full existence in the 1980s and had just moved to consider sport and physical activity as a system of patriarchy and gender relations. When I began my examination of aerobics, feminist sport sociology became "a theoretically informed, critical analysis of the cultural forces that work to produce the ideological practices that influence the relations of sport and gender" (Birrell 1988:492). In my ethnography this stage is evident through my many references to aerobics as a patriarchally constructed practice that is penetrated by masculine ideology. In early 2000 feminist sport studies, along with sport sociology in general, has embraced poststructuralism, critical ethnography, postcolonial and postmodern theory (McDonald and Birrell 1999). While my ethnographic study hints at this development, I, too, have changed with the theoretical climate of feminist research.

My guiding question for my ethnographic study on aerobics stemmed from a contradiction between my personal experiences within aerobics and the researchers' readings of (mediated) aerobics. My study demonstrated further contradictions within the world of aerobics; aerobicizers recognized the oppressiveness of the narrowly defined body ideal, yet worked relentlessly toward that ideal. Relying on a Foucauldian feminist perspective, I aimed to explain how such a contradiction was possible. While I still find Foucauldian theory very persuasive and would still argue that for many aerobicizers the contradictory relationship with their bodies remains, I have become increasingly troubled with the absence of my own body experience in my research text. I aimed to include individual aerobicizers' voices through direct quotes, but there is little evidence of the promised dialogue between me, the researcher, and "them," the objects of my study. Rather, my absence constructed me as the distant, objective, observer that I was determined to counter with an ethnographic study of women's experiences. The realization that my relationship with my body is rife with contradictions similar to the other aerobicizers' body experiences despite my feminist consciousness has driven me deeper into the Foucauldian feminist theory of discursive control, and, to further understand women's cultural conditions and aerobics, I have embarked into critically evaluating my personal experiences through evocative writing (Markula 2002). In addition, my inability to break my own controlling gaze even when armed with feminist theory of resistance and empowerment has led me to reconsider the possibilities for change through individual resistance that I optimistically endorsed through my ethnographic work. I have continued to examine the changes of women's fitness that have occurred within the past decade.

After completing my ethnography, I moved to New Zealand to take up a position as a lecturer in Leisure Studies. However, I still remain a subscriber to the *IDEA Health and Fitness Source* (an official magazine for IDEA Health and Fitness, Inc., the leading American organization for fitness professionals) to keep up with the latest trends in the ever-changing aerobics or groups exercise, as it is now titled, scene. Some early 1990s aerobics trends, like slide, have since vanished from the fitness industry, and other sport-based forms such as spinning (indoor cycling) have evolved. IDEA (2001) establishes that two types of fitness practices grew particularly fast during 2001: the martial arts-based group exercise (boxing and strength training) at the one end and so-called mindful fitness forms (yoga, Pilates, and Tai Chi) at the opposite end of the large spectrum of group fitness exercise forms. These trends are strikingly similar to my earlier classification of aerobics into serious, hard sport type aerobics and softer, music-based aerobics in the early 1990s. Obviously, while the exercise class labels come and go in quick succession, the general division appears as identified in my ethnographic study. Why these types of activities appeal to the group exercise consumers is a topic for a future study. If the basic premise of group exercise classes has not changed, what about the oppressive, narrowly defined body image?

If aerobics has undergone only a superficial change, the ideal body within the fitness media has stayed exactly the same. My recent study (Markula 2001) demonstrated that while the fitness magazines now acknowledge the problems resulting from the narrowly defined body ideal in media, they are unwilling to touch the image of the perfect body. I was also reluctant to generalize my ethnographic findings beyond the American cultural context, but my analysis of the fitness images in New Zealand (Markula 1997) revealed an even more blatant and unquestioning celebration of the thin, toned, tanned, and young body ideal. Ten years of feminist research has not brought a widespread change in the fitness media.

When I now ask my students to identify effective strategies that could abolish the oppressive image, they invariably want to start by increasing awareness of individual exercisers, instructors, and fitness industry providers who can then resist and change to dominant image. Perhaps the individual resistant practices will eventually result in empowerment, but as our understanding of the complexities of power relations advances, our understanding of resistance (an individual working toward a clearly defined notion of liberation) might need elaboration. As it has become increasingly difficult to pinpoint sources of power, it is equally impossible to clearly define what constitutes resistance and empowerment. How, then, does the fitness industry change in the present cultural condition? And how can we direct that change? These are intriguing questions for future research into women's fitness, aerobics, health, and body image.

REFERENCES

Bakhtin, Mikhail M. 1981. "Discourse in the Novel." In *The Dialogic Imagination,* ed. Michael Holquist, 259–442. Austin, TX: University of Texas Press.

Baudrillard, Jean. 1983. *Simulations.* New York, NY: Semiotext(e).

Birrell, Susan. 1988. "Discourses on the Gender/Sport Relationship: From Women in Sport to Gender Relations." *Exercise and Sport Sciences Review* 16:459–502.

Birrell, Susan, and Nancy Theberge. 1994. "Ideological Control of Women in Sport." In *Women and Sport,* ed. Margaret Costa and Sharon Guthrie, 341–59. Champaign, IL: Human Kinetics.

———, and Diane Richter. 1987. "Is a Diamond Forever?" *Women's Studies International Forum* 10:394–409.

Bordo, Susan 1990. "Reading the Slender Body." In *Body/Politics: Women and the Discourse of Science,* ed. Mary Jacobus, Evelyn Fox Keller, and Sally Shuttleworth, 83–112. New York, NY: Routledge.

Boutilier, Mary A. and Lucinda SanGiovanni. 1983. *The SportingWoman.* Champaign, IL: Human Kinetics.

Chernin, Kim. 1981. *The Obsession: Reflections on the Tyranny of Slenderness.* New York, NY: Harper & Row.

Clifford, James. 1986. "Introduction: Partial Truths." In *Writing Culture: Poetics and Politics of Ethnography,* ed. James Clifford and George E. Marcus, 1–26. Berkeley, CA: University of California Press.

———. 1988. *The Predicament of Culture: Twentieth Century Ethnography, Literature and Art.* Cambridge, MA: Harvard University Press.

Cole, Cheryl L. 1998. "Addiction, Exercise, and Cyborgs: Technology of Deviant Bodies." In *Sport and Postmodern Times,* ed. Genevieve Rail, 261–76. Albany, NY: State University of New York Press.

———, and Amy Hribar. 1995. "Celebrity Feminism: Nike Style Post-Fordism, Transcendence, and Consumer Culture." *Sociology of Sport Journal* 12:347–69.

Duncan, Margaret C. 1994. "The Politics of Women's Body Images and Practices: Foucault, the Panopticon, and *Shape* Magazine." *Journal of Sport & Social Issues* 18:48–65.

Dunn, Robert. 1991. "Populism, Mass Culture, and Avantgarde." *Theory, Culture and Society* 9(8):111–35.

Eskes, Tina, L., Margaret C. Duncan, and Eleanor M. Miller. 1998. "The Discourse of Empowerment." *Journal of Sport & Social Issues* 3:317–44.

Featherstone, Mike. 1983. "The Body in Consumer Culture." *Theory, Culture and Society* 1(3):18–33.

———. 1988. "In Pursuit of the Postmodern: An Introduction." *Theory, Culture and Society* 6(5):195–213.

Fonda, Jane. 1981. *Jane Fonda's Workout Book.* New York, NY: Simon & Schuster.

Glassner, Barry. 1989. "Fitness and the Postmodern Self." *Journal of Health and Social Behavior* 30(6):180–91.

Gottlieb, Alma. 1989. "Rethinking Female Pollution: The Beng of Cote D'Ivoire." *Dialectical Anthropology* 14:65–79.

Haravon, Leslie. 1995. "Exercises in Empowerment: Toward a Feminist Aerobic Pedagogy." *Women in Sport and Physical Activity Journal* 4:23–44.

Hargreaves, John. 1987. "The Body, Sport and Power Relations." In *Sport, Leisure and Social Relations,* ed. John Herne, Grant Jarvy, and Alan Tomlinson, 139–59. London, England: Routledge & Kegan Paul.

Fitness Programs Trends Report. 2001. *IDEA Health and Fitness Source* January: 47–52.

Jameson, Fredric. 1983. "Postmodernism and Consumer Society." In *Antiaesthetic: Essays on the Postmodern Culture,* ed. H. Foster, 111–25. Port Townsend, WA: Bay.

Johnston, Richard. 1986. "The Story So Far: And Further Transformations?" In *Introduction to Contemporary Cultural Studies,* ed. David Punter, 277–313. London, England: Longmans.

Kagan, Elizabeth, and Margaret Morse. 1988. "The Body Electronic: Aerobic Exercise on Video." *The Drama Review* 32:164–80.

Kenen, Regina H. 1987. "Double Messages, Double Images: Physical Fitness, Self-Concepts, and Women's Exercise Classes." *Journal of Physical Education, Recreation, and Dance* 58(6):76–79.

Lenskyj, Helen. 1986. *Out of Bounds: Women, Sport and Sexuality.* Toronto, Canada: Women's Press.

Lloyd, Moya. 1996. "Feminism, Aerobics and the Politics of the Body." *Body & Society* 2:79–98.

Loland, Waaler Nina. 2000. "The Art of Concealment in a Culture of Display; Aerobicizing Women's and Men's Experience and Use of Their Own Bodies." *Sociology of Sport Journal* 17:111–29.

Lyotard, Jean-François. 1986. "Rules and Paradoxes and Svelte Appendix." *Cultural Critique* 5:209–19.

MacNeill, Margaret. 1988. "Active Women, Media Representations, Ideology." In *Not Just a Game,* ed. Jean Harvey and H. Cantelon, 195–212. Altona, Canada: University of Ottawa Press.

———. 1998. "Sex, Lies, and Videotape: The Political and Cultural Economies of Celebrity Fitness Videos." In *Sport and Postmodern Times,* ed. Genevieve Rail, 163–84. Albany, NY: State University of New York Press.

MacRobbie, Angela. 1984. "Dance and Social Fantasy." In *Gender and Generation,* ed. Mika Nava, 130–61. Basingstoke: Houndhills.

Madsen, Maria. 1989. "Aerobics Update '89." *Women's Sports and Fitness,* January/February:22–27.

Maguire, Joseph, and Louise Mansfield. 1998. "No Body's Perfect": Women, Aerobics, and the Body Beautiful." *Sociology of Sport Journal* 15:109–37.

Malanka, Patricia. 1990. "Aerobics Rebound!" *Health* March:59–65.

Markula, Pirkko. 1993. *Total-Body-Tone-Up: Paradox and Women's Realities in Aerobics.* Ph.D. dissertation. University of Illinois at Urbana-Champaign.

———. 1995. "Firm but Shapely, Fit but Sexy, Strong but Thin: The Postmodern Aerobicizing Female Bodies." *Sociology of Sport Journal* 12:424–53.

———. 1997. "Are Fit People Healthy? Health, Exercise, Active Living and the Body in Fitness Discourse." *Waikato Journal of Education* 3:21–39.

———. 2001. "Beyond the Perfect Body: Women's Body Image Distortion in Fitness Magazine Discourse." *Journal of Sport & Social Issues* 25:134–55.

———. 2002. "Bodily Dialogues: Writing the Self." In *Moving Writing: Crafting Movement in Sport Research,* ed. Jim Denison and Pirkko Markula, 29–53. New York, NY: Peter Lang.

Martin, Emily. 1987. *The Woman in the Body: Cultural Analysis of Reproduction*. Boston, MA: Beacon Press.

McDermott, Lisa. 1996. "Toward a Feminist Understanding of Physicality within the Context of Women's Physically Active and Sporting Lives." *Sociology of Sport Journal* 13:12–30.

————. 2000. "A Qualitative Assessment of the Significance of Body Perception to Women's Physical Activity Experiences: Revising Discussion of Physicalities." *Sociology of Sport Journal* 17:331–64.

McDonald, Mary, and Susan Birrell. 1999. "Reading Sport Critically: A Methodology for Interrogating Power." *Sociology of Sport Journal* 16:283.

Ortner, Sherry B. 1984. "Theory in Anthropology since the Sixties." *Comparative Studies in Society and History* 26:126–66.

Poole, Marion. 1999. "It's a Lovely Feeling: Older Women's Fitness Programs." In *In a Certain Age: Women Growing Older*, ed. Marion Poole and Sally Feldman, 87–100. St. Leonards, Australia: Allen & Unwin.

Radway, Janice. 1980. "Identifying Ideological Seams: Mass Culture, Analytical Method, and Political Practice." *Communication* 9:93–123.

Rosaldo, Renato. 1988. *Culture and Truth: Remaking the Social Analysis*. Boston: Beacon Press.

Rothlein, Linda. 1988. "Portrait of an Aerobic Dancer." *Women's Sports and Fitness* May:18.

Slowikowski, Synthia S., and Karl M. Newell. 1990. "The Philology of Kinesiology." *Quest* 2(3):279–96.

Spitzack, Carole. 1990. *Confessing Excess: Women and the Politics of Body Reduction*. Albany, NY: State University of New York Press.

Strathern, Marilyn. 1987. "An Awkward Relationship: The Case of Feminism and Anthropology." *Signs* 12(2):276–92.

Taussig, Michael. 1980. *Shamanism, Colonialism, and the Wild Man*. Chicago, IL: Chicago University Press.

Theberge, Nancy. 1987. "Sport and Women's Empowerment." *Women's Studies International Forum* 10:387–93.

Varpalotai, Aniko. 1987. "The Hidden Curriculum in Leisure: An Analysis of Girls' Sport Subculture." *Women's Studies International Forum* 10:411–22.

Veit, Katarina. 1992. "Bodysculpt." *Women's Sports and Fitness* January/February:52.

Weider, Joe. 1992. "Exercise: The Dance of Life." *Shape* January:14.

Wheatley, Elizabeth. 1988. *A Women's Rugby Subculture Contesting on the "Wild" Side of the Pitch*. Masters Thesis. University of Illinois at Urbana-Champaign.

White, Philip. G., and James Gillett. 1994. "Reading the Muscular Body: A Critical Decoding of Advertisements in *Flex* Magazine." *Sociology of Sport Journal* 11:18–39.

CHAPTER FOUR

☙

Cultural Expressions of African American Female Athletes in Intercollegiate Sport

TERESE M. PERETTO STRATTA

INTRODUCTION

Participation in intercollegiate sport can be a rewarding endeavor that provides skills and experiences that may benefit individuals throughout their lifetime. Despite the fact that institutions have demonstrated a commitment toward providing a quality experience for college athletes, trying to meet the needs of all groups of athletes is difficult for sport organizations that are culturally diverse in membership. More specifically, people who participate in sport are not just part of the athlete culture, but also products of other cultures (e.g., race, class, and gender), which predisposes them to viewing and experiencing life differently.

Given this state of affairs, I explored the cultural reality of African American women who participate in intercollegiate sport at one Predominantly White Institution (PWI). In deciding on a culture to investigate, I believed that it was important to identify a situation where culture would manifest most visibly. Within the female athlete culture, not only are African American women predisposed to feeling unusual isolation and seclusion on predominantly white campuses (Willie and Levy

1972), but as participants in a sport context that has been traditionally dominated by white males, African American female athletes are also least likely to find opportunities to express their culture. Moreover, African American women must exist in a society that "denigrates women of African descent" (Collins 1990, p. 22) and relegates them to subordinate status within the African American and Euro-American cultures (hooks 1990). Given this extremely stifling reality, African American women are therefore ideal for investigating the potential for cultural expression in sport.

METHODS

Ethnographic methods were employed to answer the research question: In what ways does college sport allow for African American female athletes to express their culture? The assumptions of ethnography allowed me to place African American female athletes at the center of the investigation so that I could discover their subjectively constructed interpretations and meanings in sport and society (Applebaum 1987).

In an attempt to highlight the cultural meanings of African American female athletes in a conceptual framework, this study relied on the premises of symbolic anthropology (D'Andrade 1990; Geertz 1973; Turner 1969). Symbolic anthropology provides a framework for recognizing and understanding identifiers of culture—how individuals shape their reality and communicate meanings (Harris and Park 1983). Symbol and sign systems serve as vehicles for communicating knowledge and messages, which in turn stimulate actions or ideas in people. Within a given context, these human responses take on meanings, intersubjectively shared systems of meaning, which represent the essence of culture.

I gained entrance into an NCAA Division IA intercollegiate program that is located in an urban area in the Northern United States. During this study, the university was comprised of over 30,000 undergraduate students from the following racial backgrounds: African American (20%), Asian-American (7%), Hispanic, International, Native American (3% or under), and white (67%) (Peterson's Guide, Inc. 1992). As one athlete stated, "It's not your average milky white university." The significance of this statement is that this particular university and the surrounding social setting were racially diverse. Thus the African American athlete felt more comfortable socially than she would have had she attended a PWI located in a predominantly white city. Many athletes throughout the study supported the belief that "This [sport experience] is as good as it gets."

One hundred female athletes who were members of ten sports participated in this study over a fifteen-month period. Thirty (30%) African

American athletes were the focus of this study in addition to four black athletes, who were United States citizens and who identified themselves as Caribbean. The participation of non-African American athletes was necessary to delineate cultural phenomena from athlete phenomena. Another reason for investigating all athletes was to avoid altering the natural environment or disrupting the team "balance" that existed prior to my entrance. Ultimately, all athletes who chose to participate were accepted as informants; however, the preponderance of my time was spent with African American athletes.

Collection of data occurred through fieldwork that entailed ascertaining indicators of culture through participant-observation, and structured and unstructured interviews (Spradley 1979, 1980; Strauss and Corbin 1990). After obtaining approval from administrators and coaches to conduct this study, I met with each of the ten teams to explain the scope of the study and to request that each of the athletes meet with me individually for one-half hour. The agenda during the individual meetings was as follows: to solicit athletes' questions and concerns about the study, to ascertain athletes' willingness to participate in the study, to acquire basic demographic information, to state my assumptions as a researcher, and to agree on the parameters of an informal agreement.

Although initially distant from athletes, over time I gradually gained entrance into the many dimensions of their lives. The ease in entering the multiple dimensions of athletes' lives was aided by the fact that initially there was little resistance to participation in this study (Stratta 1992). Most athletes commented about the novelty of someone being interested in the perceptions of female athletes. They added that a study of this scope and magnitude was desperately needed. It should be mentioned that I was not only required to gain entrance into a collegiate female athlete culture, but also contended with the issue of becoming an insider in the black culture as an Italian-American researcher. The fact that I had participated in intercollegiate sport as a scholarship athlete appeared to influence athletes' receptiveness to my presence in their lives. They also mentioned that they felt "comfortable" talking to me, acknowledging that I seemed to understand the historical relationship between black and white women, and the plight of African Americans in a racist, sexist, and classist society.

Through participant observation and interviews, I began to understand cultural phenomena and the meanings attached to them from the native perspectives (Geertz 1977) of African American female athletes. Consistent with a grounded theory approach (Glaser and Strauss 1962), other questions emerged as the study progressed. Investigating these questions guided future interviews and observations until all findings were verified. Data collection was not complete until a redundancy in responses occurred. Analysis and synthesis of these fieldnotes (data treatment) ultimately led to a theory of cultural expression in sport.

FINDINGS

In this section I identify the systems of symbols and signs used by African American female athletes (in other words, how they categorize or see the world), and the contexts that existed within their lives as intercollegiate student-athletes. The meanings that emerged within the sport context, in particular, reflected manifestations of an African American women's sport culture.

Theory of Cultural Expression in Sport

I determined that an expression of an African American women's culture was identifiable in intercollegiate sport; however, the salience of this culture became manifest in different manners and was highly dependent on context (see Figure 4.1). In this study expression of culture was profoundly influenced by team context, sport context, and the coach. Team context was defined as the percentage of black athletes on a team. This grouping was referred to as *black* athletes because Caribbean athletes, who also participated in African American cultural expressions, were included. A team context that consisted of less than 20% black female athletes was referred to as low representation; athletes on these teams generally experienced cultural inhibition. Six teams in this study consisted of low representation. When 20 to 50% of the team members were black athletes, the team context was considered to have medium representation; the salience of an African American culture became evident (cultural existence). Two of the sport teams were classified in the category of medium representation. Finally, cultural celebration resulted from a team context that had a high representation (greater than 50%) of black female athletes. Two of the teams were identified as high representation. This proposed breakdown of teams by percentages of black athletes represents a continuum rather than exact divisions of a cultural reality, and therefore, should be considered as a general guide.

Sport context, or more appropriately, sport contexts, consisted of socially constructed contexts (Hammersley and Atkinson 1983) where athletes were required or expected to affiliate with or be in the presence of members of their teams. In this study two broad categories of sport contexts emerged: competitive and noncompetitive. As implied by the

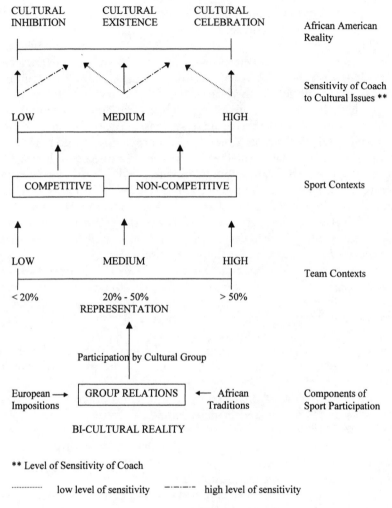

FIGURE 4.1
Theory of Cultural Expression in Sport

name, competitive sport contexts consist of the places where formal or informal sport competition occurred. These contexts included sites where practices and contests (games and meets) were conducted. Non-competitive sport contexts included locations where no formal or informal sport competition occurred while athletes interacted, yet coaches still possessed authority over and responsibility for athletes. These locations, which were either supervised or unsupervised by the coach, consisted of the following socially constructed contexts: study hall, locker rooms, training rooms, and places where team meals, lodging, travel, and leisure activities occurred.

Findings from interviews and participant-observation revealed that the coach had a profound effect on the salience of African American culture. Moreover, her/his level of sensitivity to African American cultural issues directly influenced the relative degree of safety for African American athletes to communicate expressions of their culture without being outcast by others or suffering adverse consequences. During the first academic year, the number of teams within each cultural domain (after considering the influence of the coach) was identified as follows: five teams displayed cultural inhibition, two teams displayed cultural existence, and three teams displayed cultural celebration. After a coaching change, during the second academic year the number of teams displaying cultural inhibition increased to six while the number of teams displaying cultural existence decreased to one. The number of teams displaying cultural celebration remained at three.

The domains of inhibition, existence, and celebration reflect the overall degree of cultural expression by black athletes for a particular team. Within each team context, however, I identified that black athletes experienced isolated changes in their degree of cultural expression— moments of cultural celebration and/or inhibition, for example. These subtle and contextualized changes from the overall degree of cultural expression within a team were influenced by the group relations within the sport contexts.

Investigating the nature of group relations in sport contexts assisted in theory development and in determining the salience of an African American women's sport culture. Group relations, or verbal and non-verbal forms of communication, were different in competitive and non-competitive sport contexts for black female athletes. For example, in competitive sport contexts, group interactions generally occurred with other team members whether in practice or in a contest. These contexts can also be defined as coach-controlled; that is, the athlete has little autonomy to select the group with whom she interacts. For black female athletes, cultural relations were generally peripheral in these contexts, although this finding was also influenced by team context.

In noncompetitive sport contexts, group relations generally occurred with athletes who were culturally similar. These contexts can also be defined as athlete-controlled. Moreover, athletes have a high degree of discretionary power—control over activities and the decision-making process; therefore, athletes had the freedom to choose with whom they interacted. When given a choice, black female athletes preferred interacting with athletes from the same cultural group, regardless of their team affiliation; consequently, I frequently observed groups of female athletes who were culturally segregated. Group relations were therefore culturally based and centrally located in the noncompetitive sport context.

In the remainder of this chapter, I examine more thoroughly a theory of cultural expression in sport. The degree of cultural expression in sport may be ascertained by investigating group relations among athletes. When interacting in competitive and noncompetitive sport contexts, group relations for African American athletes developed in a bicultural reality—one that is based on both African traditions and European ideals that have been *imposed* on African Americans. As important determinants for identifying where consensus of meanings exist (Tyler 1969), team and sport contexts together contributed to the emergence of a theory of cultural expression in sport. Finally, the coach's level of sensitivity to cultural issues impacted the degree of cultural expression.

Cultural Expression in Sport

A theory of cultural expression in sport reflects manifestations of the African American women's sport culture. Despite the fact that athletes of Caribbean descent shared experiences similar to those of African American athletes, I will focus on presenting the meanings and interpretations indicative of an African American cultural reality only. Group relations will be investigated in each of the domains of the African American women's sport culture: cultural inhibition, cultural existence, and cultural celebration. Each of the following sections will begin with a brief summary of contextualized relations in the sport contexts followed by examples that support the findings for each of the cultural domains.

Cultural inhibition. In a low representation team context, the cultural reality of African American female athletes was inhibited. In particular, African American female athletes were restricted from displaying dimensions of their lives that reflected their authentic cultural reality. Figure 4.2 provides a summary of how this inhibition was reinforced in sport contexts. Except for intra-team relations during contests, the competitive sport contexts were unsupportive for African American cultural expressions. For example, whether competing against teammates or opponents, black female athletes shared experiences that revealed both covert and overt forms of racially motivated encounters. The intent of these white athletes was usually to hurt an athlete (both or either physically and emotionally), and/or to get a player ejected from the competition.

The variable support for cultural expression during contests became manifest in a dualistic manner. On the one hand, African American

COMPETITIVE SPORT CONTEXT

	INTRA-TEAM RELATIONS	INTER-TEAM RELATIONS
PRACTICE	UNSUPPORTIVE	UNSUPPORTIVE
CONTEST	VARIABLE	UNSUPPORTIVE

NON-COMPETITIVE SPORT CONTEXT

	INTRA-CULTURAL RELATIONS	INTER-CULTURAL RELATIONS
SUPERVISED	VARIABLE	UNSUPPORTIVE
UNSUPERVISED	SUPPORTIVE	UNSUPPORTIVE

FIGURE 4.2
Cultural Expression in Sport Contexts
within a Low Representation Team Context

female athletes received support for their athleticism. Apparently, focusing on the task at hand, which required white athletes to join forces with black athletes to beat the competition, transcended other culturally based issues. Although African American women received much encouragement from teammates when performing in this context, when they encountered an overt form of racism from an opponent (such as a racist remark), for example, this support system suddenly disappeared. Athletes revealed that their teammates were unaware and/or not supportive of their cultural existence as members of a discrete culture.

Similar experiences were reported by athletes when participating in noncompetitive sport contexts (see Figure 4.2). Inter-cultural relations were unsupportive in both supervised and unsupervised contexts. For example, African American female athletes who interacted with black athletes from other teams encountered verbal and nonverbal feedback from non-black teammates and coaches that their behavior was inappropriate. Despite the fact that African American female athletes were only attempting to share their experiences of sport with their "own kind," the dominant white system evaluated this encounter as "fraternizing with the enemy."

While interacting with culturally similar athletes (intra-cultural relations) in noncompetitive contexts, African American female athletes experienced variable support when supervised and support when unsupervised by the coach. The variability in support in a supervised context was highly influenced by the coach's level of sensitivity to cultural issues. The support found in an unsupervised context was an outcome of the ability of athletes to engage in expressions of their culture.

The previous section provided an overview of group relations within the domain of cultural inhibition. Examples of cultural components that support these findings will be presented in the following paragraphs.

Language, which is the primary means through which people learn their culture (Werner and Schoepfle 1987), was one dimension of the lives of athletes that recurrently emerged throughout the study. Overall, three dialects of the English language were discussed by African American female athletes: "white," "black," and "ghetto." The etic terms for these dialects are Standard American English, the vernacular, and ghetto, respectively. The term "ghetto" is used in its emic form because it connotes more than spoken language. "Acting ghet-*to*" is probably more appropriate as it represents both the verbal and nonverbal symbols associated with this term.

I became acutely aware of the use of different dialects when walking with an athlete in her hometown. During our conversation, she passed a friend and said, "Hey, what up?" Her friend responded in a similar dialect (the vernacular). As we continued walking, Andrea experienced similar encounters. It occurred to me that she spoke differently to her hometown friends than she did to me. I inquired about her change in language.

TERRY: Why don't you talk like that to me?

ATHLETE: Because you're like school.

TERRY : You don't talk like that [the vernacular] in school?

ATHLETE : Yeah, but not all the time.

TERRY : Why not?

ATHLETE : Because it's not right.

TERRY : Well, when do you talk "right?"

ATHLETE : In class, like when I'm talking to a professor or when I'm talking to someone in the athletic department.

TERRY : Who in the athletic department?

ATHLETE : The trainers, coach, and other people like that.

This encounter, which occurred early in the study, initially made me aware of the extensive use of dialects by African American athletes. Rather than viewing the vernacular in the pejorative—as a correct or an incorrect usage of language—other athletes further clarified this interpretation, stating that "there's a right and a wrong *time* [emphasis added] to talk black." Nearly all African American female athletes spoke "black" in all contexts of their lives except when they encountered authority figures and white people in general. Given the fact that this dialect was described as their *native* language, encounters that necessitated that they speak Standard American English were considered antithetical to their cultural existence, and consequently, a European imposition. As members of low representation teams, African American athletes' use of Standard American English occurred in all sport contexts—competitive and noncompetitive—except for one, the noncompetitive, unsupervised sport context where athletes were interacting with athletes from their own cultural group. Since athletes spoke predominantly "white" when they were members of these teams, this context was therefore considered culturally inhibiting. This finding is further reinforced by the fact that when these athletes were outside the sport context (when they interacted with African American friends who were not teammates), they spoke almost exclusively in the vernacular.

The disproportionate number of white athletes in this team context resulted in them ultimately defining *the reality,* one that inhibited the cultural expression of African American athletes in many ways. For example, conversations among team members were usually restricted to topics that were important within the white culture. Not only were topics that impact the African American culture virtually ignored, but this context also made it difficult for the African American athlete to socialize extensively with her teammates. As one athlete stated, "Sometimes at dinner, I don't understand their [white teammates] conversation. . . . They'll say something and laugh and I don't think it's funny." When asked why she didn't initiate conversations that were important to her cultural existence, Sadonia replied that no one, except her one black teammate, would understand why she discussed the topic. In addition, a fear existed among African American athletes that discussing culturally relevant issues among a group of white people may be interpreted in a manner that inadvertently perpetuated stereotypes about African American people. For example, politics was one frequently cited topic that athletes were reluctant to discuss. Given the fact that African American athletes were acutely aware of the stereotype that "all blacks are Democrats," they were reluctant to contribute to general discussions that reflected support for a Democratic platform (welfare issues, other issues relevant to people from a low socio-economic status). Consequently, the conversations of African American athletes in both competitive and noncompetitive sport contexts were usually limited to sport-related events and to the lived reality of white athletes.

African American athletes in a team context of low representation were also less likely than athletes in other team contexts to acknowledge racial issues or tensions that arose. They may have recognized these issues, but were more cautious about verbalizing their thoughts. For example, Jade, a member of a team with three African American teammates, was complaining to Dallese about the racism that she had recently encountered in practice. Dallese, one of two African American athletes on another team with low representation, responded by saying, "We don't have time to think of race. I'm not going to deny it, it does exist, but we try to keep that stuff off the field." In the next statement Dallese contradicted herself. She continued, "It does come on the field, but you can't let it bother you because there's just one mission and that's to win."

Two common themes are salient in these quotes. The statement "we try to keep that stuff off the field" conveys the message that she chose not to discuss the racism because the only other person that may understand and support her perspective was her African American teammate. Secondly, Dallese communicated a response that was frequently heard among African American athletes when she stated, "you can't let it bother you because there's just one mission and that's to win." Athletes were inhibited from expressing culturally relevant concerns because if they *bring it onto the field,* it may cause a disruption, which in turn may *hurt the team.* This paradoxical situation can be labeled as *sacrificing the culture for the good of the team*—a theme that was dominant in the lives of African American athletes who participated in sports with a low representation team context. It reflects the struggle of athletes between defending the culture and *doing what is best for the team.* In response to this struggle, athletes usually chose to remain silent and thus were culturally stifled. The coach, on the other hand, has the authority to change this context so that African American athletes are no longer silenced when confronting racial issues. For example, by fostering a *safe* environment that is conducive for athletes to *speak out* on all issues, the coach provides the necessary support for communication that would otherwise be considered unimportant and counterproductive to the mission of the team.

Other information was discovered that supports the thesis that little *space* or opportunity was available for diverse cultural expressions in a low representation team context. One informant shared an example of a commonly stated type of cultural inhibition:

When I was growing up, I got this all the time. "Cheryl, you're one of the good black people. You're not like the rest of them. . . ." It's like pure racism. They see one black person and they're like, "She's a good one." I'm like "No, we're all good. People are bad." They just don't get it.

This quote, which illustrates one type of racism that athletes must contend with during their entire lives, reinforced the belief that athletes who have the ability to function in a white reality were viewed as *non-blacks* as opposed to being recognized for their cross-cultural abilities. Suggesting that *you're one of us* revealed marginalization of and disregard for the cultural reality of the African American athlete.

One response to the cultural inhibition experienced by African American athletes in this context was to form bonds or close relationships with teammates and/or athletes from other teams (African American and non-African American) who share the same cultural perspective. This grouping of athletes frequently occurred in unsupervised, noncompetitive sport contexts; however, it also occurred in a supervised sport context. As one athlete stated, "If it wasn't for Jaresse and Tonda [who are teammates], I don't know what I would do." This comment, which was frequently heard from athletes on low representation teams, was stated to reinforce the point that no one really understood her plight as an African American woman in intercollegiate athletics except for her African American teammates.

Having the opportunity to communicate with other black athletes (African American and Caribbean) appeared important for survival in a team context of low representation since these athletes served as their primary means of support in a predominantly white team context. Interestingly, *preserving* the opportunity to communicate with their "own kind" transcended personal conflicts that occurred between African American athletes. Athletes appeared to be more accepting and more tolerant of each other within this team context. For example, during Dana's first year, she was one of three African American athletes on a team. She admitted that the low number of African American teammates persuaded her to be more patient with Shana, one of her African American teammates. But during her second year, with five African American female athletes on the team, she no longer felt compelled to talk to Shana. Although this theme of being more tolerant of culturally similar athletes generally held true for African American athletes in this context, one athlete admitted, "there's just some things you just can't tolerate . . . we didn't get along as people. We were two different types of people completely." This quote illuminates the point that even though interacting on the basis of shared cultural perspectives was initially an important factor for developing and sustaining intra-cultural relationships in an inhibiting context, the personalities of athletes had to be compatible for personal relationships to endure.

In a low representation team context, a change in sport context generally did not affect the salience of culture. More specifically, changing from a competitive to noncompetitive context did not change the cultural inhibition except when athletes were grouped intra-culturally. A change in the coach (from white to black) or in a coach's level of sensitivity to cultural issues (from low to high), however, did appear to have a profound effect on the salience of culture. Two African American coaches improved the degree of African American cultural expression within their respective teams so that I frequently observed signs and symbols of cultural expression from African American athletes. During the subsequent year, this same degree of expression had virtually disappeared on one of the teams. The only difference in the team context from one year to the next occurred in a coaching change; the African American head coach was replaced with a white coach who exhibited a limited understanding of African American cultural issues. Interviews with African American athletes supported the thesis that the context was not as supportive and as safe for the expression of culture after a new head coach was hired. They added that a coach's awareness and understanding of an African American reality in social institutions and society in general was a crucial element impacting their degree of cultural expression in sport.

Cultural existence. When approximately 20 to 50% of the team members consisted of black athletes, symbols and signs of an African American culture began to emerge. The increase in participation of black athletes resulted in the emergence of a system of support, which can be characterized as an increase in the number of *safe spaces* or opportunities for cultural expression in a given context. Consequently, not only were African American athletes more likely to communicate cultural phenomena, but also non-African American athletes appeared more willing to participate in similar expressions of the African American culture. For example, amidst this system of support, all athletes, regardless of race, were more likely to request music that originated from the African American culture (such as rap or hip-hop).

Despite the increase in opportunities for cultural expression, the great amount of variability that existed within the competitive and non-competitive sport contexts reflects the tremendous ability of the coach to influence contextual relations (see Figure 4.3). On the one hand, the coach can suppress forms of cultural expression, resulting in cultural inhibition; yet on the other hand, the coach can foster a supportive environment, one where athletes from diverse cultural groups are allowed to mutually express their cultures.

COMPETITIVE SPORT CONTEXT

	INTRA-TEAM RELATIONS	INTER-TEAM RELATIONS
PRACTICE	VARIABLE	VARIABLE
CONTEST	SUPPORTIVE	UNSUPPORTIVE

NON-COMPETITIVE SPORT CONTEXT

	INTRA-CULTURAL RELATIONS	INTER-CULTURAL RELATIONS
SUPERVISED	VARIABLE	VARIABLE
UNSUPERVISED	SUPPORTIVE	UNSUPPORTIVE

FIGURE 4.3
Cultural Expression in Sport Contexts
within a Medium Representation Team Context

Similar to other team contexts, sport contexts that were support-ive of African American cultural expressions were more likely to exist when all athletes of a team were competing against an opponent, and when African American athletes were interacting with athletes from the same cultural group. Relative to the latter context, during per-sonal interviews athletes disclosed the fact that they preferred or felt safer interacting with their "own kind" because of the enhanced understanding from a cultural perspective. As one athlete stated, "They know where you're coming from so you don't have to explain everything." Knowing where one was "coming from" appeared to improve the degree of trust and, consequently, culturally based dis-course that was not evident in other sport contexts. African American athletes received unsupportive comments from teammates and coaches when they interacted with athletes from other teams and from other cultural groups. Examples of cultural components that support this overview of the domain of cultural existence are pro-vided in the following paragraphs.

The existence of African American cultural phenomena was initially visible through the use of language. For example, African American athletes not only "talk white," but also "talk black" or spoke in the vernacular when conversing with teammates of all races. Although athletes used the following pejoratives to describe the latter dialect: "lazy," "cutting-off words," "inappropriate use of verb tenses and past participles," and "ignorant," they all admitted that speaking "this way" was part of the African American culture. In general, "talking black" can more appropriately be described as the use of words and phrases that are indigenous to the African American culture, and changes in the spoken length of words, either elongated or abbreviated, that coincide with and reinforce the intended message.

Within a medium representation team context, two main cultural subgroups or cliques emerged—usually one whose members were predominantly black and supported the interests of African Americans, and one whose members included the remainder of athletes on the team. At times, a third neutral group emerged that was comprised of athletes who, irrespective of race or cultural affiliation, were capable of "hanging" with either subgroup. Interestingly, black athletes of non-African American descent bonded with African American athletes or with members of the neutral group. One feature that was unique to teams in this context was that the dominant cultural reality of each cultural subgroup mutually existed; consequently, a variety of cultural signs and symbols were noticeable from African American athletes and their allies despite the large number of non-African American athletes in this team context.

The team operated in harmony or disharmony depending on the personalities of and camaraderie among the group's leaders, and the sensitivity of the coach to African American cultural issues. For example, if the coach was uninformed about the needs of African American athletes, disagreements occurred as a result of different cultural preferences (such as the type of music played or food consumed). Unlike African American athletes in the culturally inhibiting context, those who participated in the context of cultural existence appeared more empowered, and thus more likely to challenge the system by expressing their views—a theme that was consistent among athletes who participated in this team context. Sport context, however, played an influential role in the degree and nature of team interaction. As mentioned previously, in competitive sport contexts, team cohesion usually prevailed, especially when athletes were engaged in contests with other teams. In noncompetitive sport contexts (such as restaurants or busses), however, segregation of cultural groups was more likely to occur. In the African American cultural group, topics of discussion included issues that were important to

African American women and their lived reality. This segregation of team members was viewed differently by different subgroups. Essentially, each group located itself at the center of the team (Asante 1993) and questioned why the other group (the marginal group) did not "join the team." The group with the numerical majority—which in this context was white—was usually viewed as "the team" by white coaches. For example, one African American athlete described the following encounter that occurred during a team dinner in a restaurant: "The coach asked me why I didn't join the team. I told her I was with my teammates." The coach's question marginalized the African American athletes by locating the white athletes at the center of the team and suggesting that the black athletes (African American and Caribbean) were separating themselves from "the team," as opposed to placing responsibility on the group of white athletes, who were sitting at another table, to join "the team."

Racial tensions were more prominent in this context than in the team contexts of low or high representation. Additionally, athletes encountered racism in both competitive and noncompetitive sport contexts. In competitive sport contexts, racism occurred both overtly (verbal and physical attacks) and covertly as was seen in the differential treatment and evaluation of athletes by coaches. An athlete, who was one of three captains, commented, "She [the coach] only talked to me if the other [white] captains weren't around." In addition, racism was institutionalized. As one athlete recollected, "She [the opponent] called me a nigger in front of the ref and he didn't do anything; but if I said a curse word, I would be carded immediately."

In noncompetitive sport contexts, African American athletes experienced forms of racism that were generally more covert and sophisticated. For example, African American athletes were frequently followed by personnel in a store when traveling with their respective teams, especially when a group of black athletes entered a store together.

Athletes in this context were more inclined to react to racism than were athletes who participated in a culturally inhibiting context. At times, responding to the racism became as important as the outcome of the competitive event. For example, after being called "nigger" and receiving excessive physical abuse from a white opponent during a competitive event, one athlete recollected:

ATHLETE: Those games are, like, fun. I look at that opportunity to, like, take out frustration. You can't take out frustrations everyday of like racism and all that stuff. We get on the soccer field and you, like, totally take it out on them.

TERRY: How do you "take it out?"

ATHLETE: Just, like, being really, the Major University game was just like [that]. Afterwards I was just, like, "Whew." It was like all my anger for the month was gone. I just took it out on them. Just made them feel pain.

TERRY: How do you make them "feel pain?"

ATHLETE: Either, like, through hitting them on the field or out-skilling them. Just pissing them off. It's, like, stuff, like, that makes them mad. There's someone out there that can be better than them or stronger than them . . . like when I go into a tackle, I try to go extra hard. Just stuff like that . . . when I shield the ball from them, that pisses them off . . . I throw elbows, stuff, like, that they [the referees] can't really see . . . I get a lot of calls for me like for tripping. They trip me a lot.

TERRY: You dive a lot.

ATHLETE: Yeah, and that's, like, it pisses them off . . . and then you try to get the ref on your side if he's a good ref . . . you don't want to let them [the opponent] see you sweat. . . . You can't let them see you emotional or hurt. Because when I see someone hurt, it's like I'm one notch above them now.

This athlete responded to the racism with the intention of making her opponent "feel pain." This pain metaphorically extended beyond the physical, however. In response to racism, a new game or *game within the sport* emerged. Athletes frequently mentioned that they engaged in the following actions during a competitive event as a result of an initial racial confrontation: "out-skill" the opponent, commit minor or flagrant fouls, fake fouls ("draw a foul"), say insulting remarks ("talkin' trash"), or attempt to win support from referees. The goal of this game was to alter the opponent's normal style of play ("make her sweat") to the point where she *takes herself out of the game*. Ultimately, the winner of this *racialized game* was the one who could endure the competition, regardless of the level of violence, without showing pain. Becoming "emotional" or "hurt" symbolically represented defeat. On the level of the actual sport competition, however, victory was achieved when the opponent committed mental or physical errors, or fouled-out of the competitive event.

Winning games that were provoked by some form of racism took on special significance to many African American athletes. Actions by opponents who displayed evidence of racism were viewed not only as an attack on the individual, but also as an assault on the culture in general. A high degree of satisfaction was received from winning since African American athletes "know" that white athletes, especially those who have revealed their racial ideologies, have difficulty coping with the fact that they are physically and mentally out-played ("out-skilled") by an African American athlete.

Similar to low representation teams, any strife that occurred among African American athletes within their own teams was not openly expressed and customarily remained within the culture. As one athlete explained:

> ATHLETE: If we get mad at each other, we'll come to each other with it instead of going talking and whispering. We'll just go straight to each other like with "what's the problem?"
>
> TERRY: You're saying with black athletes on the team?
>
> ATHLETE: Yeah, I think you have to. . . . For me to go to someone white, which is my other opportunity, and whisper to them is just, it seems like kind of a betrayal. You know what I mean. It's, like, no. If it's between black people, keep it between black people. It's like something we have to work out. If we don't work it out, it just stays between us though. You know [you] don't try to bring anyone else into it because that's not right.

The betrayal mentioned by this athlete extended beyond the sport context. Sharing an intra-cultural conflict with white teammates was not only interpreted as a personal attack but, more importantly, regarded as a violation of a cultural *rule*. The purpose of this *rule* was to prevent white people from gaining *inside* information as it may be misinterpreted and used in an inappropriate and harmful manner. More specifically, athletes were acutely aware of the historical predisposition of white people to improperly generalize and to foster stereotypes about African American people. Given this knowledge, athletes remained conscious of how their actions may be [mis]interpreted as representative of the larger culture. Additionally, one theme commonly understood among African American athletes was that allowing white people to "know your business" essentially provides them with information "to find flaw with black people."

As highlighted in the previous paragraph, African American athletes frequently must *carry the burden of the culture on their shoulders*. Contributing to this extra responsibility was the fact that white athletes were generally more outspoken about racial issues, regardless of their sensitivity and education about perspectives that differed from mainstream ideologies. To avoid condoning the beliefs of white athletes and subsequently contributing to their own oppression (through silence), African American athletes frequently provided alternative perspectives. In fact, African American athletes in this context were more inclined to *speak out* than athletes who were members of teams with low representation. As one athlete recalled:

> It's like little things that you have to teach white people, like . . . we always get in these conversations like uhh, on the bus, me and Kerry got in a con-

versation about Koreans and blacks . . . I told her why there's animosity between the two races and stuff because she doesn't see it. . . . Like, I was trying to explain to her how, like, there's just this thing with Koreans getting all this money to open businesses, but blacks have been here forever and nobody gives them money to open businesses. Little things like that. . . . And with Kim and them, we talked about Malcolm X and all that stuff because she doesn't understand how anyone could like him. I tried to explain. It's just they're [white teammates] kind of oblivious to that kind of history . . . sometimes it makes you mad that I know so much [historical knowledge] about them. How come they don't know about me? . . . If you get in a discussion over just anything, affirmative [action] being reverse racism [or] things like that, you have to explain. . . . At least they'll see it in another light instead of just having one view of it. They may not agree still, but they'll see it [an alternative perspective].

This athlete provided various examples of the burden of responsibility that African American athletes frequently must endure when participating in a medium representation team context. Many athletes reinforced the fact that their views about societal issues would not be considered during team discussions unless expressed by themselves or other African American athletes. This *educating* of teammates—teaching athletes a perspective that challenges and/or contradicts their dominant white paradigms—in addition to coping with racism in general are examples of energy that was unnecessarily expended by African American athletes.

Although the context of medium representation was easier for African American athletes to discuss culturally relevant issues and safer to express their cultural reality, athletes still contended with cultural oppression. The following incident is a poignant example that illustrates the reality of cultural existence, where athletes were required to compromise their culture for the good of the team.

> I was on a roadtrip with a team. During the ride from the hotel to a contest, an African American athlete brought a tape to the bus driver so that the team could "psych-up" for the game. Without even looking at the tape, the white bus driver stated emphatically, "I don't play rap music on this bus!" The athlete replied, "It's not really rap." Needless to say, it was really rap. During the second song, the bus driver decreased the volume. Shortly after the beginning of the third song, he ejected the tape and said, "Sorry girls, this isn't music." Upon retrieving the tape, the athlete stated, "This is our culture, it's the roots of our music." The assistant coach, who was sitting in the front right seat, turned around and blurted, "It's not music!" The athlete said nothing and returned to her seat.

Despite the fact that this athlete displayed some resistance—attempting to explain the significance of the music beyond the scope of its effect on the team (as a motivational device)—she was rendered silent, ultimately succumbing to the demands of the white authority figures (bus driver, coach). Two issues that are salient in this scenario commonly occurred in a medium representation team context: 1) the signs and symbols of an African American culture were virtually stifled, and 2) the leadership abilities of African American female athletes were trivialized or ignored.

Relative to the first issue, even though the athlete felt comfortable providing some recourse to the actions of the bus driver, the argument for symbolic representation of her culture was clearly unimportant to the white authority figures. She was thus forced to compromise her culture in order to fulfill her obligation as a dutiful athlete of the team. In addressing the latter issue, I discovered in a subsequent interview that this tape was traditionally played on the bus from the hotel to a contest to motivate the team; and secondly, the tape belonged to a white athlete. Rather than viewing the African American athlete as a leader who was delivering the tape on behalf of her teammates, the bus driver and assistant coach appeared more preoccupied with her skin color and what it represented. More specifically, the bus driver assumed the music was rap when an African American woman gave him the tape rather than viewing it as music to which the entire team could listen. Similarly, the assistant coach ignored the fact that rap music was desired by the team and considered necessary for them to "psych-up" for the upcoming competition. If the African American athlete was viewed as a leader, the coach probably would have condoned the playing of the tape (for the good of the team) despite her own dislike of the music.

As depicted in the theory of cultural expression (Figure 4.1), the coach possesses the ability to enhance or inhibit the cultural expression of African American female athletes in this team context. In the previous case, for example, the coach could have insisted that the bus driver play the music for the team regardless of his musical preferences. This action would have resulted in a team context that was more accepting and supportive of the cultural values of African Americans.

Cultural celebration. When the majority of the team or the entire team was comprised of African American athletes, the diversity that exists within the African American culture became visible. The dynamics within the team reflected the athletes' abilities to *define* the contextual reality, as opposed to existing in an unfamiliar and alienating one. In this context of cultural celebration, athletes were uninhibited about displaying the range of behaviors, attitudes, beliefs, and traditions possessed by each person and reflective of an African American existence. So in general, I observed multiple dimensions of athletes' personalities and their cultural reality. Similar to the team context of medium representation, the increased salience of cultural expression resulted not only from the increased number of African American athletes in the context but, more importantly, from the system of support that became manifest with their presence. As one athlete stated, "I look forward to practice and being with my friends. It is like my escape [from white people]."

As noted in Figure 4.4, support for cultural expression was found in all sport contexts except when African American athletes interacted with athletes from other sport teams and other cultural groups. With reference to group relations in the competitive sport context, the occurrence of inter-team conflict with opponents was not seen as frequently as with teams that had medium or low representation. One reason for this change in behavior was that athletes in a high representation team context were usually competing against teams whose membership also consisted of a high percentage of black athletes. This context was identified as variable, however, because the incidence of inter-cultural conflict increased as the racial composition of opposing teams became dissimilar, thus resulting in less support for African American cultural expression.

COMPETITIVE SPORT CONTEXT

	INTRA-TEAM RELATIONS	INTER-TEAM RELATIONS
PRACTICE	SUPPORTIVE	SUPPORTIVE
CONTEST	SUPPORTIVE	VARIABLE

NON-COMPETITIVE SPORT CONTEXT

	INTRA-CULTURAL RELATIONS	INTER-CULTURAL RELATIONS
SUPERVISED	SUPPORTIVE	VARIABLE
UNSUPERVISED	SUPPORTIVE	UNSUPPORTIVE

FIGURE 4.4
Cultural Expression in Sport Contexts
within a High Representation Team Context

As one athlete recalled, "We were running side by side and this [white] girl's like 'Ohh, don't touch me. Don't touch me, you're black!' Like it's gonna rub-off." Similar to other team contexts, inter-cultural relations were considered variable in a supervised context and unsupportive in an unsupervised context. Examples of cultural components that support this overview of the domain of cultural celebration are provided in the following paragraphs.

Similar to previous cultural domains, language served as a powerful purveyor of culture in the team context of high representation. In addition to the vernacular, which was expressed almost exclusively, a third dialect was spoken, "talking ghetto." "Talking ghetto" (also referred to as "gutter") was not frequently recognized as a dialect by African American athletes as it extended beyond the spoken word. In fact, "acting ghet-*to*" was more recognizable by athletes, and thus a better descriptor of this form of cultural expression. In addition to "speaking loudly," "using harsh tones," and "cursing," for example, acting ghetto was also identified by many nonverbal signs. As one athlete stated:

> There are a lot of people on campus that are very ghetto. And a lot of people that are from nice families act ghetto. You know—colored hair, not like all colored, like one spot; or blue hair with pink and green. That's so ghetto and that's what's accepted. . . . Girls come with big ol' Rashida earrings [hoop earrings]. And the people that are, like, in, a lot of them are, like, very materialistic and everything. So you think you have to be part of the Jones.

Other nonverbal indicators of acting ghetto include "goose-necking" or moving one's head from side-to-side while talking, and an extensive use of the hands and fingers—one hand on the hip and the other with a finger extended and moving side-to-side—in conjunction with the spoken words.

Although "acting ghet-*to*" was recognized as a dialect within the African American culture, athletes considered this behavior inappropriate as it connotes ignorance and a lack of sophistication when it is performed *out of context* (outside an informal gathering of African American people). For example, while walking to dinner one night, (a noncompetitive sport context), I observed Deidre talking loudly to her teammates who were walking across the street. In a later interview a teammate, Tasha, recalled the incident to explain the concept of "acting ghet-*to*" and to voice disapproval with the behavior of Deidre. Even though Tasha recognized the fact that her teammate was just "having fun," she believed that talking loudly while walking down the street of a small white town reinforced negative stereotypes about African Americans as being loud and obnoxious. On the other hand, in a team context that consisted of all black representation, athletes frequently interjected "ghetto" verbals and nonverbals during conversations when only teammates were present. Using the dialect during these discussions was imperative for reinforcing a message that would have been otherwise incomplete if not conveyed in this manner.

Hairstyles and clothing were also visibly more diverse and reflective of an African heritage in a high representation team context. For example, in addition to a range of relaxed hair styles, athletes wore their hair naturally and in braids. Athletes openly discussed hair care, frequently asking each other "Who did your hair?" Physical appearance, in general, was an important cultural value in the lives of African American athletes. The fact that athletes were more comfortable than in other contexts wearing a variety of hairstyles and clothing, in addition to speaking a variety of dialects, reinforces the thesis that a higher degree of safety for cultural expression existed in this context.

In contrast to athletes who participated in other team contexts, African American athletes in this context did not display behavior that revealed a sacrifice or compromise of their cultural existence. The beliefs and behaviors of athletes in this context constituted *the reality*. For example, during a study hall session, seven athletes were sitting in a group discussing events that pertained to their sport experiences and to life in general (such as not studying). All new thoughts were initiated by one of the five African American athletes. In addition, athletes spoke exclusively in the vernacular with use of "ghetto talk" when appropriate to reinforce a message. Whenever the two white athletes participated in discussions, their contributions were limited. At best, they could be considered as passive participants (for example, laughing along with their teammates). Sitting away from the group, I suddenly noticed that not only was the conversation of African American athletes central, but also they were physically located in the center of the group, while white athletes sat on the periphery. In fact, two of the African American athletes had to turn around in their chairs to see the white athletes. For athletes in a high representation team context, these group interactions occurred on a consistent basis, but did not occur with African American athletes in other team contexts.

As highlighted in the previous example, athletes in this team context were generally more outspoken, conversing about issues that were important to African Americans. Many of the discussions pertained to cultural signs and symbols portrayed in the media. For example, athletes frequently talked about the content of television shows that particularly appealed to an African American audience (such as *A Different World, Martin, In Living Color,* or *Russell Simmons' Def Comedy Jam*). The latest music releases, in particular rap music, were also frequently discussed. Lyrics from this music were commonly interjected into conversations—"What up?" or "What's your man got to do with me?" I frequently observed athletes discussing and imitating the latest dance moves by musicians who performed on music videos and commonly heard conversations about local forms of entertainment (such as dance clubs) that appealed to an African American clientele. Finally, athletes discussed the content of articles in magazines that were popular in the African American culture (such as *Ebony, Essence, Jet*).

Athletes' increased freedom of expression was additionally seen through their use of humor. Although joking was also heard in other contexts, in the team context of high representation athletes appeared less inhibited to interject *racially based,* humorous comments. For example, when the movie *White Men Can't Jump* began to play, the track team initiated the expression "White Girls Can't Run." Joking also occurred intra-culturally, and was frequently referred to as "dogging" someone. The nature of this joking was usually based on values and norms within the African American culture. In the following paragraph I describe an encounter that typifies this intra-cultural joking.

> At the end of practice, I was "hanging" with a team that was stretching. During a discussion, Charese invited me to her home where she was modelling in a lingerie show. When I asked her where she lived, Shorty, her teammate, blurted out, "You go down two blocks and turn right at the trash can." Both athletes then started laughing.

I concluded two things after this conversation: 1) Shorty was communicating that Charese lived in the ghetto; and 2) this conversation, and the subsequent laughing, would not have occurred in a sport context if both athletes did not feel safe about expressing multiple dimensions of their culture. The frequency and visibility of racially-based humor provided another example of the high degree of safety that existed within this team context.

As in other team contexts, the concept of safety appeared to be an important factor in determining the degree to which athletes express cultural phenomena; however, the definition and meaning of safety in this context were more encompassing. As demonstrated in the previous example, a *safe* sport context can be characterized as one where athletes share culturally relevant information (provide criticism) without offending their teammates. Within this team context, essentially a high level of respect and trust existed among teammates. The information exchanged between athletes would not normally be offered in other contexts, especially those in which white people were present. Finally, a *safe* context was one where the message was perceived and understood as intended, and not distorted by those who participated in the exchange of information.

The increased sense of freedom of expression experienced by athletes resulted in a context where a greater number of African American athletes were more frequently contributing to conversations. I frequently observed discussions among athletes where two to four conversations were occurring at the same time. Unlike other team contexts, African American athletes in this context were initiating and/or participating in at least one of these conversations. This increased participation in discussions, however, resulted in a greater propensity for intra-cultural and inter-personal conflicts to occur among African American athletes. One explanation for this increased incidence of conflicts is that the diversity of norms that exist in the larger African American culture are more salient within a high representation team context. So in addition to becoming more outspoken, African American athletes who participate in this team context tend to be more critical of one another.

Another explanation for the intra-cultural conflict may be related to a change in the social needs of athletes. In a context that is supportive of diverse cultural expression, the need to "hang together" is no longer as crucial to survival as in other contexts where African American athletes are the numerical minority. Athletes appeared less tolerant of others' actions and more willing to communicate their dissatisfaction with teammates. Although this intra-cultural conflict may be considered problematic for the individual, within a high representation team context these behaviors can be interpreted as manifestations of the cultural freedom experienced by African American athletes. More specifically, group relations more closely mirrored the African American culture and thus reflected the diversity, whether supportive or problematic, that is present in the larger society. This conflict, therefore, was viewed as a normal outcome of intra-cultural relations as opposed to imposed or oppressive conflict that results from existing in a bicultural reality.

Interestingly, when African American athletes interacted in a context where they were no longer the numerical majority (noncompetitive, unsupervised sport context), their actions mirrored those of athletes who participated in low and medium representation team contexts. For example, during a roadtrip, I accompanied two athletes while they were shopping in a predominantly white town. When talking among the group, athletes spoke in the vernacular; however, after entering a clothes store, they immediately began speaking Standard American English to the white saleswoman. During subsequent interviews, athletes shared with me knowledge that they had learned from past experiences. Although not the *rule,* speaking "white" usually improved the service they received and/or deterred white salespeople from following them throughout the store. On other occasions, however, white store attendants could not "get past" their skin color, thus athletes were closely scrutinized while browsing through the store. Even though athletes in this team context experienced cultural celebration in some sport contexts, they inevitably could not escape societal racism that pervades the lives of African American people. As one athlete stated, "It's like a popular song on the radio. You keep hearing it over and over everyday."

As in other team contexts, the coach may influence the salience of an African American culture in sport. In a high representation team context, however, the coach may only inhibit the level of cultural expression as it is usually at an optimal level.

SUMMARY

This chapter presented a theory of cultural expression in sport that is reflective of an African American women's sport culture—one where athletes must exist in a bicultural reality. Two main contexts, the team context and the sport context, greatly influenced the degree of cultural expression in sport. Additionally, the coach's level of sensitivity to cultural issues can either enhance or diminish the degree of cultural expression in sport.

Analysis of group relations in team contexts revealed three domains of cultural expression. More specifically, a team context that consisted of low representation (less than 20% black athletes) resulted in cultural inhibition. Basically, athletes were subjected to existing in a "white" reality—one that was based on European traditions. In the medium representation team context (20 to 50% black athletes), symbols and signs of an African American culture became manifest. Additionally, non-African American athletes revealed signs of appreciation for African American cultural phenomena. Finally, in a high representation team context (greater than 50% black athletes), African American athletes defined contextual relations. In this context of cultural celebration their culturally based interactions and expressions were optimal, thus revealing the diversity that exists within the African American culture.

Within each team context, athletes experienced a variety of support for cultural expressions that were highly dependent on specific sport contexts and the influence of the coach. Ultimately, the degree of cultural expression revealed by African American athletes was impacted by the level of safety that was perceived by athletes in any given context.

African American female athletes are hindered by norms, values, and rules that are inconsistent with their lived reality as African American women in society, yet pervade intercollegiate sport. Given the limited opportunities for these athletes to celebrate their culture, I propose that African American female athletes are predisposed to feeling like *athletic intruders* when participating in predominantly white team contexts (low and medium representation). Except for a high representation team context, where athletes are more prone to experience cultural celebration and empowerment, African American athletes must sacrifice and compromise their culture to *fit in* to the existing cultural system of intercollegiate sport. Given this alienating and disenfranchising experience, I conclude that the social institution of sport does not allow for culturally diverse groups, such as African American women, to freely express their culture.

REFERENCES

Applebaum, H. 1987. "Symbolic and Humanistic Anthropology." In *Perspectives in Cultural Anthropology,* ed. H. Applebaum, 477–87. Albany, NY: State University of New York Press.

Asante, M. K. 1993. "Location Theory and African Aesthetics." In *The African Aesthetic: Keeper of the Traditions,* ed. K. Welsh-Asante, 53–62. Westport, CT: Greenwood.

Collins, P. H. 1990. *Black Feminist Thought: Knowledge, Consciousness, and the Politics of Empowerment.* Boston, MA: Unwin Hyman.

D'Andrade, R. G. 1990. "Cultural Meaning Systems." In *Culture Theory: Essays on Mind, Self, and Emotion,* ed. R. A. Shweder and R. A. LeVine, 88–119. New York, NY: Cambridge University Press.

Geertz, C. 1973. *The Interpretation of Cultures.* New York, NY: Basic Books.

———. 1977. "'From the Native's Point of View': On the Nature of Anthropological Understanding." In *Symbolic Anthropology,* ed. J. L. Dolgin, D. S. Kemnitzer, and D. M. Schneider, 480–92. New York, NY: Columbia University Press.

Glaser, B. G., and Strauss, A. L. 1967. *The Discovery of Grounded Theory: Strategies for Qualitative Research.* Chicago, IL: Aldine.

Hammersley, M., and Atkinson, P. 1983. *Ethnography: Principles in Practice.* New York, NY: Tavistock.

Harris, J. C., and Park, R. J. 1983. "Introduction to the Sociocultural Study of Play, Games, and Sports." In *Play, Games & Sports in Cultural Contexts,* ed. J. C. Harris and R. J. Park, 1–36. Champaign, IL: Human Kinetics.

hooks, b. 1990. *Yearning: Race, Gender and Cultural Politics.* Boston, MA: South End Press.

Peterson's Guide, Inc. 1992. *Peterson's Guide to Four-Year Colleges.* Princeton, NJ: Peterson's Guide, Inc.

Spradley, J. P. 1979. *The Ethnographic Interview*. Fort Worth, TX: Holt, Rinehart, & Winston.

———. 1980. *Participant Observation*. Fort Worth, TX: Holt, Rinehart, & Winston.

Stratta, T. M. 1992. "Crossing Racial Lines: Gaining Entrance in Ethnographic Research." Paper presented at the annual conference of the North American Society for the Sociology of Sport, Toledo, OH.

Strauss, A., and Corbin, J. 1990. *Basics of Qualitative Research: Grounded Theory Procedures and Techniques*. Newbury Park, CA: Sage.

Turner, V. 1969. *The Ritual Process*. Chicago, IL: Aldine, 1969.

Tyler, S. A. 1969. *Cognitive Anthropology*. New York, NY: Holt, Rinehart & Winston.

Werner, O., and Schoepfle, G. M. 1987. *Systematic Fieldwork: Ethnographic Analysis and Data Management*. Newbury Park, CA: Sage.

Willie, C., and Levy, J. 1972. "Black is Lonely." *Psychology Today* 5 (October):50–80.

CHAPTER FIVE

Beauty or the Beast:
The Subversive Soma

ANNE BOLIN

INTRODUCTION

This chapter undertakes a textual analysis of Western women's bodies that is politically engaged. The body as relation, as reflection, and as reform is articulated through the phenomenon of competitive women's bodybuilding, which offers insight into the multivocality and contradiction embodied in the muscular soma. The bodybuilders' contours are contextualized and discussed as a script of gender relations embedded in a struggle between notions of strength and weakness, doing and display, and presented metaphorically as beauty or the beast. Despite cultural frosting with symbols of traditional "feminine frailty" that pervade the public realm of competitive bodybuilding, it is argued here that the women's muscular physiques are critical, rebellious, and reforming. This chapter locates "the beast" in women's competitive bodybuilding in spite of the beauty.

RE-READINGS OF THE BODY

The goal of this research is to contribute to an apparently burgeoning interest by anthropology inspired and fired by the symbolic approach of the body as metaphor in the work of Douglas (1973) and the bio-political interpretations of Foucault (1985) (cf Armstrong 1983). As a consequence of the efforts of the latter, a new synthesis has arisen between anthropology, history, and literature (cf Armstrong 1983; Gallagher and Laqueur 1987; Turner 1984), leading to the "centrality of the body" as a recent foci in contemporary scientific discourses (Gallagher and Laqueur 1987:vii).

Since my purpose is not an encyclopedia of the history of scientific thought on the body, at the risk of glossing, it is perhaps not unreasonable to characterize Western scientific paradigms as encoding intellectual moiety systems that have polarized mind and body. This has been clearly represented in the Durkheimian (1961:29) notion of homo duplex, wherein reason and passion have respectively resided. Polarization, in part, has harkened back to the Christian tradition of spirit and flesh, sacred and secular, as well as Cartesian mind-body dualism (cf Turner 1984). The Christian and Cartesian discourse on the body subsequently became medicalized by the end of the eighteenth century into a full-blown object, and crystallized in the nineteenth century, according to Foucault, as an object of power (Armstrong 1983:xi,2).

Twentieth-century social theorizing has witnessed the body as a biological organism in the works of Social Darwinists and Functionalists (such as Parsons), as a system of needs and sites of subjugation according to the Marxists, as desire by the Freudians, and as choreographed in the writings of the symbolic interactionists (Turner 1984:2). Feminist and postmodern perspectives have surpassed the structural and modern view of the body as encoding and transacting binary oppositions such as nature and culture, femininity and masculinity, passivity and power, yet preserve the importance of difference in the face of co-optation as suggested by Mascia-Lees, Sharpe, and Cohen (1989a and 1989b). These approaches have also transcended theories of a purely "monolithic body," offering rather a syncretic analysis where power, privilege, and "difference" operate inside and outside postmodern blurring and contradiction (Mascia-Lees, Sharpe, and Cohen 1989b:31).

". . . [F]eminist thinking conjoined with postmodern[ism] . . . has suggested provocative new paradigms in anthropology from which to encounter the physical self, rendering the body in greater contextuality, complexity and as more reflexive" (Bolin 1992b:379; Bolin 1997:185–86). The body is regarded as encompassing a gender blending of natural and cultural symbolism, as meaning is extrapolated from morphology and social forms reiterate and reflect the physical form. In this regard Douglas (1973:93) suggests that:

> The social body constrains the way the physical body is perceived. The physical experience of the body always modified by the social categories

through which it is known sustains a particular view of society. There is a continual exchange of meanings between the two kinds of bodily experiences so that each reinforces the categories of the other.

Or in the words of Turner (28), ". . . gender is a social construct that mediates another social construct of biology." And according to Flax (637), ". . . gender can become a metaphor for biology, just as biology can become a metaphor for gender."

As a discourse on Western gender, the contemporary soma (including that of bodybuilders) reflects and reifies relations of hegemony and hierarchy, of power and privilege, and in keeping with a postmodernist mood, that which lies in-between, in the junctures and crevasses where gender is lived and negotiated (Bolin 1997, 1998, and 2001).

Of late anthropology has experienced a shift of interest and re-interest in complex societies—for example, Martin's (1989) study of immunology as a medical discourse on gender. "Ethnography is moving into areas long occupied by sociology, the novel, or avantgarde cultural critique (Clifford 1981), rediscovering otherness and difference within the cultures of the west" (in Clifford 1986:23). The field of anthropology may be on the frontiers of a new culture concept more appropriate to the interpretation of complex societies as suggested by Barth and postmodern feminists such as Mascia-Lees, Sharpe, and Cohen (1989a and b). These authors share a sentiment that maintains a concern for power relations, patriarchy and privilege, yet incorporates the ambiguity of postmodern society and the multiplicity of experience, ethnicity, and position. In concurrence with a contemporary thrust suggested by Barth (1989:134), the "distributive" and heterogeneous context of complex society is therefore acknowledged in the inscription of the soma.

In the study of the body research must go well beyond simplistic notions of isomorphism between ideology and social structure, and must trace the diverse threads of meaning in the body as text within a text, written about and written upon. Yet the concern for the roots of oppression and the propagation of patriarchy through inequalities in resources, power, and prestige must be maintained. The contemporary female body is more than mere reflection of and reaction to patriarchy; it is also proactive. Here the question of the relations between "macro-level social process and micro-level aspects of textual form" (Hanks 1989:100) is not only begged but must be answered.

Theory and Method

My theoretical compost consists of influences from symbolic and interpretive anthropology and elements of postmodernism—the body as a text of representational pluralism and underlined with issues of privilege and power. Goffmanesque symbolic interactionism was also found to be a particularly appropriate interpretive tool in this synthesis because bodybuilders, by the nature of their sport, are necessarily hyper-aware of the bodies they manage and present. This study incorporates these theoretical themes in an analysis of the athletic female soma as it publicly incorporates yet privately opposes, and as it portrays and finally betrays femininity in the culture of beauty, power, and privilege. I argue this occurs through a public and private splitting in which the public somatic text or frontstage, displayed in magazines, in television, and in contests is presented through a lens of femininity, and the private somatic text or backstage is, in contrast, a script of subversion. The public text continues to be rewritten by elements from the private that push the perimeters of what is regarded as feminine in women's bodybuilding (Bolin 1998).

The discourse analysis undertaken here incorporates dialogue from formal and informal interviews with bodybuilders, content analysis of bodybuilding magazines and newsletters and National level competitions on ESPN's *Muscle Magazine* show, as well as interpretation and comparison of two television programs on weight training: Cory Everson's *Bodyshaping Show* and Lee Haney's *Animal Workout* (ESPN). These discourses are embedded within the broader framework of the ethnographic context.

Fifteen years of participant-observation in the sport subculture of competitive bodybuilding forms the ethnographic basis for this research. Ethnographic observation took place in the bodybuilding communities of two different areas in the United States. Methods included immersion in the locker-room society of "hardcore" gyms, participation in health clubs and spas, training with both male and female "partners," backstage interaction on the pit crews of various male and female competitors, my own contest preparation in both the Amateur Athletic Union (AAU) and National Physique Committee (NPC) bodybuilding contests, and training as an AAU judge.[1]

Before beginning, it is important to identify the subject and the population. Bodybuilding is defined as working out with weights to reshape the body (Weider and Weider 1981:8), not just tone it. Unlike male bodybuilders, women bodybuilders, in the majority of cases, are either active competitors or have aspirations to compete. In responses from 205 women bodybuilders registered with the International Federation of Bodybuilders, 74% were active competitors, and many others were sidelined due to injury or were anticipating their first competition (Duff and Hong 1984:375).

THE GENDERING OF SPORT: RELATION, REFLECTION, AND REFORM

Bodybuilding for women is a sport that textualizes gender relations, reflects traditional notions of femininity, actively rebels against these in terms of challenging the cultural construct that muscularity and femininity are mutually exclusive, and finally contributes to the ongoing larger redefinition of femininity and womanhood (Bolin 1998:200–4).

Women bodybuilders wholeheartedly pursue what has traditionally been a male imperative: to lift weights, become strong, and demonstrate that strength through editing the body (developing muscles). Like the larger text of athletics for women, competitive bodybuilding challenges the construct of the "weaker sex" but also incorporates elements of traditional femininity to neutralize stigma associated with sports that are perceived as male/masculine. Bodybuilding is an unusual sport in that the majority of the athletic component (lifting weights) that underwrites the display of muscularity in a contest is not presented—it is rather re-presented. While bodybuilding is a sport of display, and conventionally women have "displayed" while men "do," what they are displaying, muscles, are clearly a reinscripting of male somatic strength and agonic power onto the female form. Muscles are agonic in the sense they textualize threat or potential for force (Freedman 1986:72).

How You Do It

Because display for the male gaze is intimately associated with women and the culture of beauty (Freedman 1986, Banner 1983), "Critics asked if it is was a beauty contest or a sport" (Freedman 1986:161). It is through the gender complex of the equation of women, beauty, and femininity that the oppositions and contradictions in the sport of women's bodybuilding reflect and reiterate a system of inequality and male privilege in the economic, political, social, and physical arenas. Male privilege to act is expressed in the freedom to be physical and to feel physically efficacious in the environment. It is well documented that the history of the female soma (until recently) has been one of constraint and restraint from the experience of physical autonomy through the sanction of femininity. Women bodybuilders from the sport's beginnings were faced with the dilemma of how to be taken seriously as athletes while maintaining their femininity. One avenue to ward off the dreaded label of "unfeminine" has been for women spokespeople of bodybuilding to redefine femininity to include strength and muscularity. It comes as no surprise that in 1979, after winning the first major women's bodybuilding competition, Lisa Lyon went on record stating that ". . . women can be strong, muscular, and at the same time feminine" (Gaines and Butler 1983:67, Cohn 1981:153). And to prove her point, she promptly posed for *Playboy* (Freedman 1986:161). But the gender bending inherent in the sport of women's bodybuilding would not go away even with such acts as this.

The woman bodybuilder's soma is a text within a broader text of sport. The athletic soma subverts the essentialist schema that the weaker sex is a "natural" construct. Despite this rather recent contestation, sports continue to be gendered. First, sports (particularly team sports) as a generic activity may have emerged as a vehicle to validate manliness after the closing of the frontier. American sports have evolved as a rite of passage for males to instill characteristics necessary for success as adults (see Fiske and Beisser in Hart 1972). Secondly, sports are polarized along traditional gender lines, reflecting a history of male action orientation and power in the environment as well as the equation of beauty and femininity associated with womanhood (Bolin 1998:206).

Henricks's (personal communication) research of student perceptions of athletics found that sports were gendered through the use of adjectives that are semantically sexed. The "more aesthetically" pleasing sports (Freedman 1986:162), such as iceskating and gymnastics, were labeled with stereotypically feminine adjectives denoting grace and beauty, flexibility, composure, and expressiveness, while male sports were rated with terms denoting strength, speed, aggression, and task orientation.

Del Rey (1977, 1978) has reported that women athletes, particularly those engaging in sports associated with masculine characteristics, may experience role conflict resulting in attempts to apologize and "feminize" their participation with obvious insignias of femininity such as jewelry, makeup, and accessories. Calhoun (1981:172) and Hart (1976:176–82) have suggested that women in nontraditional sports feel athletic ability is inconsistent with traditional notions of femininity. Indeed, women's athletic movements have a long history of association with women's liberation and continue to be important in forging new conceptions of femininity at the macro-level, and in facilitating the enhancement of self-esteem for women individually and collectively (see Duquin 1982, Snyder and Kivlin 1975, Snyder and Spreitzer 1976). In this regard, Ogilvie and Tutko (1971 in Snyder and Spreitzer 1978:114) have noted that women athletes were ". . . more independent, creative, and autonomous than male athletes." Increased self-esteem, a sense of "power" in the world, and related identity issues such as autonomy are subversive to inequality and patriarchy (see Snyder and Spreitzer 1978:115–18). In addition, sports hold the opportunity not just for instrumentality but for the fulfillment of expressive needs as well, thereby encompassing the potential for true "epicenism," the quality of being held in common by both sexes (Duquin 1978:103) and being beyond gender.

The sport of women's bodybuilding is rumored among competitors to be in decline and this is attributed to an absence of clear guidelines in the judging of women and the related concern over steroid use. The judging issue is focused on the question of the degree of muscularity acceptable for a woman contestant. Unlike the male competitor whose masculinity is unmarked, the female competitor is required to display femininity conterminously with her muscularity. At the local and at the national level, in both amateur and professional contests, and even in the Ms. Olympia contest (the pinnacle of bodybuilding achievement for women), the judges are accused by the bodybuilding community at-large of giving mixed messages to the women about the criteria for winning (Bolin 1998:200–4). Since judging the women has little in the way of formal standards—there is no written definition of what characteristics constitute femininity—the judges' criteria is embodied in the somatic styles of the women they select as winners.

Bodybuilding is a big business that depends primarily on servicing the snowballing fitness needs of middle America and athletes in general, with competitive bodybuilders representing only a small part of a much larger body of consumers. As an industry with a profit motive, the national organizations and the promoters must respond to somatic representations and images marketable to the wider public through the mass media, including competitions, television broadcasts of shows, and magazine sales. At the local and state level, competitions consist of two phases, in the morning where the majority of the judging decisions are made, and in the evening when the finalists and winners are announced and awarded. A judges' meeting will occur prior to the competition in the morning show. This meeting is an important site for brokering informal standards into actual embodiments that ultimately impact the economy of the sport. It is here that the judges discuss guidelines and trends in judging.

Recently at a local show, a heavily muscled competitor, who was the obvious choice of the audience, was given second place to a less muscled woman. The audience loudly voiced its disapproval of the judges' decision, and the angry competitor returned the trophy to the promoter, declaring: "I don't deserve this!" At the judges' meeting earlier that day, it was stated that in support of the NPC position against steroid use, the judges were requested to avoid selection of competitors for first place whom they assessed were obvious steroid users. This decision could not be based on hearsay about a competitor, but only by visual inspection. Needless to say, this ruling was applied to the women, not the men, if selection of winners at this show was any criterion.

Bodybuilders, judges, and others in the know feel they can spot "heavy" steroid users who have used "bulking drugs." However, interviews with bodybuilders on this subject indicate that detection isn't always so obvious with users who are "going light," who have just begun the use of steroids, or who have or are using "cutting" as opposed to bulking drugs.[2] I am not going to argue about the extent of steroid use among bodybuilders, but must note that the question of judging extends beyond the drugs and their obvious association as "unnatural" for women. My research indicates that the issue of steroids emerged first in women's bodybuilding as part of a wider discourse on beauty and femininity, not as one of health (although the health issue did enter subsequently). This was clearly articulated by Jim Manion, NPC President, who stated that the women ". . . were looking too offensive for the networks" (in Mollica 1986:66). Drug testing was implemented at the national and professional level among the women to keep the beasts at bay. However, extremely large muscles on a woman contest the female-femininity equation regardless of the source of those muscles. Women with large muscles may be suspected of steroids and "unnaturalness" by the public at large as well as bodybuilding cohorts.

The question of muscularity and femininity or how much beast can be tolerated in the beauty has been going on since the inception of the sport, prior to widespread reports of steroid use among women. The muscularity/femininity debate was central in the late 1970s when women's bodybuilding was a bikini contest and Gloria Miller Fudge (Douglas 1990:9) first kicked off her high heels. Or when Cammie Lusko, competing in the first "Miss" Olympia in 1980, presented a "hardcore muscular routine," which drove the audience wild, but judges didn't even allot her a placing (Cohn 1981:94).

But something new was on the horizon for women and it was subversive. Although Rachel McLish, with a lean and well defined but muscularly diminutive physique, was pronounced the winner in this first "Miss" Olympia, some of the other women ". . . showed muscles, big, veiny, chunky, standout ones" (Gains and Butler 1983:65). Over time the contestants have become increasingly muscular. This may be attributed to the convergence of several factors: the competitors have been training over a longer period of time; as the competitors age, their muscle also matures; the sport has enjoyed an explosion in scientific research on training techniques and nutrition; instead of, or in addition to, the purported role of anabolic steroids. Despite concern by judges and other gatekeepers, the women competitors continue to expand the boundaries of muscularity well beyond what was conceived as possible for the female soma eleven years ago in the "Miss" Olympia (Bolin 2001:149–50).

Anabolic steroid use has just flamed what is an essential dichotomy in Western paradigm of femininity = woman = female and masculinity = man = male (Devor 1990:147–49). The competitive woman's muscular morphology contests this formula. This equation is the deep structure underlying women competitors' concern over judging standards. Criteria in judging is frequently phrased in terms of a debate between muscularity and symmetry (proportion.) At the extreme end these standards are considered mutually exclusive in terms of degree. Too much muscle and bulk is not considered symmetrical (Vedral 1989:127). For women bodybuilders, symmetry has come to denote femininity.

Cory Everson, six-time Ms. Olympia winner, is said to represent the ideal combination of femininity displayed in a "spectacular" symmetry and muscularity. But Everson is not recognized for having exceptionally large muscles. Conversely, in the 1989 competition, the second-place winner, Sandy Ridell, and the third-place winner, Bev Francis, are competitors well known for their large muscles and size, although their symmetry is not considered as well-balanced as Everson's. In several interviews subsequent to the 1989 Ms. Olympia, Everson attacked the judges on their inconsistency over the symmetry and muscularity question, citing the lineup of contestants and their relative scores on symmetry, muscularity, and posing. She noted that in the 1988 Ms. Olympia the judges announced that excessive muscularity would count against a competitor, but

> . . . in the contest (the 1989 Ms. Olympia), it seemed that the judges had reversed their criteria on the issue of excessive muscularity. . . . The athletes received mixed signals: Muscularity is good, muscularity is bad; definition is good, definition is bad (Everson 1990:126).

Nine years earlier, Cammie Lusko's words echo the endurance of this discourse: "When you compete your muscularity is all, but the judges insist on looking womanly. They try to fudge the issue with garbage about symmetry, proportion, and definition. What they really want is tits and ass" (in Cohn 1981:93–94).

What lies beneath the lines of this debate is a dialogue on beauty and the beast (Bolin 2001:149–50). Symmetry, in bodybuilding parlance, refers to a particular shape or contour that the judges look for in what is the first stage in a competition: the symmetry round. In this round the bodybuilders must stand feet together, semi-flexed but looking relaxed.

By taking quarter turns to the right, the competitors present the judges with a full-face view, a right and left side view, and a back view. The ideal contour for the female bodybuilder is an "x" as opposed to the traditional hourglass. Wide shoulders, wide lats (latissimus dorsi), narrow waist, and hips flaring out to wide and well-developed quadriceps are the sine-qua-non of the bodybuilders' morphology.

The symmetrical woman must present all this in addition to being "hard and ripped"; that is, she must reduce her bodyfat and diet so that the muscle separations and striations are clearly visible. The contour of the V-shaped upper body, narrow hips, flared legs, and "hardness" is obviously a hegemony of masculine somatology embodying metaphors of strength and power. But the woman bodybuilder cannot follow the "masculine" imperative too far, for she must maintain a seemingly ineffable quality of "femininity" that is never defined or clearly articulated. This is indeed one of the few sports in which a competitor can be too good; she can have too much muscle.

The women competitors are self-aware manipulators of their physical selves and they know that "femininity" lies beyond muscle. Competitors will deliberately offset hypertrophied muscles with attributes associated with conventional femininity: pink posing suits, blond hair color, long and fluffy hairstyles, magazine layouts in which they hold tiny weights. While the traditional aspects of femininity and women's bodybuilding have been identified (Bolin 1992a, 1998), it is the subversive elements and the relationship of the treasonous to the traditional that are emphasized here—the beasts in the beauties.

BEASTS WITHIN THE BEAUTIES

The female competitive soma is indeed a recent one in a young sport that has been wrestling to set parameters for female bodies that appear to hemorrhage into domains regarded as uniquely masculine. The muscular morphology of the woman competitor co-opts attributes that are regarded as typically male secondary sexual characteristics, such as greater muscularity and less body fat. These characteristics have been regarded in the medical and sexological texts as demarcating "natural" boundaries between the sexes. Women bodybuilders have contributed to pushing flexed muscles into a state of cultural flux. The flexed bicep is gaining as a synecdoche for power cross-cutting genders.[3]

Muscles are on the move so much so that an article in *Time* magazine proclaimed, "Work That Body! Fewer Curves More Muscles. Across the country, women are working out, running hard, even pumping iron. And they are doing it not just to look attractive but also to gain strength and a sense of self-sufficiency" (Donnelly 1990:68). The athletic soma has emerged as an option for women where previously it was the privilege of men (Bolin 2001:147–49).

However, women still voice distress over the potentially stigmatizing effect of too much muscle (Donnelly 1990:68). To offset the hegemony of masculinity with muscularity, women bodybuilders have opted for deliberate efforts at manipulation of their images in the public sector. I propose that there is a significant fissure between the frontstage presentation of self in contests and in the media, and the private and mundane backstage one in the hardcore gym.

My research strongly suggests that women bodybuilders, amateur and professional alike, compete to win, not just for the experience. Competitors seek information on the ephemeral standards in judging from a variety of sources: reading the somatic styles of winners, talking to judges, and consulting the professional journals. From this evidence, femininity emerges as a salient feature and the competitor resorts to manipulation of obvious insignias of femininity widely available in our culture. In this sense the competitive body produced for the stage is an engram of oppositions.

I have found a variety of techniques used for the public persona of competition and/or media. The neotonic trait of blondness is rampant among bodybuilders; for example, the top six contestants in the 1989 Ms. Olympia have blonde hair. Long and fluffy hair is de rigueur for shows, along with artificial fingernails. Of the eighteen contestants in the 1989 Ms. Olympia, only one wore a short hairstyle. Participant-observation reveals a flurry of activity around these concerns the week prior to a competition. The competitors will make arrangements to have their hair styled and colored, their nails manicured and polished, false fingernails and professional makeup applied. They will put effort into selecting the "right" color and texture of their posing bikini. No jewelry is allowed in the morning show except engagement and wedding rings, but for the evening show, small earring studs may be worn and women will often decorate their hair with ribbons or other hair accessories, akin to the "evening gown presentation" of a beauty contest.

Inasmuch as these symbols have in the past denoted frailty, on the athletic body such symbols can be jarring, for they clearly point to the cultural construction of femininity as opposed to a "natural constitution." This contradicts the dominant Western gender schema, which posits a biological foundation to what is a cultural and symbolic process of attributing gender and then de facto presuming genitalia and genes (see Kessler and McKenna 1978; Devor 1989 on the gender attribution process.)

Beauty is the common denominator the competitive bodybuilder uses to guide her contest presentation and negotiate the pollution of masculinity inscribed by muscles. Because beauty is equated with femininity, in order for females to participate in a sport of muscularity, they may re-enfranchise their at-risk identities with these "feminine insignias." It is posited here that women bodybuilders' superscript of femininity over muscularity is neutralization strategy (see also Duff and Hong 1989:517).

These efforts at taming the beast are but a shallow surface. Underlying the "putting on" of femininity are years of hard training and muscle-building, a putting on that is far more resilient than the artifice added prior to the competition. As a consequence, there is an irony, so that as a construct of naturalness, femininity is subverted to a category of contrivance, and in its mixing metaphorically a redefinition of femininity is provoked so that a competitor comments: "I am a woman and therefore I am feminine whether I have muscles or not."

Contest posing represents another arena of insubordination and transformation superscripted by femininity. Although both male and female competitors must present the same set of mandatory poses, gendering segregates the posing. Women are allowed extended legs on two of the poses and are required to extend the leg on the front double biceps pose. This provides an aesthetic and obviously feminine appeal for a pose that is known as a "muscle shot." In addition, women's posing includes more flourishes and hand and body movement preparatory to actually striking the pose.

In a recent posing session with Doctor Iron, the mentor of the hard-core gym I belong to, the 214-pound competitor instructed me in posing femininely despite my small muscles, stating: "OK, Now you turn, breathing in and gracefully pulling your hand around as you turn, as softly as a baby's breath." And he cautioned: "be careful how you extend that leg, you don't want it to look like a big heavy horse plopping its foot down, remember softly, softly." Male bodybuilders, as well, are aware of the judges' hidden agenda of femininity. And women bodybuilders will deliberately construct what they perceive to be the judges' notions of femininity.

Posing also inscribes transgression. Placed in historical context, women's posing initially involved fluid presentations in which flexed muscles were seldom seen. But in 1980 some of the first Miss Olympians posed differently, showing the front double biceps pose, which was previously prohibited to women (Gains and Butler 1983:65). The front double bicep, a movement germane to male displays of strength from childhood through adulthood has subsequently evolved into a mandatory pose for women. The "most muscular" pose (in which every muscle is tensed) has also been regarded as a male "muscle shot" but is now used as a secondary mandatory for close "calls" in the evaluation of women in this research.

Women's posing has impacted men's traditions in the choreographic and musical aspects of the posing routine (Douglas 1990:12). It is because of women's influence that the expectation for men has been elevated considerably, adding an important element of the expressive to the typically male instrumental free posing routine. The men's posing has undergone significant changes in this direction over the last ten years.

Finally, bodybuilding and exercise subverts Western essentialist constructions of women's sexuality as "naturally" reluctant and passive. To illustrate its prevalence, this notion has even been revisioned as a contemporary scientific discourse in some of the socio-biological theorizing. This research is cited prolifically by the mass media as substantiation of what the public suspected all along.[4]

Research associating women's enhanced sexuality with exercise is particularly relevant in defying the image of women's sexual reticence. For example, Whitten and Whiteside's (1989:42, 44) study of women swimmers correlates exercise with enhanced self-esteem and sexual enjoyment. They conclude that exercise "can make you sexier" (1989:42). Other research indicates that women who exercised experienced an increase in the ability to be aroused sexually and their "sexual confidence" was enhanced (Sare 1989:73). De Villers's survey of eight thousand women on the effects of exercise on women's sexuality found that 31% of the population who exercised regularly reported an increase in sexual frequency, 40% noted enhanced arousal, and for 25% orgasm was more easily achieved (Porterfield 1990:33).

While this research was quickly cited in the " muscle magazines" as a solid generic reason for people to work out and hence support the economy of fitness, it was retranslated for woman bodybuilders, who are after all well known for taking a good thing too far. In an article entitled "Love, Lust and Muscles" (Townsend 1990:81–82, 196, 200–1), women's bodybuilding is textualized as sexually insurgent.

This "muscle dynasty" story stars rock-hard Rick and spouse equivalent Annie, a petite blond. Problems arose when Rick began training with a woman bodybuilder named Joan and found himself attracted to her:

> There were striking physical differences between Joan and Annie . . . Joan had a female bodybuilder's sexual energy and sensuality. She was physical. Annie was blond, Joan was brunette [of course]. Annie had big breasts, Joan's breasts were medium. Joan had well-formed glutes from her bodybuilding (Annie did not). Joan knew she was built well and flaunted it. . . . She was tight and very muscular, and Annie soon seemed to Rick to be soft and flabby by comparison. . . . (Townsend 1990:81–82)

"Joan, appreciating bodies and muscles, began to flirt with Rick." She was "[p]roud of her own sexuality" and "worked out in tight leotards." With this combination, it came as no surprise that Joan and Rick ended up in bed (Townsend 1990:82).

> Joan was sexually aggressive, a reflection of her individuality, expressed as a woman bodybuilder in a man's world. Rick said that coupling with Joan was an altogether different, hedonistic experience than making love to Annie. . . . He could not resist Joan's sexuality and that body. He thought he was in love, but he was in bodybuilding lust. It happens. (Townsend 1990:82)

As this sexual soap unfolded, Rick became increasingly critical of Annie's soft feminine curves and her passive sexuality, asking why she never initiated sex. He also became ". . . interested in sex all the time and wasn't treating her [Annie] with the respect he once had" (Townsend 1990:82).

Several themes are interwoven throughout this discourse. The sexually aggressive brunette represents a vigorous sexuality that violates traditional conceptions of women's sexuality as reluctant, shy, and legitimized within the framework of love. The article concludes with Annie and Rick's relationship terminating because "Rick's immaturity and confusion of lust for love were too much . . ." (Townsend 1990:82, 196, 200).

Annie's soma denotes conventional femininity while Joan's denotes anti-femininity and participation in a "man's world" (82). The muscular woman's morphology has opened the door for a dangerous symbolic redundancy: an assertive sexuality raided from the male domain. The woman bodybuilder's soma in this narrative transcribes conventional male and female love into lust. In addition, recent trends in sexual conservatism reiterating political and larger societal concerns over AIDS are also embodied in this discourse, whose tone promotes the relative merits of sex within committed and loving relationships over those based on lust alone.

However, the obvious moral to this story is ironic. As somatotypes that write an alternative women's sexuality, the competitive contour announces the instability of essentialistic views of sexuality as well as power of gendered complexes to intertwine traits and behavior. And ultimately there is also an open titillation in the description of Joan and her "coupling" with Rick. It may not be far from the "Garden of Earthly Delights" by Hieronymus Bosch (active ca 1480–1516), in which the hell of hedonic sex may indeed have its "up" side.

SUBVERSION BACKSTAGE: GENDER IN THE GYM

Turning from the public arena in which femininity and beauty frost a subversive soma is a backstage of bodywork and further contestation.[5]

The backstage of competitive bodybuilding includes phases of training and preparation for a contest. This includes a pre-contest and contest phase as well as an off-season phase. While competitive bodybuilders train toward their competitions throughout the year, this training, as well as their diet, varies as their contest(s) approach. Despite the fluidity in judging criteria for women, both women and men try to acquire as much muscle as possible by training as intensely as they can off-season in a gym in which they are part of a subgroup of competitive male and female "lifters." A "hardcore gym" in which there is a serious atmosphere is considered essential for maximum athletic performance and muscle growth. Although gyms are public in a sense, they are also the backstage of competitive bodybuilding. The hardcore gym of which I am a member, referred to here as Heavy Metal, has a sense of privacy, as people who are not "serious" about their lifting are discouraged from participating, gym memberships are not actively marketed, and the structure is not clearly identified as a gym. Onlookers are discouraged.

Although bodybuilding as a phenomenon is produced by capitalism and male privilege, it has nurtured the seeds of a somatic insurrection by women (cf Abu-Lughod 1990). The hardcore gym is a site that spawns the subversive soma. The 1970s witnessed an eruption of the fitness industry in which women entered gyms for the first time (Douglas 1990:9; Donnelly 1990:68; Bolin 1996, 2001). While health clubs and spas have targeted women through offerings of aerobics classes, sales of fashion activewear, color-coordinated locker rooms with vanities and amenities such as blow driers and curling irons, hardcore gyms distinguish themselves symbolically through characteristics associated with the masculine and antagonistic to what is regarded as "prissy." Local hardcore gyms in the area (N = 4) are typically without showers, locker rooms are austere, and decor is nonexistent. In fact, when Dr. Iron wanted to paint the equipment in Heavy Metal Gym red and repaint the walls, the men objected, saying it would look like a health spa and ruin the intense atmosphere.[6]

The majority of lifters in the local hardcore gyms are males. Heavy Metal Gym has a rostered clientele of about two hundred people and an active "hardcore" group of around sixty lifters. The women members who work out regularly consists of three retired competitors, four active contest competitors, and four women who work out to keep in shape.

The frontstage of the contest demands that male and female competitors lose weight to paradoxically create a stage illusion of enhanced muscle size by revealing greater definition. But backstage in the gym, the goal of the competitor regardless of gender is to acquire bigger muscles. The ethos of working out in the gym is one of developing muscles and training intensely. The public contest persona of bodybuilding inscribes the female soma as beautiful and feminine, its backstage and its association with muscle and strength, with power and potency, is about the beast and pushing the somatic perimeters of gender. This translation is evident when the act of "lifting" is taken from the backstage fully into the frontstage of the media through two television programs on working out: Lee Haney's *Animal Workout,* featuring the seven-time Mr. Olympia winner, and Cory Everson's *Bodyshaping Show,* starring the six-time winner of the Ms. Olympia.

꩜

Haney's *Animal Workout* stands in stark contrast to Everson's *Bodyshaping.* Everson's show rewrites "working out" into an activity satiated with symbols of conventional femininity as it transfigures the backstage of weightlifting to the frontstage for public consumption. As Everson demonstrates the exercises, she uses light weights, dresses in fashionable fitness wear, with her hair worn long and flowing, despite its obvious inconvenience to her movement. Everson has deliberately manipulated her muscularity into a softer, less striated morphology that one woman bodybuilder referred to as "an aerobic instructor appearance." It is a superficial denial of the muscular body as a location of a struggle.

In comparison, Haney lifts heavy weights that cause him to strain, trains in tank tops and other workout clothes that are designed for movement and displays a physique that is nearly contest-ready. Haney's program transcribes the private backstage of bodybuilding into the public with little change. The title of his show, *Animal Workout,* is an accurate metonymy for the work of the sport of competitive bodybuilding.

In Heavy Metal Gym specifically, and hardcore gyms generally, "seriousness" of desire and training is a metatext that overrides the issue of gender.[7] The sartorial system reiterates the body. In opposition to Everson's aerobic-wear, Haney dons what is characteristically worn by men and women alike in the hardcore gyms of this research: tank tops, tee shirts, sweatshirts, sweatpants and shirts, and baggies designed for the workouts. Custom dictates that workout clothes are modified with scissors as a further identity peg. While spandex tights for both sexes have found their way into Heavy Metal Gym, these may be modified to inscribe "bodybuilder" upon the wearer. For example, one woman has cut a series of two-inch cuts up the sides of her spandex tights, while others might add a cutout sweatshirt or some other insignia of the status. Bodybuilding tribal attire is underwritten by the ethnotheory that "you are in the gym to train, not be seen or socialize." Women bodybuilders, and men for that matter, who want to be regarded as dedicated athletes do not wear "aerobic" style of clothing in the gym. Aerobics is associated with masses who work out in health spas and are not "serious" athletes by bodybuilders.

Both Cory Everson's *Bodyshaping Show* and Lee Haney's *Animal Workout* also present a text on training relationships. Everson is usually assisted by a less muscular, slender woman or sometimes an aerobically fit man (not a hardcore bodybuilder) to demonstrate variants of the exercises. The interaction of Everson and her assistant is also a public translation of the backstage training partnership, considered a salient relationship among bodybuilders. This is represented in the frequently heard adage "You're only as good as your partner." The training partner provides a safety net for heavy lifting, motivates his/her partner to extra "reps" or movements of the exercises, and is generally an important part of the lifters' support system for high-intensity exercise.

Everson publicly transmutes this relationship. In a recent program she encouraged her assistant to do a few more leg curls by saying "just a few more now" and then looked to the audience and said, "She's going to kill me after the show." In contrast, Lee's Haney's *Animal Workout* is a public discourse on the kind of training that is experienced in the backstage of the gym among "serious" training partners. On Haney's show male and female partners yell and encourage each other with typical bodybuilder training partner talk such as "Let me see that huge back," "C'mon Lee, show me one more," "rock and roll, big guy." Bodybuilding is characterized by the pursuit and "enjoyment" of pain. Bodybuilders are quick to defend, "You want the pain, you want to be sore afterward, . . . if you can't feel the muscle, if it doesn't hurt you won't grow." The training partner helps push one into extending the pain threshold and hence growing more muscle. The interaction between Everson and her assistant is clearly a gendered script that draws on a history in which physical exertion is discrediting to femininity.

Backstage, resistance occurs through redefinition as well. Bodybuilders regard muscles and hardness as a generic quality, not a gendered one, desired by both men and women alike. This neutering is transcribed in a variety of ways as they admire and comment upon the physiques of their cohorts. As a form of morphological mutiny, men will admire a woman's "abs" or "delts" (abdominal or deltoid muscles) or openly state "I'd be happy to have a peak like that," or women will unabashedly covet a man's "lat spread" (wideness of a male competitor's back). Although this degendering supports wider trends for the "reshaping" of the feminine soma to include tone, bodybuilders have prodded this trend to include hypertrophied, well-defined muscles with visible vascularity (veins). This private subversion supports the rewriting of the public text by pushing the perimeters of gender every year.

Competitive women's bodybuilding is a form of persistent resistance rather than a large-scale revolution (cf Abu-Lughod 1940:41). It is nevertheless transgressive and transformative and participates in much broader societal changes in the cultural typing of the female soma.

CONCLUSION

The sport of bodybuilding evolved dramatically from its inception in the late 1970s, when women wore high heels and the women's bodybuilding contests were nothing more than beauty pageants (Douglas 1990:9; Bolin 2001) It was not until the 1980s that women's bodybuilding came into its own through the legitimization of women's contests as bonafide events in their own right, not just as sideshows for male bodybuilding contests.

In conclusion, women's bodybuilding is a postmodern phenomenon in which the dominant gender schema of naturalness is contested through a blending and blurring of gender boundaries. The muscular female soma challenges "incorrigible propositions" about the essential nature of gender (cf Kessler and McKenna 1978:4). While the public and frontstage discourse of women's bodybuilding maintains the traditional dichotomy of beauty as the female purview, it also enlarges the gender schema by adopting muscularity in juxtaposition to beauty, and co-opts instrumentality from the traditional male domain in the backstage arena of the sport. The muscular soma is a proactive text of gender ideologies and relations that disputes an inequality of the physical self based on the idiom of the "weaker sex." The muscular soma also expands the definition of femininity to include strength and power and de facto whatever else a woman chooses to include, while promoting the view that conventional femininity is an illusion. The "beauty" sustains male privilege, but the "beast" challenges it.

The woman bodybuilder's soma is a textual critique of what lies within or "inside" the physical self. At the micro-level, lifting weights with concomitant increases in strength and its referent muscularity enhances self esteem, facilitates an attitude of mastery, and physical efficacy of the environment (Snyder and Kivlin 1975, Snyder and Spreitzer 1976). It is the last frontier of the resistance of the self. In this sense, the muscular morphology of the female bodybuilder is subversive. The competitive woman bodybuilder's soma does indeed talk of treason.

NOTES

1. The term "hardcore bodybuilding" was coined by Robert Kennedy and caught the imagination of the bodybuilding community (Douglas 1989:10). I

suspect it became popular as a marker to distinguish "the bodybuilder" from the flood of fitness enthusiasts in the 1980s who flocked into health clubs to work out with weights and Nautilus-types of equipment.

2. This tactic will eliminate "heavy " steroid use at the local level, although I doubt if it will eliminate steroid use altogether.

3. When discussing my research with women colleagues and others, an almost invariable response is that I am asked to see their bicep flex and acknowledge their muscularity. Images in magazines of women working out and the increase of females involved in lifting weights and working with machines indicate women want to have muscle tone (Duff and Hong 1984:374; Freedman 1986:43). The beauty ante has apparently been upped from thin to include toned (see Bolin 1992).

4. Statistics on intercourse (premarital, marital, and extramarital) testifying to these gender differences in American coital activity (Frieze and Parsons et al. 1978; Kinsey et al. 1948, 1953; Masters et al. 1982:196–97) are garnered as evidence that men and women are "really," meaning biologically, different in their sexual needs and interests. That such differences may be culturally constituted by the sexual double standard is demonstrated by recent changes in women's sexual behavior that may be attributed in part to the feminist movement and the sexual revolution of the 1960s. Although Masters et al. (1982:222) see an ideology of equal sexual opportunity beginning its ascent, it is perhaps still not unfounded to suggest the dominance of an essentialistic theme of a passive female sexuality that must be won over by men. This gender schema of female sexuality that is "controlled" and "interior" is opposed to a male sexuality that is potentially "out of control" and nearer the "surface."

5. My conclusions refer to the hardcore gyms and health clubs of the two areas in which I researched—a southern state and a midwestern state. Other sites I have investigated include: South Carolina, Pennsylvania, Georgia, and California.

6. In fact, the only hardcore gym that has decoration in terms of a minimal attempt at a color theme has been questioned by the "lifters" of Heavy Metal Gym as to its "authenticity" of atmosphere.

7. Class is clearly a salient factor in the male bodybuilder's identity. However, this subject bears further scrutiny and research. Originally "seriousness" as an athlete was obviously gendered as masculine prior to the advent of women in sports. My preliminary research indicates it may be in the process of being neutered, at least in some bodybuilding communities and some sports.

REFERENCES

Abu-Lughod, Lila. 1990. "The Romance of Resistance: Tracing Transformations of Power Through Bedouin Women." *American Ethnologist* 17(1):41–55.

Armstrong, David. 1983. *Political Anatomy of the Body*. Cambridge, MA: Cambridge University Press.

Barth, Fredrik. 1989. "The Analysis of Culture in Complex Societies." *Ethos 54* (3–4):120–42.

Beckworth, Carol. 1983. "Niger's Wodaabe: People of the Taboo." *National Geographic* 164(4):483–509.

Beisser, Arnold R. 1972. "The American Seasonal Masculinity Rites." *Sport in Socio-Cultural Process,* ed. Marie M. Hard, 259–60. Dubeque, IA: Wm. C. Brown Co.

Blacking, John. 1977a. "Preface." In *The Anthropology of the Body,* ed. John Blacking.

———. 1977b. "Towards an Anthropology of the Body." In *The Anthropology of the Body,* ed. John Blacking 1–28. New York, NY: Academic Press.

Bolin, Anne. 1988. *In Search of Eve: Transsexual Rites of Passage*. Amherst, MA: Bergin and Garvey.

———. 1992a. "Vandalized Vanity: Feminine Physiques Betrayed and Portrayed." In *Tattoo, Torture, Mutilation, and Adornment: The Denaturalization of the Body in Culture and Text,* ed. F. Mascia-Lees, 79–99. Albany, NY: State University of New York Press.

———. 1992b. "Flex Appeal, Food and Fat: Competitive Bodybuilding, Gender and Diet." *Play and Culture* 5(4):378–400.

———. 1996. "Bodybuilding." *The Encyclopedia of World Sport: From Ancient Times to the Present*. Vol. 1, 125–34. Santa Barbara, CA: ABC-CLIO.

———. 1997. "Flex Appeal, Food and Fat: Competitive Bodybuilding, Gender and the Diet." In *Building Bodies,* ed. Pamela S. Moore, 184–208. New Brunswick, NJ: Rutgers University Press (originally published 1992).

———. 1998. "Muscularity and Femininity: Women Bodybuilders and Women's Bodies in Culturo-Historical Context." In *Fitness as Cultural Phenomenon,* ed. Karin Volkwein, 187–212. New York, NY: Waxmann (published in America and Germany).

———. 2001. "Women's Bodybuilding." In *The International Encyclopedia of Women and Sport,* ed. Karen Christensen, Allen Guttmann, and Gertrude Pfister, 125–34. New York, NY: Macmillan.

Brain, Robert. 1979. *The Decorated Body*. London, England: Hutchinson & Co. Pub. Ltd.

Calhoun, Don. 1981. *Sports, Culture and Personality*. West Point, NY: Leisure Press.

Clifford, James. 1986. "Introduction: Partial Truths." In *Writing Culture,* ed. James Clifford and George E. Marcus, 1–26. Berkeley, CA: University of California Press.

Cohn, Nik. 1981. *Women of Iron*. U.S.A.: Wideview Books.

Del Rey, Pat. 1977. "Apologetics and Androgyny: The Past and the Future." *Frontiers* 3:8–10.

———. 1978. "The Apologetic and Women in Sport." In *Women and Sport: From Myth to Reality,* ed. C. A. Oglesby, 107–11. Philadelphia, PA: Lea and Febiger.

Devor, Holly. 1989. *Gender Blending: Confronting the Limits of Duality*. Bloomington, IN: Indiana University Press.

Donnelly, Sally B. 1990. "Work that Body." *Time* 136(19):68.

Douglas, Mary. 1973. *Natural Symbols*. New York, NY: Vantage Books.

Douglas, Steve. 1990. "Muscle Go Round." *Muscle Magazine International* 95:9–13.

Duff, Robert W., and Lawrence K. Hong. 1984. "Self Images of Women Body-builders." *Sociology of Sport Journal* 1984(1):374–80.

Durkheim, E. 1961. *The Elementary Forms of Religious Life*. Glencoe, IL: Free Press.

Duquin, Mary E. 1982. "The Importance of Sport in Building Women's Potential." *Journal of Physical Education, Recreation, and Dance* 53:18–20, 36.

Everson, Cory. 1990. "In Defense of Winning in 6th Olympia." *Flex* 8(2):58, 126, 128.

Fisher, H. 1978. "The Clothes of the Naked Nuer." In *The Body Reader,* ed. Ted Polhemus 180–93. New York, NY: Pantheon Books.

Fiske, Shirley. 1972. "Pigskin Review: An American Initiation." In *Sport in Socio-Cultural Process,* ed. Marie M. Hart, 241–58. Dubuque, IA: William C. Brown Company.

Flax, Jane. 1987. "Postmodernism and Gender Relations in Feminist Theory." *Signs* 12(4):621–43.

Foucault, Michel. 1985. *The Use of Pleasure*. New York, NY: Vintage Books.

Freedman, Rita. 1986. *Beauty Bound*. Lexington, MA: Lexington Books.

Frieze, Irene H., Jacquelynne E. Parson, Paula B. Johnson, Diane N. Ruble, and Gail L. Zellman. 1978. *Women and Sex Roles*. New York, NY: W. W. Norton & Co.

Gaines, Charles, and George Butler. 1983. "Iron Sisters." *Psychology Today* 17:65–69.

Gallagher, Catherine, and Thomas Laqueur. 1987. *The Making of the Modern Body*. Berkeley, CA: University of California Press.

Hall, Edward T. 1966. *The Hidden Dimension*. Garden City, NJ: Doubleday.

Hanks, W. F. 1989. "Text & Textuality." *Annual Reviews of Anthropology* 18:95–127.

Hanna, Judith L. 1987. *To Dance Is Human: A Theory of Non-Verbal Communication*. Chicago, IL: University of Chicago Press.

Hart, M. 1976. "Stigma or Prestige: The All American Choice." In *Sport in the Sociological Process*, ed. M. Hart, 176–82. Dubuque, IA: William C. Brown.

Hoskin, F. 1979. *The Hoskin Report on Genital and Sexual Mutilation of Females*. Lexington, MA: Women's International Network News.

Kessler, Suzanne J., and Wendy McKenna. 1978. *Gender: An Ethnomethodological Approach*. New York, NY: John Wiley & Son.

Kinsey, Alfred C., Wardell B. Pomeroy, Clyde E. Saunders Martin, and Paul H. Gebhardt. 1953. *Sexual Behavior in the Human Female*. Philadelphia, PA: Saunders.

———. 1948. *Sexual Behavior in the Human Male*. Philadelphia, PA: Saunders.

Marcus, George E., and Michael M. V. Fischer. 1986. *Anthropology as Cultural Critique*. Chicago, IL: University of Chicago Press.

Martin, Emily. 1989. "The Cultural Construction of Gendered Bodies: Biology and Metaphors of Production and Destruction." *Ethnos* 54(3–4):143–60.

Mascia-Lees, Frances E., Patricia Sharpe, and Colleen Ballerino Cohen. 1989b. "The Postmodern Turn in Anthropology: Cautions from a Feminist Perspective." *Signs* 15(1):7–33.

Masters, William, Virginia Johnson, and Robert C. Kolodny. 1982. *Human Sexuality*. Boston, MA: Little, Brown and Co.

Messing, Simond. 1978. "The Non-Verbal Language of the Ethiopian Toga." In *The Body Reader*, ed. T. Polhemus, 251–57. New York, NY: Pantheon Books.

Mollica, Mae. 1986. "Body and Soul." *Flex* 4(2)64–68, 71.

Polhemus, Ted, ed. 1978. *The Body Reader: Social Aspects of the Human Body*. New York, NY: Pantheon Books.

Porterfield, Kay Marie. 1990. "Fitness Report: A Sexual Second Wind?" *American Health* 9(1):33.

Postal, Susan. 1978. "Body Image and Identity: A Comparison of Kwakiutl and Hopi." In *The Body Reader*, ed. Ted Polhemus, 122–33. New York, NY: Pantheon Books.

Sare, Chris. 1989. "Exercise Makes You Sexy." *Muscle and Fitness* 50(12):72–73, 174.

Snyder, Eldon, and Elmer Spreitzer. 1978. *Social Aspects of Sport*. Englewood Cliffs, NJ: Prentice Hall.

Snyder, E., and S. Kivlin. 1975. "Women Athletes and Aspects of Psychological Well-Being and Body Imagy." *Research Quarterly* 46:191–99.

———, and E. Spreitzer. 1976. "Correlates of Sport Participation Among Adolescent Girls." *Research Quarterly* 47:804–9.

Townsend, Peter J. 1990. "Love, Lust, and Muscles." *Muscle and Fitness* 51(8):81–82, 196, 200–1.

Tress, Daryl McGowan. 1988. "Comment on Flax's Postmodernism and Gender Relations in Feminist Theory." *Signs* 14(1):196–203.

Turner, Bryan S. 1984. *The Body and Society*. Oxford, England: Basil Blackwell.

Vedral, Joyce. 1989. "Ms. O. Contestants: Sexier this Year?" *Muscle and Fitness* 50(7):124–27.

Weider, Betty, and Joe Weider. 1981. *The Weider Book of Bodybuilding for Women*. Chicago, IL: Contemporary Books.

Whitten, Phillip, and Elizabeth J. Whiteside. 1989. "Can Exercise Make You Sexier?" *Psychology Today* (April):42, 44.

CHAPTER SIX

A Woman's Place is in the . . . Cardiovascular Room?? Gender Relations, the Body, and the Gym

SHARI L. DWORKIN

> . . . at no time has the muscled woman been regarded as a paragon of beauty.
>
> —Anne Bolin, *Tattoo, Torture, Mutilation, and Adornment*

INTRODUCTION TO KCF FITNESS SITE

After handing an I.D. card to a KCF fitness center employee, a short beep signals that I am allowed to push my way through a cold, metal turnstile that leads into a modern, spacious, well-lit fitness site. Off to the immediate right is a series of glass windows that allows viewing access into the weight room. Continuing just a short distance down the red, carpeted main hallway, a set of vast, burgundy weight room doors are open, inviting my gaze.

The Weight Room

Glancing in, the buzzing weight room scene appears: the vast majority of men and women are clothed in gym shorts and a t-shirt or tank top,

131

although some women are wearing lycra tops and tights. One can hear the clang of weights, mostly male grunts, the swish of air from air cam Nautilus stations, the murmur of music from speakers overhead, and the low hum of collective voices. Stories, laughter, and yells are exchanged among lifting partners, well-intentioned verbal jousts are passed back and forth, and the loud smack of "high fives" celebrate members' personal bests. Upon closer examination, surveying the bodies in motion, the fact that this is male terrain quickly becomes clear. The proportion of men to women in the weight room at any given time is approximately eighty/twenty or ninety/ten.

Aerobics and CV Rooms

Leaving the weight room, walking five feet down the hall, just outside the aerobics room doors, there is a glass case that contains fitness articles. One of the articles shows a picture of a fit, slender, white woman who is seated next to a scale in shorts and a tank top, and she is chained to the scale via her left foot. She has her hand on her forehead, she is visibly upset, and the caption reads: "Don't Let Weight Control You." Putting the picture into context, thinking about the scarcity of women in the weight room, peeking in to see that the aerobics classes are usually 100% female, I travel down the hall a few more feet and enter the cardiovascular room (The CV room). The CV room is predominantly filled with women, but proportionately more men enter this space than women enter the weight room. The paradox of simultaneous empowerment and constraint for women in fitness becomes more evident. Despite the fact that many fitness activities make women feel more physically powerful, their experiences are limited by fit, slender, toned bodily ideals that do not come naturally or easily. As we will see, bodies are carefully constructed through strategic selection and repetition of particular fitness practices.

This project is a pilot study of one fitness site and is part of a much larger, ongoing, multi-site exploration of women in fitness. Using a combination of ethnography (participant-observation) and intensive interviews to explore women's daily fitness choices in a local gym, I begin with the question: Why do women do what they do at the local gym? Why do so few women use the weight room while spending long doses of time in the CV and aerobics rooms? These questions point to issues of individual and structural agency and constraint such as: Is fitness truly empowering for women on site, providing an arena for strength and resistance against narrow constructions of femininity, or is it highly constraining? Is it both? How do beauty, the body, hegemonic masculinity, and emphasized femininity play a role in explaining why (Connell 1987, 1995)?

SPORT/FITNESS, GENDER, BODIES

Sport and fitness are complex sites of multifaceted gender, race, class, and sexuality dynamics. Embedded within and thus similar to other aspects in U. S. society, the institution of sport has historically been found to be a site for the enforcement and maintenance of masculine hegemonies, serving the interests of patriarchal ideology,[1] wrought with homophobia (Bryson 1990; Blinde and Taub 1992, 1992a; Cahn 1994; Griffin 1992, 1998; Hargreaves 1994; Kane and Disch 1993; Lenskyj 1986, 1987; Messner 1988; Nelson 1991; Pronger 1990; Theberge 1987) and race and class inequality (Birrell 1990; Messner 1992; Messner and Sabo 1990; Smith 1992).

Researchers who focus on bodies in sport/fitness have also shown that these arenas are sites of struggle where the meaning of gender has been negotiated and contested, and where many women have been empowered by the self-definition of their own bodies (Bolin 1992a; Cahn 1994; Gilroy 1989; Hargreaves 1994; Messner 1992; McDermott 1996; Theberge 1987). That is, researchers do not simply report that women in sport and fitness are oppressed objects who are subject to a totalizing patriarchal grip. Increasingly, research highlights the more subjective aspects of women's sport and fitness participation, such as women's physicality and bodily empowerment, which offers numerous benefits including the ability to ward off attack and heal past bodily victimization and abuse (Guthrie and Castelnuovo 1998; Heywood 1998; McDermott 1996). Most recently, the focus has moved to the simultaneous coverage of both the object status of women in sport and fitness and their subjectivity and agency (Bolin 1992a; Heywood 1998; Messner 2000). Thus, we can say that sport and fitness are institutions within which power is shifting and continually at play (Messner 1992, p. 14).

Historically speaking, however, while men's participation in numerous sport and fitness rituals has generally reinforced dominant conceptions of masculinity and heterosexuality, women's participation in many sport and fitness activities has worked in the opposite direction (Cahn 1993; Kane 1995; Lenskyj 1987; Nelson 1991).[2] That is, much cultural energy is expended to ensure that female athletes are perceived as heterosexual (Hargreaves 1994, p. 159). Backed by powerful institutions for compulsory heterosexuality, there exists widespread stigmatization for female athletes who move "too far" outside the accepted boundaries of femininity (Blinde and Taub 1992, 1992a; Cahn 1993; Griffin 1998; Kane 1995; Lenskyj 1986). The same phenomenon is seen within (shifting) media representations where images of strong women in sport and fitness are still framed ambivalently at times through sexualizing and trivializing their athletic performances (Duncan and Hasbrook 1988; Kane and Greendorfer 1994).

Are women sexualized by external forces or do they "choose" this body work and sexualization on their own? Or both? And why do it? Some feminist research focuses on how many women in fact choose to construct a body that embodies dimorphic gender difference while idealizing dominant ideals of femininity due to the plentiful cultural rewards that are offered (Butler 1990; Lloyd 1996).[3] Relying heavily on Foucault (1979) and his ideas of bodily surveillance, Bartky (1988) focuses on women's bodies as docile bodies, practicing endless diet and fitness routines as self-discipline in "obedience" to patriarchy (Bartky 1988, p. 81).[4] Although compelling, this position can be said to over-conceptualize women as objects, leaving little room for resistance and human agency. Both Bordo (1993) and Foucault (1979) attempt to avoid this danger by conceptualizing power as simultaneously oppressive and constitutive, and as always accompanied by resistance.[5]

Connell (1987) provides useful concepts that link individual women's choices to ideology and social structures. He defines hegemonic masculinity as a structurally supported system where masculinity is constructed in relation to various subordinated masculinities in an overall system of male domination over women. His concept of "emphasized femininity" refers to compliance with women's subordination in such a system by "accommodating the interests and desires of men" (p. 183).[6] Connell leaves room for women's agency and resistance and argues that women can push and challenge definitions of femininity, so long as they make concessions to emphasized femininity.

Research on women's bodybuilding is especially adept at demonstrating the above concepts. Bolin's work (1992, 1992a) reveals that women's bodybuilding is both transgressive of and containing with regard to femininity. In her exploration of women's bodybuilding culture, she asserts that although muscular women are empowered, and it is acceptable for women to carry more muscle mass over time, the size of the bodybuilder must be mediated by "beauty." Here, judges have been found to penalize women for their muscle size (drug free) and reward them for bodily adornments (dyed and highlighted hair, lipstick, painted fingernails, breast implants) and muscle size consistent with culturally prescribed "femininity."

Indubitably then, the body is central to research on women in sport and fitness and stands at the particularly conflictual nexus of nature/culture debates. Dworkin (2001) has noted that there are a growing number of studies that have examined a range of female bodies, from female bodybuilders (Balsamo 1994; Bolin 1992, 1992a; Daniels 1992; Guthrie and Castelnuovo 1992; Heywood 1998; Holmlund 1994) to anorexics

(Bordo 1986, 1993). Indeed, little work explores the more everyday women in fitness. The fact that we have many more male than female bodybuilders and many more female than male anorexics in U.S. culture is illustrative of cultural constructions of masculinity and femininity and of the performative nature of gender (Butler 1990). However, there is an important and obvious distinction between the two—although weak anorexic women may be said to be strong through their empowered sense of control, they do *not* contest physical power as a solely male prerogative, whereas female athletes often do (Messner 2000). Needless to say, strong and muscular women still pose a unique threat to ideologies of natural male superiority in U.S. society today (Messner 1992).

All too often, it is common for U.S. society to take what we think we see as women's "lesser" athletic performance, skill, or muscled bodies and use them as evidence of the "fact" of natural male superiority (Lorber 1994). This chapter acts explicitly against such a notion and uncovers women's strategic fitness choices that are used to construct particular bodily forms within socially constrained (and enabled) choices. I find it essential to conceptualize a continuum of bodies—those with extreme size and muscularity on the one hand, those with extreme thinness on the other, and the many in-between.[7] In order to flesh out issues of agency and constraint, I ask how women are consciously structuring their fitness activities to get to a place on this continuum, and what determines how far women can and do go in either direction. I use such a continuum in this pilot study to allow for an overlap of bodies and athletic performances between women and men (Kane 1995). I also use it to open up the possibilities for future research to explore any of the several axes that might impact where various women might fall on such a continuum (gender, sexuality, race, age, or others).[8]

PARTICIPANT-OBSERVATION AND STARTING WHERE YOU ARE

I employed participant-observation over the course of ten months, three days a week, for two to six hours a day in a local university gym from 1995 to 1996, and carried out eleven in-depth interviews with undergraduate and graduate women.[9] Lofland and Lofland (1995) inspired me to choose this topic through their suggestion of beginning research where one already is. The gym has been and still is a second home to me since my days of high school track (1982–1986). Engaged in both cardiovascular and lifting activities over the past sixteen years, I have worked out regularly (at least three days a week) in approximately ten gyms across five states. There were many pros and cons to starting where one has been for so many years. The main pro of choosing this site as a place of research was that I had a great deal of familiarity with and understanding of gym culture. Knowing how to do the many exercises combined with a familiarity of the lingo, rules, and etiquette allowed for an ease of talking to others and a fluidity of physical movement within and between rooms. At other times, these very factors were liabilities, such as not remembering how long it might take some individuals to feel comfortable in the setting.

It was useful to be continuously self-reflexive and ask myself how I had learned various activities, how much time it took me to maneuver in fitness settings, and what feelings were provoked and why. This awareness proved helpful in leading me to be sensitive not only to women's current experiences, but their past ones as well. Although many women stated in interviews that they would feel more comfortable in the gym if more women were present, one woman commented that she wondered if one of the intimidation factors was "those few women in there who can crank." I shuddered to myself that I was perhaps one of "those." Indeed, pointing to the overlapping continuum of strength between women and men (Kane 1995), I was quickly reminded that men aren't the only intimidating aspects of the weight room.

INTERVIEWEES—THE WOMEN

Six of the eleven women used to be involved in organized sport, but none of the eleven is currently involved. Not unlike many of the women in the fitness site, all eleven of the women I interviewed currently "choose" to do heavy doses of cardiovascular work when they go to KCF gym (four to seven days a week ranging from thirty minutes to two hours). Four of the eleven lifted weights regularly (two to three times a week, thirty to sixty minutes), three of the eleven women lifted irregularly (perhaps once or twice a month), one used to lift heavily in the past but had stopped, and three have never lifted. Of the women who were interviewed and lifted, all of them were graduate students, and the women who did not lift currently were all undergraduates.[10] It is fruitful to explore why there may be some reasons for this possible divergence by age, although it would be unwise to generalize using a pilot study with a very small sample size.

The sample of women ranged in age from nineteen to twenty-eight and was anywhere from the second year of undergraduate school to nearly completing their Ph.D. programs. Eight were white (and came from a middle-class background) two were African American (one from the middle class, one from the working class), and one woman was Asian-American (middle class). One woman was married; the rest were single. I asked women at the end of the interview to self-identify their sexuality—two came out as lesbian, one self-identified as bisexual, and the rest identified as heterosexual. In terms of the racial distribution of women of color in the weight and CV rooms, recent data shows that there indeed is a disproportionately small number of African Americans who use the KCF fitness center when compared with percentages in the campus population.[11] This may be related to the historically lower rates of participation in sport in general among women of color (Smith 1992), and is likely to be impacted by historical race, class, and gender dynamics.[12] Just as it has been found that anorexia is overwhelmingly a white, upper-middle-class woman's disease (Bordo 1993), the dominant patterns found at KCF are likely due to race and class homogeneity within the site.

Examining the interviews and ethnographic elements of this project, we will see that many women are highly conscious of the latest images/constructs of the fit woman (for example, Karen Voight) and work to move towards it. To move towards this image, we will see how many women on this particular site spend long periods of time on cardiovascular equipment while limiting activity in the weight room. *Most* women stay out of the weight room for the common reason that they feel intimidated but also because they don't want to "bulk" or get bigger. Although women today may find it more allowable to acquire muscle mass than in the past, bulkiness is often a powerfully feared transgression. I argue that it is *not* the case that women can't get big muscles, but rather many *know they can* and frequently structure fitness activities so as to avoid this bodily outcome. We will soon explore the agency and constraint of women who use the CV room, those who steer clear of the weight room, and also those who dare to venture in.

THE CV (CARDIOVASCULAR) ROOM

Once the CV room is entered, there is a noticeably different feel from the weight room. This room is smaller, the ceiling is much lower, there are no windows offering a glimpse outdoors, and the space feels more confined. Many more people here find ways to keep to themselves through reading newspapers, magazines, books, or articles for classes as they work out. Asking around as to why people read during CV work, I find that busy students think this a good way to get in their studies or enjoy reading. Several state that they want to work out, but don't want workouts to take away much time from their schoolwork.

Whereas the weight room seems to buzz from talking, laughing, grunts, and the clanging or swishing of weights and weight machines, the most prominent noise in the CV room is often the whir of Stairmaster motors. Several fitness participants wear Walkmans, and few talk to one another. Off to the side of the CV room, many people stand, sit, or do situps or leg exercises on a blue mat. Signs are posted that ask people to limit their workouts to fifteen minutes, and I note that few people follow the rule. Many stay on their equipment for thirty to forty-five minutes, and some stay on much longer. Unlike the weight room, those who are "hardcore" in the CV room are most often women.

The mode of dress for the CV room is also slightly different from that in the weight room. For the most part, the men wear gym shorts and t-shirts. Several women wear this too, but many wear what might be called (hetero)sexualized aerobicizer outfits—cropped, tight tops and tight shorts or spandex with thongs. At times, I am struck by how little differentiation there is in body size from woman to woman as I look down the rows of Stairmasters and bikes. Indeed, some of the women from the CV room drift over to the weight room, but many do not.

The CV room has four reclining bikes, sixteen Stairmasters, two rowing machines, and one crossaerobics (seated aerobic leg press) machine. The proportion of women to men in the CV room is approximately seventy/thirty across the course of my participant observation. KCF differs from private gyms outside of university settings, where there have been varying age, race, and class distributions. At these other sites, participation rates for CV and lifting activities are somewhat more even between women and men.

WHY ENGAGE IN FITNESS ACTIVITIES?

When I ask women at KCF why they work out, many of the interviewees immediately engage with a health discourse. Consistent with the irony presented by Glassner (1990, 1992), many engage in "health talk" even when their actions are both healthy and antithetical to health. Five of the women are vegetarian, ten say they have always "been active," nearly all state that they "watch their fat intake and sodium level," and many offer that they "don't smoke or drink or take drugs." I note the similarity in health talk across different women, and how it slides effortlessly out of mouths like a cultural mantra. At the same time, several women are also willing to talk about how they work out when sick, in pain, or with injury. During both formal and informal ethnographic interviews, women discuss feeling emotionally overwhelming pressures to look good, and several say they work out when hungry, sick, or injured, that they "bind" themselves to Stairmasters or bikes, or "force" themselves to go to aerobics classes. A few women equated their long cardiovascular workouts with torture.

Along with heath talk and torture talk, all of the women attest to a long list of welcomed benefits thought to be derived from routine fitness, such as: gaining a clearer mind, destressing, being able to sleep better, feeling energized, maintaining a higher level of work and/or school productivity, maintaining a healthy weight, and enjoying the effect it has on their bodies. Can we ever get more specific than this seemingly broad and general engagement with a health and fitness discourse? The answer is yes, and rests with "the look."

YOU'VE GOT THE LOOK? . . .
THE RANGE OF LOOKS, AND THE BODILY CONTINUUM

Consistent with Featherstone (1991) and Featherstone and Turner (1995) who argue that body maintenance has become an obsession (and product) of consumer culture, many women state that they work out in order to attain a certain "look." Unlike research that claims that there is a single dominant image of beauty, the women in this project call up a range of images and looks that are acceptable for themselves and/or considered "ideal." The "ideal" is not particularly broad, but it does entail a range. Rejection and/or acceptance of bodily ideals is a complex process, as discussed by Markula (1996). Ironically, no matter what women express about bodily ideals and/or whether or not they aspired to move closer to it, numerous women chose the same fitness practices—long cardiovascular workouts—while simultaneously avoiding or limiting weight room time.

Let us imagine a continuum of bodies with very thin, nonmuscular bodies on the left and large, muscular bodybuilders on the right. When I ask women to describe what they want their bodies to look like, the description lands near the left-hand side of the continuum (but not all the way left), and women rarely describe themselves as creeping up (or wanting to go) past the middle of the line. I define the middle of the line to the interviewees as a mesomorph—a medium-sized person with moderate muscularity.

When I ask each interviewee to specifically describe the body they want to have, four mention female supermodels as examples—those who are on the very thin side with few or no muscles. Four women describe what Bordo (1993) might call the solid muscular, athletic minimalist look—that is, female aerobic instructors who are fit and trim with some muscle—but not "too much." I consider this a move to the right, away from thin, along the bodily continuum, and this body might rest halfway between the far left side of the line and the middle of the line. Lastly, three women cannot precisely pinpoint the look they want to have, but come up with a range of looks that moves from the aerobic look described above to a mesomorphic on the other. Ironically, half of them seem to already look like the body they claim to not have. As we will see, the look is especially instructive because it is one of the key factors that shapes women's decisions regarding their fitness activities.

WHY DON T MORE WOMEN USE THE WEIGHT ROOM?

I use a mixture of open-ended conversation and direct structured questioning. Some of the direct questions I ask during participant-observation and in interviews are whether participants use the weight and/or cardiovascular rooms and, if so, how much, how often, and for what reasons they do or do not. I also ask if they notice any trends in participation rates in the various rooms and why they think these trends occur. During interviews, ten of the eleven women offer an unprompted description of the weight room that is similar to what some women might say about a male-dominated occupation—it is an "intimidating" space where they do not feel comfortable. This lack of comfort may be related to the alienating feeling that several women describe that comes with being "practically the only woman there." This is consistent with Kanter's findings (1977) of token women's experiences in male-dominated occupations. However, the territory is not just intimidating because it is dominated by men, or because some of the actions some men and women partake in lead to discomfort for women. The territory is also intimidating because of a gendered knowledge gap.

That is, those who enter the weight room later in life and with a lack of knowledge are likely to be women (and a few men), and those who are veterans are likely to be men (and a few women). Women must often therefore frequently "catch up" in the space upon entering—find out the "how-tos" of the equipment, formal and informal rules, etc. Some of the gap may be due to women having less encouragement to use their body physically in childhood (Young 1990) and having fewer opportunities to engage in organized sport than men. Indeed, many of the women who had organized sports experience cited sport as the place where weightlifting was first learned. This playing "catch-up" isn't unlike Thorne's (1993) findings that knowledge gaps exist between boys and girls in math and science at school. She shows how these gaps are culturally set in motion and perpetuated through time, and then get reified as "natural differences."

But aside from a lack of experience, why else might women stay out of the weight room? Several women on site state that they just "don't feel motivated to lift," "just aren't interested in strength," or "just haven't felt the need to prove their strength" to anyone.[13] How-ever, many women seem to be very motivated to spend long periods of time on Stairmasters, bikes, and in aerobics classes, and seem very interested in "strength" if strength is defined in a cardiovascular endurance sense. Why are so many women seemingly interested in bike and Stairmaster strength and not weight lifting strength? This leads me to embrace a line of questioning about strength and muscularity. What's good or bad about having muscles? Is having muscles empow-ering, constraining, or both?

STRENGTH IS EMPOWERING, BULK IS "THE STIGMA," AND ENSURING WHAT THE BODY IS "SUPPOSED" TO DO

All eleven women cite physically empowering benefits of both cardio-vascular and weight room strength. In terms of CV strength, women at KCF are happy that working out gives them endurance to do other things they enjoy such as hiking, Rollerblading, mountain bike riding, dancing, walking, and more. It also helps several women psychologi-cally—they feel they could flee an attack situation in the streets or catch a bus that was pulling away. Most women cite enjoyment in the feeling of strength and power that results in their bodies from CV work.

Similarly, many women cite reasons as to why weight room activi-ties are physically empowering. Some of these reasons include: being able to carry grocery bags independently, move furniture, lift boxes, carry computers, stereos, or other equipment at the time of a move or purchase. Not unlike some of the CV narratives, several share that they like the fact that lifting may help them to "hold their own" in an attack situation if they could not flee the danger.[14] One of the women who doesn't lift now but did in the past describes how much she misses her powerful body. Several relay pleasure in not having to ask for help from others, and a few express joy at "blowing people's minds" as to how much they can do physically. Overall, the tone was consistent with other researchers who show how strength is unquestionably related to a feel-ing of agency, strength, independence, and physical power for women (Blinde, Taub, and Han 1994; Gilroy 1989; Hargreaves 1994; Heywood 1998; Messner 1992). However, ironically, recognition of the benefits of weight lifting does not necessarily translate into *doing*[15] it, or doing it more,[16] since we have already seen that many women on this fitness site do not lift.

So what do we make of this paradox? Why do the majority of women on this site steer clear of the weight room and why do those who do lift weights choose to "not lift much?" I learn from interviews that part of the reason women are not "interested" in weight lifting strength lies in a feared bodily masculinization that is often described as a fear of bulk. Most women I spoke to on site and interviewed expressed fears that if they lifted (at all or too much), they might gain too much muscle and become too bulky. Women express that it is "bad" to bulk, talk about fears of getting bigger, and do not want to gain much muscle or look bigger in their clothing, etc. Muscle is described using the following words: "I don't need it," "I don't want it," "I don't want to carry it," "it's excess," "it's too much," or "it's not necessary."[17] More extreme words are also used to describe muscular bulk as being ugly, or "too masculine." Here, we turn to Celeste, who touts a common description of bulk:

> CELESTE: I don't want to be bulky, but thin, lean, hard. I don't like it when flesh jiggles.
>
> SHARI (interviewer): Do you think that bulk is stigmatized somehow?
>
> CELESTE: Yes, definitely, that's definitely *the* stigma—I think women try to get to the opposite end—really thin, *not* to be really muscular.

Celeste is a very thin woman who was a bodybuilder a mere two years ago and also states during her interview that when she used to compete she "looked great," but that she "had to lose all the muscle" when her current modeling contract required that she "get rid of it." Perhaps muscles and (much of) modelling still do not mesh together well in today's fashion industry. Since Celeste has been on several different places on the bodily continuum, I wondered, does she feel she "naturally" falls onto the place where she is now on the continuum, or does she think she consciously works to place herself there—or both? When I ask her why she now does two hours of cardiovascular activity seven days a week, her reply sheds some light on this question:

> . . . it's just that I want to be really thin . . . I mean I want a really good body, I want to be really satisfied with my body, and I don't think, I mean, I have a very healthy diet, I am a vegetarian and I eat fabulous, I don't drink, I don't smoke, but I don't really think I'm doing this thing for my health, I just do them, like, because that's what it takes to be thin.

Here, equating "good body" with "thin body," I learn that Celeste considers a thin body to be an attractive one and a "satisfying" one. The stigma mentioned above is perhaps one that equates bulk with *dis*satisfaction and unattractiveness. Interestingly, her narrative both establishes health talk and deconstructs it—she admits to having a "very healthy" diet and yet also states that she doesn't "do this" fitness regimen for her health, but rather, to be thin. As such, Celeste is seemingly quite aware of the constructionist notion of the body; that it is not "natural" for her to be this thin, but she will do "whatever it takes" to get there. Apparently, "what it takes" is an intensive combination of eating and exercise practices—"eating fabulous" and an avoidance of the weight room while choosing to do long cardiovascular workouts seven days a week.

In order to try to understand whether it is *strength* or *size* or both that are stigmatized, I offer all of the women I interviewed a "deal"—I state that in the deal, they can get much stronger *without* getting any larger and ask if they would accept or reject the deal, and why. All but two enthusiastically accept the deal, and one woman says she'd like the deal even better if she could "get thinner *and* much stronger." So perhaps it is not strength per se that is stigmatized, but size (muscle or fat) that are powerfully feared. A more muscled body, past the center and towards the right side of the bodily continuum, seems to be the symbol of strength that many women wish to avoid. Indeed, Jacki sums up the general trend of voices:

SHARI: Do you want to be stronger?

JACKI: No.

SHARI: Why?

JACKI: I dunno, I guess I don't have a need for it for one, but I think that if I could be stronger and look the same I wouldn't fight it off. I would worry that if I was getting stronger that it would mean that I am getting bulkier.

It is both intriguing and telling that popular culture frequently touts that women "can't" get big, yet Jacki and many others express how they have to "fight off" the size that comes with weightlifting and increased strength. Furthermore, it is also telling that no interviewee expresses corollary fears of "fighting off" thinness, carrying too much thinness, doing too much cardiovascular activity, or burning "too much fat."[18] We have already met Celeste, a woman who went from being a body-builder at 160 pounds two years ago to a 125 pound model today. As she describes the moves up and down the scale to me, she makes no mention of the discomforts of fitting into her (smaller) clothing on the way down the scale, but expresses being very uncomfortable with her body and (larger) clothing when moving up the scale.

There certainly are women at KCF who do lift weights, yet there are similar tensions expressed by many of these women. Here, many women who lift weights make a clear distinction between "toning" and "lifting to get bigger." Few women lift to get bigger (unless feeling weak or very skinny), and most are interested in toning. In fact, many women cite using specific weightlifting strategies such as "keep the weight light," "do high repetitions with light weight," or "be very careful about how much" they try to lift. In addition, ethnographic interviews with personal trainers also reveal perceptions that women are "holding back" on weightlifting. What is striking and central to interview narratives is the fear of bulk, the conscious choice to hold back on or avoid weightlifting, and a desire to ensure that the body is becoming leaner and more taught, with an allowance for some muscular tone and size, but not "too much."

Following the logic that it is unnatural and unlikely for women to be muscular, many men and women inside and outside of fitness sites argue that women "*can't* really get bulky" unless they spend hours and hours in the gym. However, half of the interviewees in this small sample do *not* spend many hours (if any) in the gym and plainly note, rather unenthusiastically, that they gain muscle "really fast." For many women, then, there are tensions between wider cultural ideologies about what's *natural* (possible) for women's bodies to do, what women's bodies should do, and what their bodies actually do. That is, engaged with a discourse on what bodies should do, but knowing that their actual bodies may do something entirely different, many women in fitness use workouts to ensure that bodies do what bodies are "supposed" to do. Since many women feel that their bodies are not supposed to have big muscles, and in fact fear them, workouts are structured accordingly, with *much* more time (and many more days a week) spent on cardiovascular activity than in the weight room (if any). But what if a woman's body naturally "does" otherwise, or she *chooses* to structure her practices to do otherwise? That is, what if women and women's bodies do what they're not "supposed" to do? And who or what is telling women what they are supposed to do?

THOSE WHO DARE TO LIFT, THE THREAT OF A STRONG WOMAN, AND WHOSE GAZE IS THIS?

Of the women I interview who "dare" to lift, it is clear that there is a rejection of femininity when it is perceived as the equivalent of frailty or dependency. Words such as "power," "strength," "independence," and even outright "rebellion" are often used to describe weightlifting. One example is Vicky, a tall but very slight and muscular, 5'7" 115-pound woman who boldy declares her bodily strength, desires bodily bulk and strength, and says she is "tired of being tiny." Here, she shares how much she enjoys pushing the boundaries of what people expect of her physically:

> . . . the other day I bought a computer, and there was this huge guy at the desk. He puts this huge box on the counter and just looks at me. He didn't offer any help and I was not going to ask for any. I said thanks, hiked the

box on my hip, on my side, and left with it under one arm. He was looking at me the whole time like "I gotta see this." And the guy in line behind me brought a friend with him, and his friend helped him carry his computer out. Fuck that. So there. They look at me like "she can't carry that" and I'm like "fuck that, come here, I'll carry you up four flights of steps." I just just love to step outside the boundaries of what people expect me to be able to do . . . (she laughs)

SHARI: Do you think people expect less of you than you are able to do?

VICKY: Yes. Always. They cannot believe how strong I am.

SHARI: Do men or women tell you that, or both?

VICKY: Both.

Throughout the interview, she and Nicole, who is also seeking bulk, express their frustration with people expecting them to be weak since they are relatively small women. Both equate strength with independence, express a distaste of having to rely on others for help, and reject femininity as frailty or weakness. Both discuss how lifting weights and being strong gives them the ability to carry out independently many of life s physical tasks.

Despite a desire by some women to seek increased strength and size, most women also express a sense of fear—they are fearful not only of becoming too big but also of becoming too much of a "threat." Researchers have long noted the threat that female athletes offer to presumed ideologies about male physical superiority and female inferiority in the gender order. This leads to other questions, such as who strong women might be threatening to, and/or whether or not some women contain their own strength so as to prevent the perception of being threatening.

Although this study is exploratory, my fieldwork, interviews, and discussions with personal trainers lead me to believe that many women are not even close to knowing how strong they can physically become. Not unlike Young's (1990) "inhibited intentionality," college-aged women may not even entertain the thought of finding out one's physical limits—many express shame, disgust, or a fear of rejection on the heterosexual dating market when they were told that they were strong. Here, Jacki explains:

When I get positive reinforcement for being strong, I feel like an ox. Like I helped someone move the other day, and I picked up a table, and my friend said "oh my god, you're so strong." I mean, it was in a positive way, but I felt like I was Babe the blue ox from Paul Bunyon or something. I was like, what are you trying to tell me? Like I wanted to ask what do you mean? I mean, sometimes its flattering, but sometimes I feel defensive, like it feels like it is something bad . . . if I was really thin then I wouldn't mind being told. I'm strong, but I'm not thin, and I'm not fat, so when people tell me I am strong, I don't like it . . .

Darcy shares another aspect of the same sense of shame/fear: "I hide that I lift, from people. I don't want them to know."

There is some question, then, as to whether women might downplay or hide their physical strength, or become afraid to show physical strength again in the future if they've shown it in the past. When I ask Nicole how others view her "strength" that she mentions earlier in her interview, she replies: ". . . anyone I ever dated loved it [my being athletic and strong]. . . ."

SHARI: Were they athletic?

NICOLE: Yes. Males who were not athletes found my strength daunting.

SHARI: Daunting?

NICOLE: Yes, threatening.

SHARI: How did you know that?

NICOLE: They told me.

SHARI: What did they say?

NICOLE: "I think you're too strong for me" or "I can't believe how strong you are" or "How are you so much stronger than I am?"

SHARI: Were they interested in you romantically?

NICOLE: Yes.

SHARI: Did it work out?

NICOLE: Well, no, it didn't work out, for them, because, well, egotistically speaking, I was too much for them [physically].

Nicole appeared to be quite thin, trim, and fit. She didn't look big at all, yet she states that she thinks that her physical strength poses a threat to men who are romantically interested in her. Her existence counters the assumption that men are categorically naturally physically superior to women and reminds us of an overlapping continuum of strength and athletic performances by gender. I originally thought that maybe since Nicole was so small, this made her strength less visible and thus less threatening; this was not the case. And it is interesting to note her statement that many men find her small body with "hidden" strength attractive. However, her small body with *overt* displays of strength is seemingly unattractive at times, once "discovered," even though her body conforms to the widely sought-after taut, fit, trim ideal.

Other women also describe the threat that strong women can be to men. For example, Charlotte states:

> . . . Lots of guys I've dated do nothing [athletically] and then *instantly*, they'll work out too. The last guy was like, "God, I can't believe what great shape you're in, you're in better shape than I am. . . ."

SHARI: Was he upset?

CHARLOTTE: Oh God, yeah. Threatened.

SHARI: How did you know this, exactly?

CHARLOTTE: He said so.

Another interviewee, Fiona notes:

> . . . this one guy used to flirt with me like crazy . . . all the time, he really liked me. Then, one day, he pissed me off, and I put him in a headlock, and man, was he surprised when he couldn't get out. He didn't flirt with me after that . . . (laughter)

There indeed seem to be times when men lose romantic interest in women if women outperform them athletically. At the same time that women fear being perceived as a threat, all eleven interviewees enjoy telling stories of athletically beating some men themselves—or seeing other women do this. Lillian laughs with me that she can hear men harassing one another in the gym when they are "beaten by a girl" and happily shares that she can pass her husband on the bike at times when they ride on the weekend. Of course, it is not clear as to what level of proficiency or years of training women have when they outperform men (nor is it known how much the man is training); however, it may be the case that many individuals still erroneously expect all men to be categorically stronger than all women.

Since women may recognize the threat that being strong and/or muscular can provide, it may be the case that women fear rejection on the heterosexual dating market. Thus, perhaps women self-monitor in order to comply with what they think meets the approval of what many researchers call a male gaze.[19] If a heterosexual woman wants to be appealing on the dating scene, she might consider how strong or threatening she seems to be and downplay her strength. This may be part of the conscious decision for some women to limit the development of their muscular strength. Although ideology may play a powerful part in defining such a limit, it seems that women's experiences with individual men (or women) also play an important part. This may especially be the case on a college campus where an active social life may overdetermine one's social status, quality of life, and self-esteem.

However, my ethnographic work also highlights that gazes and internalization of gazes are much more complicated than the popularly discussed woman who adjusts her bodily look to be pleasing to the "male gaze" (Bartky 1988; Bordo 1993). First, whose gaze are we talking about? Not all women (no matter what their sexuality may be) are trying to satisfy a male gaze; some women desire to satisfy only a female gaze, and some desire to satisfy both. Several heterosexual women I spoke to during ethnographic work stated a desire to look good for women as well as men. And the heterosexual women I interviewed sometimes expressed that their male partners wanted them to have *more* muscles or size, or liked when they rejected aspects of emphasized femininity such as not wearing makeup or dresses. However, these same women rejected these challenges and thoroughly embraced numerous aspects of emphasized femininity regardless of what their partners thought. Furthermore, it is popularly assumed that lesbian and/or bisexual women aren't attempting to satisfy a male gaze, but, indeed, several lesbian and bisexual women I spoke to on site stated that they do in fact seek a look that satisfies a male gaze. Lastly, there is some suggestion that there may be differing notions of femininity across different races and classes. Thus, while several researchers have suggested that women are disciplining their bodies for men, or internalizing a generalized patriarchal gaze, my preliminary ethnographic work and interviews reveal that day-to-day living and power relations may be more dynamic than suggested.

Connell (1987) explores concepts that may help link hegemonic masculinity to the gaze and the more nuanced aspects of power mentioned above. He notes that although hegemonic masculinity is the dominant form of masculinity in a given time, and many men can and do benefit from it, not all men directly practice it. Here, Jacki sums up this point:

> I think certain notions I have about the way I look and the way I want to look are based on what I think men like. I think I have the kind of legs and ass a man likes, so I like it too. I think my wanting my breasts to be bigger, for instance, is what I think a man would want. But no man has actually ever said these things to me. I have an idea in my head about what I think a man wants.

In some instances, as I have already noted, male partners may desire for their female partners to have larger muscles while their female partners themselves accept more of what might be considered dominant ideology (that women shouldn't lift too much). In the above case, it appears that ideology may be more powerful in influencing how women think about their bodies than what actual individual men express. This points to the need to explore further the relationship between cultural ideologies, individual beliefs, and why (men and/or) women do or do not embrace emphasized femininity. Although this pilot study points to some dynamics that may be at work, a more nuanced analysis of the gaze needs to be explored regarding women's fitness practices and choices. Common assumptions around gazes and sexual identities may be false, and further work needs to explore this complexity.

FEAR OF LESBIAN STIGMA

Another reason for an upper limit on women's muscular size and strength, or an avoidance of bulk and a downplaying of strength, is that many women fear being labeled a lesbian. Although straight and lesbian bodies likely span a wide array of body types and fitness practices, many women associate strong or muscular bodies with "looking like a lesbian." Lillian, who has been previously introduced, helps illuminate this point:

> . . . I like being strong and having big muscles, but maybe a lot of women don 't want that appearance because they think they will look masculine or be unattractive to men, or threatening in some way . . . like in rowing, I don't wanna keep harping on this, but like in rowing, a lot of women were really big and strong, like six feet tall, very strong, and a lot of those women ended up I think . . . I dunno (hesitation) . . . you know, some were gay . . . and some were not, and some were with each other . . . um . . . lots of the big tall men had, it seemed, tiny girlfriends, so like, a lot of the men I think were, in a lot of ways, interested in that . . . [small women]

Lillian makes several noteworthy points. First, she highlights how many women are complicit in constructing bodies that are smaller than men's—or not threatening to men. These conscious bodily constructions help maintain the appearance of a dimorphic gender order that is often considered the basis for a heterosexual order where "opposites" attract.

Of course, the fear of a lesbian label and the ensuing precautions that women take reveal the trap in U.S. discourse and practice that erroneously assumes automatic links between sex, gender, and sexuality (Lorber 1996). Heterosexual femininity seems to remain unquestioned if women are thin and not-too-muscular (typically tagged as "feminine"), but is challenged if women are larger with more muscularity (typically tagged as "masculine"). Future empirical explorations could examine whether or not and how lesbian, bisexual, or queer women are more or less likely than heterosexual women to reject certain aspects of emphasized femininity. In the meantime, the lesbian label serves to divide heterosexual and lesbian women, and leads many women to fear their own strength and bodily muscularity through a loss of social approval.

CONCLUSIONS

It is still frequently believed in U.S. culture that women can't get strong and muscular—as strong and muscular as "men." However, as we collect the reasons why so many women do not lift weights—or do not lift heavier weights—we begin to point to the pervasive power of historically specific cultural ideologies and practices. These ideologies and practices are often invisible to the naked eye but are integral to shaping, maintaining, and changing bodies in fitness. From interviews, we learn how many women on site enact fitness practices that reinforce the popular idea that women cannot "naturally" acquire large muscles despite the fact that *actual* bodies can and do get muscular. This project attempts to reveal that there is little that is arbitrary about women's fitness decisions, and, in fact, a sociology of gender, sport/fitness, and the body can be used to explain the central patterns. These patterns are shaped by complex power relationships where gender, race, class, sexuality, and age are likely central.

Tensions between agency and constraint lead to negotiations around the "look," which is vital in explaining why women do what they do at the gym. Results reveal that even though many women cite benefits that come from weightlifting and express that it is good to be strong, the look has *upper* limits in terms of what women should *not be*—bulky, larger. Faced with a paradox between what bodies should do and what they actually do (if one regularly lifts weights), many women in KCF frequently avoid or cut back on weightlifting while engaging in long cardiovascular workouts. These practices are consistent with the range of bodily ideals that have moved beyond thin to include toned, lean, and somewhat muscled bodies (Bolin 1992; Bordo 1993; Hargreaves 1994). Perhaps this ideal exemplifies the current definition of heterosexual feminine attractiveness. Most women will "allow" a little bit of muscle, some more than others, but a multitude of women fear and avoid large or even moderate bulkiness. Since there is more acceptance of muscles on women today than in the past (see Dworkin, 2001; Heywood and Dworkin, Forthcoming), it is especially noteworthy that so many of the women I observed at the KCF center do long cardiovascular workouts, only lift lightly, or steer clear of the weight room. It is telling that the aesthetics of women's bodies are one primary factor in influencing their fitness choices, and this is consistent with the long tradition of feminist works that explore how women are defined but through their bodies.[20]

At the structural level, women may be at a disadvantage to having access to information that teaches weightlifting, since women still have lower levels of access to organized sports than do men.[21] Future research needs to track the relationship between Title IX progress and the fitness boom to see if fitness participation is related to the accessibility of locally organized sport. Research should also explore how both individuals and institutional structures play a role in setting up and maintaining a knowledge/skill gap between women and men in sport and fitness, and how to continue to narrow that gap.

These findings are not unlike women's current position in the U.S. economy, whereby women are frequently funnelled or self-selected into female-dominated occupations and are not well represented in male-dominated fields. We may see similar outcomes among women who venture into male-dominated occupations and women in fitness who venture into the weight room to seek muscular strength. Some similarities include difficult access, a subtle backlash for the few who do enter, and defining an upper limit. Is it possible that just as women in male-dominated occupations hit a glass ceiling on professional success, so do many women in fitness who seek muscular strength and size? That is, do women in fitness find their bodily agency and empowerment limited not by biology but by ideologies of "emphasized femininity" (Connell 1987; Dworkin, 2001) that structure an upper limit on "success"? How might different women experience such a ceiling and how might varying time periods affect its negotiated placement? As challenges to natural male superiority are forged in the twenty-first century, questions that center around female athletes, fitness participants, and their bodies will continue to provide compelling ground for exploring "contested ideological terrain" (Messner 1988).

NOTES

1. Kandiyoti (199 1) notes that patriarchy is perhaps the most overused and, in some respects, the most undertheorized concept in feminist theory (p. 104). Here, I use the term not to imply a universal and fixed notion of men's oppression over women. Rather, I am aligned with Hargreaves (1986), who notes that there is a dynamic relationship between men and women that moves with great speed at times (p. 115).

2. I prefer to deconstruct the claims that individuals can consistently identify a heterosexual (or bisexual or homosexual) woman (or man) in the media or public at large. Queer theorists and others have revealed how U.S. culture automatically (and erroneously) links sex, gender, and sexuality according to a widely adhered-to triad. Two brief examples that are contrary-to these automatic assumptions are the existence of both lipstick lesbian women and butch gay men. The sociology of sport has only begun to probe this kind of analysis— see Broad (2001); Messner (1996); Sykes (1998). Also see Heywood and Dworkin (forthcoming) for an analysis of contemporary acceptance of female masculinity within current athletic iconography.

3. One example would be receipt of more product endorsements. For instance, Heywood (1998) has shown how women have flocked to female body-building to move into fitness contests. Ms. Fitness contests feature women who are toned, cut, and athletic while adhering more closely to emphasized femininity than do densely muscled bodybuilders. Unlike bodybuilding, female fitness contest participants combine light to moderate muscle gains with a number of cheerleading and gymnastics moves, and also compete in a beauty round with evening gowns where emphasized femininity is more rigidly adhered to. Heywood notes how the prize money for fitness contests has already outpaced that of female bodybuilding in a very short period of time.

4. Far before Foucauldian thought, however, feminism is acknowledged to have articulated a version of the docile body in the late 1700s through the work of Mary Wollstonecraft. See Bordo (1993, pp. 17–18).

5. I do not embrace this type of resistance as a thorough social activism. After all, while some women are empowered in the United States by their sport and fitness participation, their Third World sisters are busy stitching Nike swooshes on more privileged women's sneakers (Cole and Hribar, 1995; Dworkin and Messner, 1999; Sage, 1996).

6. Consistent with Connell (1995) and Chodorow (1994), my desire is to not conceptualize femininity and masculinity as singular, but rather as plural entities—femininities and masculinities. Connell's (1987) work acknowledges the existence of hegemonic masculinity and many subordinated masculinities, yet he limits his discussion of femininity largely to emphasized femininity. Research can and should push towards the plurality of femininity, and I hope that this work begins to carve such a space.

7. I am aware that my continuum is lean-centric and needs to add a vertical dimension of body fat on it in order to make it more inclusive of bodies that are not lean. Such minimalist biases on the body are referenced by Bordo (1993). I am grateful to Michael Messner for improving my upcoming analysis of women, fitness, and bodies through the suggestion of a U-shaped curve with body fat on one end and muscle on the other.

8. Lorber (1996) makes the suggestion to deconstruct assumptions that automatically link sex, gender, and sexuality in research. She challenges researchers to consider instead analyzing data by adding categories beyond those mentioned above (or creating altogether new ones) and/or acknowledging multiple dimensions of reality.

9. After several more years of fieldwork and interviewing, my works in process now entail coverage of three fitness sites and thirty-five interviews.

10. This trend shifted three years later when I returned to the same site. More and more women enter the weight room to lift heavily since the university had increased the number of weight-lifting classes offered. Increasingly, these classes became female-dominated on campus. Perhaps it is no accident that this trend occurred after the 1996 Year of the Woman Olympics and the introduc-

tion of the WNBA in 1997. Further shifts are likely after the 1999 World Cup victory and the formation of the WUSA.

11. Although university data shows that a higher proportion of African American women are on the basketball team than in overall university demographics, athletes have their own workout facilities. Thus, these numbers relate to fitness enthusiasts at the KCF Fitness Center, not university athletes and university athletic facilities.

12. Indeed, femininity is classed, racialized, and sexualized. Cahn (1994) provides an excellent historical overview of racialized and classed constructions of femininity that shaped and were shaped by white, African American, and working-class women. Little work within the history and sociology of sport has been done on Asian-American, Native-American, or Chicano women of color, as noted by Birrell (1990).

13. Strength and muscularity are integral to many men's self-definitions (Wacquant 1995). It is less fathomable to imagine most men saying the statements about just not being interested in strength (if defined as muscular strength acquired in the weight room).

14. This is consistent with Heywood (1998), who argues that weight lifting is a feminist strategy to physically self-empower or heal past bodily victimization and abuse.

15. There is indeed a difference between ideology and actual behavior. A fine example of this is Hoschild's (1989) widely read work on the gendered division of labor in the household, where couples often hold the belief that parties should share the work equally. Despite this belief, she shows that in reality women disproportionately manage household tasks.

16. My doctoral work, which spans several fitness sites and years of fieldwork, reveals that approximately 25% of women on sites do not lift, 65% lift lightly and hold back for fear of having bulging muscles, and 10% or less of women lift heavily. See Dworkin (2001) for further discussion.

17. In 1999 I guest presented on this topic at a local university, and one young woman in the audience raised her hand and asked: "In a culture of violence, how can having muscle and physical strength be viewed as unnecessary for women?"

18. However, years later in other sites I did find several forty-something aged women who spent the 1980s fitness boom days in aerobics rooms. These women stated that burning off all that body fat vithout weight lifting left them feeling skinny and weak. Weights came to the rescue for these women to increase size and strength—but the desire to not get too big remained.

19. I am grateful to Faye Linda Wachs for highlighting that perhaps the gaze is a cultural aesthetic that is no longer gendered.

20. Postmodern feminist thinkers such as Grosz (1994) might disagree with this emphasis. She argues that women are no more subject to this system

of corporeal production than men; they are no more cultural, no more natural, than men (p. 144). This is not to say that she sees the process as symmetrical, but indeed it seems that she does not want to look at corporeal production in terms of who is more or less oppressed or privileged. Rather, she asserts, "it is a question not of more or less but of differential production" (p. 144). The danger here is leaving out both an analysis of power and important aspects of gendered privilege and inequality.

21. As has been noted, a mediating variable may be weight-lifting classes. Also, increasingly, women learn how to lift weights from personal trainers, and this may help close some of the knowledge gap. At the same time, the cost of personal training and the body knowledge passed between trainers and clients raises several new issues that I do not have room for here.

REFERENCES

Balsamo, A. 1994. "Feminist Bodybuilding." In *Women, Sport, and Culture*, ed. S. Birrell and C. Cole. Champaign, IL: Human Kinetics Publishers.

Bartky, S. L. 1988. "Foucault, Femininity, and the Modernization of Patriarchal Power." In *Feminism and Foucault: Reflections on Resistance*, ed. I. Diamond and L. Quinby. Boston, MA: Northeastern University Press.

Birrell, S. 1990. "Women of Color, Critical Autobiography, and Sport." In *Sport, Men, and the Gender Order*, ed. M. A. Messner and D. F. Sabo. Champaign, IL: Human Kinetics Books.

Blinde, E. M., D. E. Taub, and L. Han. 1994. "Sport as a Site for Women's Group and Societal Empowerment: Perspectives from the College Athlete." *Sociology of Sport Journal*. 11:51–59.

Blinde, E. M., and D. E. Taub. 1992. "Women Athletes as Falsely Accused Deviants: Managing the Lesbian Stigma." *The Sociological Quarterly* 4:521–33.

———. 1992a. "Homophobia and Women's Sport: The Disempowerment of Athletes." *Sociological Focus*. 2:151–66.

Bolin, A. 1992. "Vandalized Vanity: Feminine Physique Betrayed and Portrayed." In *Tattoo, Torture, Mutilation, and Adornment: The Denaturalization of the Body in Culture and Text*, ed. F. E. Mascia-Lees and P. Sharpe. Albany, NY: State University of New York Press.

Bolin, A. 1992a. "Flex Appeal, Food, and Fat: Competitive Bodybuilding, Gender, and Diet." *Play & Culture*. 5:378–400.

Bordo, S. 1986. "The Body and the Reproduction of Femininity: A Feminist Appropriation of Foucault." In *Gender/Body/Knowledge: Feminist Reconstructions of Being and Knowing*, ed. A. M. Jaggar and S. R. Bordo. New Brunswick, NJ: Rutgers University Press.

————. 1993. *Unbearable Weight: Feminism, Western Culture, and the Body.* Los Angeles, CA: University of California Press.

Broad, K. 2001. "The Gendered Unapologetic: Queer Resistance in Women's Sport." *Sociology of Sport Journal* 18(2):181–204.

Bryson, L. 1990. "Challenges to Male Hegemony in Sport." In *Sport, Men, and the Gender Order,* ed. M. A. Messner and D. F. Sabo. Champaign, IL: Human Kinetics Books.

Butler, J. 1990. *Gender Trouble: Feminism and the Subversion of Identity.* New York, NY: Routledge.

Cahn, S. K. 1994. *Coming On Strong: Gender and Sexuality in Twentieth Century Women's Sport.* New York, NY: The Free Press.

Chodorow, N. 1994. *Femininites, Masculinities, Sexualities: Freud and Beyond.* Lexington, KY: University Press of Kentucky.

Cole, C. L., and A. Hribar. 1995. "Celebrity Feminism: Nike Style Post-Fordism, Transcendence, and Consumer Power." *Sociology of Sport Journal* 12(4):347–69.

Connell, R. W. 1987. *Gender and Power.* Stanford, CA: Stanford University Press.

Connell, R. W. 1995. *Masculinities.* Berkeley, CA: University of California Press.

Daniels, D. B. 1992. "Gender (Body) Verification (Building)." *Play & Culture* 5:378–400.

Duncan, M. C., and C. A. Hasbrook. 1988. "Denial of Power in Televised Women's Sports." *Sociology of Sport Journal* 5:1–21.

Dworkin, S. L., and Michael A. Messner. 1999. "Just Do What?: Sport, Bodies, Gender." In *Revisioning Gender,* ed. Judith Lorber, Beth Hess, and Myra Marx Ferree, 341–64. Thousand Oaks, CA: Sage.

Dworkin, S. L. 2001. "Holding Back: Negotiating the Glass Ceiling on Women's Muscular Strength." *Sociological Perspectives* 44(3):333–50.

Featherstone, M. 1991. "The Body in Consumer Culture." In *The Body: Social Process and Cultural Theory,* ed. M. Featherstone, M. Hepworth, and B. S. Turner. London, England: Sage.

————, and B. S. Turner. 1995. "Body & Society: An Introduction." *Body & Society* 1(1):1–12.

Foucault, M. 1979. *Discipline & Punish: The Birth of the Prison.* New York, NY: Vintage Books.

Gilroy, S. 1989. "The Embody-ment of Power: Gender and Physical Activity." *Leisure Studies* 8:163–71.

Glassner, B. 1990. "Fit for Postmodern Selfhood." In *Symbolic Interaction & Cultural Studies,* ed. H. Becker and M. McCall. Chicago, IL: Chicago Press.

———. 1992. *Bodies: Overcoming the Tyranny of Perfection.* Los Angeles, CA: Lowell House.

Griffin, P. 1998. *Strong Women, Deep Closets: Lesbians and Homophobia in Sport.* Champaign, IL: Human Kinetics.

———. 1992. "Changing the Game: Homophobia, Sexism, and Lesbians In Sport." *Quest* 44:251–65.

Grosz, E. 1994. *Volatile Bodies: Towards a Corporeal Feminism.* Bloomington, IN: Indiana University Press.

Guthrie, S. R., and S. Castelnuovo. 1998. *Feminism and the Female Body: Liberating the Amazon Within.* Boulder, CO: Lynne Rienner Publishers.

———. 1992. "Elite Women Bodybuilders: Model of Resistance or Compliance?" *Play & Culture* 5:378–400.

Hargreaves, J. 1986. "Where's the Virtue, Where's the Grace? A Discussion of the Social Production of Gender Relations in and through Sport." *Theory, Culture, and Society* 3(1):109–21.

———. 1994. *Sporting Females: Critical Issues in the History and Sociology of Women's Sport.* New York, NY: Routledge.

Heywood, L. 1998. *Bodymakers: A Cultural Anatomy of Women's Bodybuilding.* New Brunswick, NJ: Rutgers University Press.

———, and S. L. Dworkin. Forthcoming. *Built to Win: The Rise of the Female Athlete as Cultural Icon.* Minneapolis, MN: University of Minnesota Press.

Holmlund, C. A. 1994. "Visible Difference and Flex Appeal: The Body, Sex, Sexuality, and Race in the *Pumping Iron* Films." In *Women, Sport, and Culture,* ed. S. Birrell and C. Cole. Champaign, IL: Human Kinetics Publishers.

Hochschild, A. 1989. *The Second Shift.* New York, NY: Avon Books.

Kandiyoti, D. 1991. "Bargaining with Patriarchy." In *The Social Construction of Gender,* ed. J. Lorber and S. A. Farrell. London, England: Sage.

Kane, M. J., and L. J. Disch. 1993. "Sexual Violence and the Reproduction of Male Power in the Locker Room: The 'Lisa Olson Incident.'" *Sociology of Sport Journal* 10:331–52.

———, and S. Greendorfer. 1994. "The Media's Role in Accommodating and Resisting Stereotyped Images of Women in Sport." In *Women, Media and Sport: Challenging Gender Values,* ed. Pam Creedon. Thousand Oaks, CA: Sage.

Kane, M. J. 1995. "Resistance/Transformation of the Oppositional Binary: Exposing Sport as a Continuum." *Journal of Sport and Social Issues* 19(2):191–218.

Kanter, R. M. 1977. *Men and Women of the Corporation.* New York, NY: Basic Books.

Lenskyj, H. 1986. *Out of Bounds: Women, Sport, and Sexuality.* Toronto, Canada: Women's Press.

———. 1987. "Female Sexuality and Women's Sport." *Women's Studies International Forum* 4:381–86.

Lloyd, M. 1996. "Feminism, Aerobics, and the Politics of the Body." *Body & Society* 2:79–98.

Lofland, J., and L. H. Lofland. 1995. *Analyzing Social Settings: A Guide to Qualitative Observation and Analysis.* Detroit, MI: Wadsworth.

Lorber, J. 1996. "Beyond the Binaries: Depolarizing the Categories of Sex, Sexuality, and Gender." *Sociological Inquiry* 66(2):143–59.

———. 1994. *Paradoxes of Gender.* New Haven, CT: Yale University Press.

Markula, P. 1996. "Firm But Shapely, Fit But Sexy, Strong But Thin: The Postmodern Aerobicizing Female Bodies." *Sociology of Sport Journal* 12(4):424–53.

McDermott, L. 1996. "Towards a Feminist Understanding of Physicality within the Context of Women's Physically Active and Sporting Lives." *Sociology of Sport Journal* 13(1):12–30.

Messner, M. A. 1988. "Sports and Male Domination: The Female Athlete as Contested Ideological Terrain." *Sociology of Sport Journal* 5:197–211.

———. 1992. *Power at Play: Sports and the Problem of Masculinity.* Boston, MA: Beacon Press.

———. 1996. "Studying Up on Sex Sociology." *Sociology of Sport Journal* 13:221–37.

———. 2000 "Theorizing Gendered Bodies: Beyond the Subject/Object Dichotomy." Unpublished research.

———, and D. F. Sabo. 1990. "Towards a Critical Feminist Reappraisal of Sport, Men, and the Gender Order." In *Sport, Men, and the Gender Order,* ed. M. A. Messner and D. F. Sabo. Champaign, IL: Human Kinetics Books.

Nelson, M. B. 1991. *Are We Winning Yet?: How Women are Changing Sports and Sports are Changing Women.* Random House: New York.

Pronger, B. 1990. *The Arena of Masculinity: Sports, Homosexuality, and the Meaning of Sex.* New York, NY: St. Martin's Press.

Sage, G. H. 1996. "Patriotic Images and Capitalist Profit: Contradictions of Professional Team Sports Licensed Merchandise." *Sociology of Sport Journal* 13(1):1–11.

Smith, Y. 1992. "Women of Color in Society and Sport." *Quest* 44:228–50.

Sykes, H. 1998. "Turning the Closets Inside/Out: Towards a Queer-Feminist Theory in Women's Physical Education." *Sociology of Sport Journal* 15:154–73.

Theberge, N. 1987. "Sport and Women's Empowerment." *Women's Studies International Forum*. 10:387–93.

Thorne, B. 1993. *Gender Play: Girls and Boys in School.* New Brunswick, NJ: Rutgers University Press.

Wacquant, L. 1995. "Why Men Desire Muscles." *Body & Society* 1(1):163–80.

Young, I. 1990. *Throwing Like a Girl and Other Essays in Feminist Philosophy and Social Theory.* Bloomington, IN: Indiana University Press.

CHAPTER SEVEN

Women Who Ride:
The Bitch in the Back is Dead

BARBARA JOANS

"My butt hurts. My butt really hurts. I'm not going to be able to walk or sit down."

Debby shouted this bit of information to me as we stopped for a red light on the way to Apple Jack's Saloon.

"My cunt hurts too." I shouted back. "My cunt really hurts. I'm not going to be able to walk or sit down either. Hey Deb, how many men do you think ever get to say this while they're riding?"

Stopped in the middle of a feeder highway on the way to Sky Londa, we rocked with laughter. Each time we yelled some female complaint, Ken, our riding companion and my husband, rode a bit faster. He definitely appeared to want to get away from us. When females bond around bodily functions, men quickly disappear.

"Well, a guy *could* say his cunt hurt," I replied, "if he was packing and treating her like shit." The light changed and we took off down the highway.

Debby and I are riding buddies. While a lot of women have helped me gather the courage to brave the bike, if it weren't for Debby, I wouldn't be riding. It's scary. Women are not raised to ride motorcycles. Riding is so contradictory to the traditional forms of femininity that finding "riding" women on the road is truly astounding.

Women bikers. Women riding buddies. Women's passenger clubs. These words bring up mixed images. Women riding motorcycles? In the distant past it was pretty common. In the recent past, it is almost unknown. Today, it raises eyebrows if not hackles. This chapter is about women who find it necessary to change the definitions of femaleness and femininity in order to ride—women riders who push the boundaries of stereotypic femininity and dare to ride the wind.

In the 1920s and 1930s women rode. Milwaukee created motorcycles, and women, as well as men, took to them. Women were pictured riding, passengering, and hanging out in the biking world. In the early days men and women both rode; and, while it took daring to do so, women as well as men were daring. By the late 1940s the motorcycle world changed. The men, returning from World War II, wanted a different kind of woman, and most women obliged.

The biking woman became the biker's woman. Known in less polite circles as the "bitch on the back," she rode only with her man. The biker was male, and the woman's place was behind him in the bitch seat. That seat, usually small, was extremely uncomfortable, and the woman's position precariously perched (almost as an afterthought in both actuality and symbolization). The biker's woman was necessary and peripheral to the biker world. She was a necessity as a subordinate sexual companion. The biker's woman was often interchangeable with other women, and frequently nameless.

The biker's woman was the groupie who drove to bike rallies in cars, snuck into the festivals carrying food, drink, and drugs, and was often dismissed at dawn. If she loved bikes or bikers and survived the biker's bitch stage, she could settle down with her biker, who invariably expected her to fulfill her female role within the male biker world. She would be soft and submissive, sexual and subservient. Her weakness made him look strong, his unequal complement.

In every era and in each generation there were, however, extraordinary and remarkable women who rode motorcycles. They rode independently, in their own way and in defiance of the stereotypes. Sometimes they rode with men, sometimes with other women. Mostly they rode alone, choosing a solitary and unforgettable path. They became the stuff of legends, but they did not become the leaders, for the remarkable biking women of this generation. Perhaps they were too few in number or too individual in tastes and choices. For whatever reasons and regardless of how exemplary their behaviors, they remain outside the main arena of women on motorcycles. By the close of the 1940s, most women, if they appeared on motorcycles at all, rode the rear.

Women who ride today are a relatively new phenomena. There are many groups, clubs, organizations, and chapters of riding women that grow stronger and larger each day. In Santa Cruz, California, *Thunder Press* (a biker newspaper) puts on an event called "A GATHERING OF WOMEN MOTORCYCLISTS." Last year, two hundred women attended the run. There are women's motorcycle festivals, parties, rallies, and gatherings. The only entrance requirement is a bike. Women can ride or passenger, although most who participate in these events ride their own.

The women who ride cover all arenas of the riding continuum. They are rich, poor, young, and old. They are hetero, they are lesbian. They are rural, urban, working class, and professionals. They are big, they are small—mothers and childfree. They have mates, they are single. They all, however, share some similar traits. Whether they ride in the front or on the back, they all have challenged the historical roles of women in the biking world. None of them is the "bitch in the back."

In this context, *all* these women have broken with stereotypical femininity. They have rejected, consciously or unconsciously, the written and unwritten rules of female behavior. They have rewritten the rules because they had to do so and because these women hold anomalous positions in a dangerous and predominantly male world. In this world the language, rituals, and rites-of-passage are male-defined, and all women bikers ride the roads at risk.

As a field anthropologist, I follow my people. I never expected, however, that I would actually enter the world of bikers. For the past five years I have been doing just that. I started this research from the back of my husband's bike, but then I moved to the front seat of my own Honda Rebel. Eventually, I bought a Harley Sportster and now ride my own Harley Low Rider. The progression is about weight, handling, and power. The Honda weighed about 300 pounds, handled like a large bicycle, and had enough power to speed up or down hill. (I loved it.) The Sportster added about 200 pounds and was extremely difficult to handle but had all the power I would ever need. The Low Rider weighs in around 650 pounds, glides like a champ, and holds steady in the wind.

As a working anthropologist I am never without a people to study, a community to investigate, a subculture to join, or a counter-culture in which to play. The rules are simple: participant-observation, taking field-notes, and analysis. The rules remain simple: love, respect, and appreciate those with whom you hang out. Identify with them *for the duration of the work* and never, never betray their confidences. If this requires keeping three sets of books, so be it. If it means burning your notes, bring marshmallows. If you stop liking the folk, leave. Riding with men and women in the California motorcycle community has been among the most exciting fieldwork of my life. This is one community I could only have entered on a bike. The fieldwork took place at runs, rallies, swap meets, biker rodeos, campouts, and other gathering places. It was through my study of this community that I learned that women brave enough to ride the wind were also brave enough to redefine femininity and male/female relationships.

This research focuses upon a number of related topics: the differences between women and men riders; women's self perceptions; and how the rest of America sees riding women. The research was gathered on both the back and the front of a bike, at rallies, through interviews, and always with the full knowledge of the community.

While there are many different types of male riders, the world at large rarely sees those differences. The riders might ride Harleys, Sports bikes, or European motorcycles. They might be poor, rural, and outlaw, or they might be urban, sophisticated, and middle class. They might be rich and politically well connected. The general public, however, sees *biker,* and expects only the worst.

Among male riders, there are differences. Sports bike riders, riders of the very colorful Hurricanes and Ninjas, are usually young and hip and tend to see Harley riders as middle-aged, rough, old fashioned, and hardcore. A typical remark addressed to the Harley crowd is: "There goes another asshole on a Harley." The bikes are seen as loud and poor performing. Harleys are very loud and troublesome, but Harley riders consider themselves Kings of the Road and make it very clear that all the rest is "Jap crap." Harleys are seen by riders of Yamaha, Honda, Suzuki, and Kawasaki Sports as "down and dirty bikes." This is a cultural appraisal of the Harley image, not a description of the often polished, gleaming bike. Outlaw clubs almost always ride Harleys, and this continues to contribute to the "hard-assed" image of such riders.

European bike riders (those who ride Moto Guzzis, BMWs, Ducatis, and Triumphs) usually separate from both other groups in terms of class, education, money, and style. European riders most typically refer to themselves as motorcyclists, not bikers, and reject the working-class sensibilities of most of the other groups. They rarely appear with noticeable tattoos, visible piercing, dangling earrings, or ripped leathers. Then there are the dirt-bike riders, the racers and solo riders of all types. They cross all lines and affiliate with many different groups. Sometimes they go it alone.

All groups are snobs. Each tends to ride with their own kind. When they do bond, they are held together by a number of integrative mechanisms including both negative and positive forces. High on the negative list are the public attitudes, laws, and sanctions against bikers. These range from ideological disapproval to legal oppression. Every year, there are more laws limiting a rider's freedom of movement and choice of road gear. Many mountain roads and desert dirt trails have been closed to off-road motorcyclists. Many states have adopted the dreaded and hated helmet laws requiring its continual wearing. All groups face negative stereotypes by the general public. Having the "General American Society" as an enemy creates strong bonds. High on the positive list are shared biking values, a common road culture, magazines, rallies, and a profound love of riding on two wheels.

Riding clothes help reinforce the negative stereotypes. While most bikers ride "leathered up," there is a large proportion of riders who wear black leather on almost all parts of their bodies. From the leather jackets to leather chaps, the clothing leaves a distinctive impression. While it may look like something out of the movies, it is functional riding gear. Nothing survives a spill like leather and nothing protects against road rash like leather. It is worn by both men and women. It looks formidable, but it works.

Riding down the road in shades and leathers creates that distinctive biker image. *And it is a male image.* While it is extreme, it does no fundamental damage to the stereotypical male look. He is still, basically, in pants, jacket, and boots. Masculinity, in all its traditional forms, has been upheld. In fact, it has been enhanced, reinforced, and pushed to its limits. While it appears as an exaggeration, it reflects qualities of strength, ruggedness, and toughness. The look promotes the "in your face" attitude held by some bikers and *believed,* by the general public, to be held by all. "General American Society" expects bikers to be crass, crude, and boorish. To the general public, a nose-picking, publicly fornicating, street-pissing biker would not be seen as a contradiction. In fact, such behavior would only reinforce the already negative stereotype. It is always a male stereotype because bikers are always assumed to be male.

Since the 1940s bikers have had bad press. While some of it was deserved, most of it was not. From movie roles as boorish and sadistic outlaws to magazine articles as criminals and rapists, bikers have been stereotyped as the bad guys. Yet the public has a strange love/hate fascination with bikers. As a symbol representing both the unknown and the unallowed, bikers make a great study in contrasts. They are seen as heroes of the *id* and villains of civilization—the rampaging rogue males, raping, marauding and pillaging as they go. These are men who are "manly" enough to grab what they want and thumb their noses at the forces of civilized law and order.

There is just enough truth in the myth to keep it alive. There is so little truth in the myth that most folk within the biker community think it's funny as hell. But male bikers are not above playing off the myth and using the bad-ass stereotype to their advantage if it gets them a faster table at a local bar, quicker service in the gas station, and groupies at gatherings.

Bikers (always seen as male) serve as lightning rods for both hatred and wish-fulfillment within America. Biker stereotypes are larger-than-life myths, but they function within the greater society. They provide, at a distance, a target group to both hate and envy. Most Americans are uptight about sex. Bikers are seen as super studs. Most Americans feel locked into uninspiring jobs. Bikers reject such obligations. Most Americans feel trapped. Bikers ride free. Most Americans feel afraid in their homes. Bikers fearlessly ride the open roads. In short, many Americans *think* bikers do what many Americans wish they could do and cannot. In an uptight, rigid, scared, problem-ridden, overburdened society, bikers are a symbol of freedom. Most Americans both love and fear freedom. Both are part of our cultural heritage. Freedom represents the wild, the uncontrolled, the unsafe, the untamable, the unknowable, and the irresistible. In a fearful, insecure country riding a speeding motorcycle down a winding road is seen as courageous, dangerous, and nuts. Most Americans will not commit such an act. Many Americans wish they could. Since most Americans do not commit the feared and desired act of biking, they punish, with stereotypes, those who do.

The punishment takes many forms. Besides the stereotypes, attitudes and behaviors towards bikers reflect part of this punishment. Bikers are treated as scum. The retention of the persistent "Wild One" image is part of it. Behaviors towards bikers are another part of this punishment. Laws grow more restrictive and punitive every day—from the inappropriate and dangerous helmet laws to the ever more threatening legislation that can be seen looming on the horizon. Bikers may soon have to wear neon colored vests, restrict their riding to designated roads, and become uninsurable. Bikers are convenient scapegoats for frustrated mainstream ambition.

While the above biker descriptions are part of the stereotypic mythologizing, most bikers, in truth, are no more "free" than the rest of America. They carry the same mortgages, job problems, and family obligations as the rest of the population. They work, marry, raise kids, and worry about taxes along with everyone else. They do all this *and* they ride motorcycles.

Women, in the biker world, must deal with all of the typical negative stereotyping plus several new ones. These are women in a male terrain. They have stepped over some invisible boundary and invaded male territory. Women are riding where they do not belong. They are sitting on a bike. If the general public rarely sees differences between male riders (all males are seen as *biker* and potential members of outlaw motorcycle gangs), the public has no problem recognizing women. In fact, gender is the only difference commonly acknowledged. Women bikers are not seen as free-living, marauding gang members but rather as *sexual outlaws* or *gender traitors*. A rider or passenger, if female, is seen as dangerous, tough, and a possibly dyke. She is so far out of the traditional norms of femininity that almost anything is possible because she breaks the patterns. Who knows how she will act? She is unpredictable, wild, and dangerous.

Women riders and women passengers are not alike. They have different needs and different desires. The public, however, is much like the historically oriented male biker and believes that if women are going to be on bikes at all, they should be on the back. To the general public, a woman passenger who willingly participates in such a dangerous and free activity as biking must certainly be no less than a *sexual outlaw*. She is the slutty seductress gracing the pages of the sexist biker's calendars. She is the ribald and ripe sex object, who is permanently in heat. She is the breast-braced bitch advertising bike parts. In short, she is odd, trashy beyond redemption, and certainly beyond acceptable society.

But if the public has contempt for the woman passenger, the real scorn is reserved for the woman rider. She is stereotyped as *gender traitor*. This woman refuses to accept the gender rules that place her on the back of the bike. She rides her own bike and it goes where she wants.

Both the woman rider and the woman passenger brave the risks of the road. Both deal with the wind, weather, traffic, animals, and unpredictability. The woman rider, however, goes it alone. She is in charge of her own destiny and has taken an assertive and risky position. She must maneuver both the bike and the male riding world. She is responsible for her own survival. Some male bikers accept her and some don't. She has dared to enter a masculine preserve that most American men are too wary to enter.

The news media focuses upon biker groupies and gossips. The general public most often categorizes her as a dyke and dismisses her. These stereotypes of biking women as *sexual outlaws or gender traitors* are ludicrous and wrong but they persist in the minds of non-biking "General American Society."

Women did not start riding in large numbers again until the middle 1980s. There were always a few, here and there, who rode and a few who thumbed their collective noses at conventions, constraints, and confinements. For the most part, however, women's riding coincided with the 1980s manufacture of a more reliable touring motorcycle. When the Harley Davidson Evolution engine was developed, women cheered. Here was a comfortable bike that could be ridden without major maintenance. Gone were the kick start, the oil leaks, the grease drips. Women, once again, took to the roads.

Who was riding? The public saw only the tough and the troublesome. In reality, women from all social groups and cultural regions started to ride. Married women, who had been passengering for years, suddenly had the urge to move up to the front seat. Lesbians, who had considered biking too campy and stereotyping, started riding. Even male anthropologists noticed this phenomena. According to Wolf:

> The newest and fastest-growing phenomenon on the asphalt highways of contemporary North America is the solo female rider. Every year more and more women are turning to motorcycles and motorcycling on their own. For the purpose of mutual companionship and support these sisters of the highway have begun to organize themselves into groups that are independent of males. The following is an excerpt from a letter to the editorial section of V-Twin magazine.

> Our name is Against All Odds MC and our patch will consist of the Queen of hearts playing card in the background. In front will be two dice showing three and four circles representing the number seven. We will hopefully show that women can ride motorcycles and still be ladies and that we actually have brains in our heads, not mashed potatoes. (*The Rebels* 1991)

Wolf goes on to add, "In addition to the emergence of individual clubs, there is a growing number of national associations for women motorcyclists, such as Women on Wheels, Leather & Lace ("Ladies of the '90s, Leather stands for our inner strength, Lace depicts our femininity"), Women in the Wind, and Ladies of Harley." In 1986 *Harley Women*, published by Asphalt Angels Publications, Inc., emerged as a magazine "dedicated to all women motorcycle enthusiasts." An increasing number of women bikers are also taking active roles in political-rights organizations such as American Bikers Aimed Towards Eduction (ABATE), pro-choice helmet legislation, Aid to Injured Motorcyclists (AIM), and National Coalition of Motorcyclists (NCOM).

When Wolf writes about the outlaw clubs, his descriptions of women bikers change. He disregards the newer female clubs and returns to the stereotypes.

> The reason women do not ride their own motorcycles or become club members in the outlaw subculture does not relate to lack of interest, ability, or desire. Rather it is because the fabrication of male and female gender identity and roles within the subculture requires female participation only in a marginal and supportive manner. A man's image of "machismo" (dominance and aggression) is achieved in part by contrasting it with a women's image of "femininity" (subservience and passivity.) From a comparative perspective, gender relations defined by outlaw motorcycle clubs are not a radical subcultural departure from, but rather, an exaggerated statement of, the traditional values that have dominated North American society for several centuries. (*The Rebels* 1991)

Among the Outlaws, according to Wolf, men's and women's relationships mimic, in exaggerated form, the rest of society. Outlaw Bikers' old ladies may be seen by American culture as Sexual Outlaws but clearly not as Gender Traitors. They ride the back of the bike but follow traditional ideas about femininity.

It was a blow to much of the male riding population when biker babes became bikers. How individual woman decided to take the plunge and ride is different for each woman. There are as many biking stories as there are women who ride. Each woman has her own tale and her own triumph. Biking women are all different, yet they share some common remarkable traits. Every one of them has had to fit her female self into a male-biased community. Each has had to overcome the negative stereotypes and sanctions of the broader society and redefine her definitions of masculine and feminine.

Traditional masculinity, in "General American Society," has been described in various ways. A man is tough, strong, independent, capable of making quick judgments and actions, self-sufficient, and competent. These traits are absolutely consistent with riding a motorcycle. Traditional femininity, in American culture, has been described as soft, gentle, nurturing, emotional, caring, and responsive. She is tender, conciliatory, and willing to negotiate solutions. These traits do not promote the biking competence. By themselves, they do not prepare a woman for the road.

In the late 1960s the negative side of femininity has been well explored. A woman is small, subservient, passive, ineffectual, and submissive. She is vulnerable, weak, unsure of herself, and has a great need for group approval and love. These traits are absolutely inconsistent with riding a motorcycle. Moreover, if femininity is defined in opposition to masculinity as it frequently is, then a woman must possess a number of feminine traits and *not* possess masculine ones.

Since the resurgence of the feminist movement in the late 1960s, the negative side of masculinity has also been described. A man is aggressive, domineering, overbearing, abusive, rarely swayed by emotions, and willing to go it alone. These traits are absolutely consistent with riding a motorcycle. Most of the time, and in most cultures, masculinity is seen to get some of its meaning in contrast to femininity. To be a man is to have a significant number of masculine characteristics *and* not have feminine ones.

Contrary to the popular stereotypes, most people in America have a mixture of both masculine and feminine traits. It is the proportions that make them significant. Very few people possess almost all the traits of one group and almost none of the other. Most of us are blends, and we identify with some core principles of our gender. We then branch out to include aspects of the opposite one. While some principles of masculinity and femininity may differ from subculture to subculture, the core beliefs remain the same. Men are seen as strong and action-oriented. Women are seen as gentle and nurturing. Men who ride bikes are seen as exaggerating their gender. Women who ride bikes are seen as denying theirs. These women are the *gender traitors*.

How does a woman who participates in the riding world combine biking with a vision of femininity? How does a woman biker integrate the inherent contradictions of riding? How does she put her self-image and the expected norms of femininity into alignment? She does this by changing the meaning of femininity by changing the social concepts and behaviors to conform to her self-image and her actions. She changes societal definitions. To some degree all biking women, to some degree, have revised, modified, and redefined the word "feminine." And they do this in an almost total absence of any feminist identification, information, or consciousness.

"The word feminine has been abused. I like to think that I'm feminine, soft, sweet and all the nice things that go with being a woman. It's a term that's been misused by the press. As riders we are seen as bitches on wheels, and we're not." Jayne Kelly de Lopez expressed her views to me one warm, sunny San Francisco day. We were comfortably seated at her law office when Pablo, her husband, came in with their lunch. Having forgotten to bring mine, we all shared. Pablo, an old-time biker, mentioned that he had had difficulty at first getting use to Jayne's riding. She was the first woman he had been with who rode her own motorcycle. Now he considers it an asset. He strongly approves of the way she looks and the way she expresses her femininity. "I like the fact that women and men are different," she continued, "feminine is different. It's a softer way of dealing. I like to think that I'm feminine. I don't like the concept, gotten from the women's movement, that says that women should be aggressive. I want to be soft and strong. The word feminine has been used, for a long time, as a derogatory term. And that is ludicrous. Feminine is lots of things, including making cookies all day Saturday 'cause your kid is in Chicago and lonesome. It's a good thing. I'd hate to give that up."

Jayne, who promises to throw the biggest party in San Francisco when she turns fifty, is an interesting study. She has had her share of difficulties along with her many accomplishments. She is the mother of six, runs her own law practice, and continues to maintain a good marriage with Pablo. She rides a big bike, a brand-new Low Rider, which she has already had modified to heighten its power, its rumble, and its angle.

Debby Lindblom, another woman biker, had to think about femininity before getting back to me. It was too big an issue to be discussed at once. Also a lawyer, she works for a private firm, rides to work, and has a reputation for both fairness and toughness. Married to Usaia, whom she met while traveling in Fiji, they are raising their baby, Joe, in the middle of San Francisco.

> We all know the stereotypes of being feminine. Some are good. Some aren't. They are nurturing, caring, sweet, quiet, demure, loving and gentle. Then there are the other things. The things we are supposed to do like cooking, cleaning, and the rest of it. On the bad side, there is the idea that we are supposed to be submissive, and, oh yes, have PMS.
>
> Those are the stereotypes. But for me feminine and masculine have become so blurred that I really only use these definitions in a stereotypical sense. It's so blurred that, in reality, I'm not sure it even exists. The idea of masculinity and femininity may just be an artificial dichotomy. I don't really believe in it. It's a false dichotomy. We are all just people. The masculine stereotype is just as bad as the feminine one. Men are usually said to be macho, aggressive, protective, strong, needing control, and sexual.
>
> I consider myself to be both feminine and masculine in both stereotypic senses. I am a woman, female and feminine. But in my personality, all the lines are so blurred, that I don't believe there really is such a separation. It's a creation of language. You create a distinction that may not be there at all. Masculine and feminine is a creation of language.

I asked Debby, my riding companion of four years, how she arrived at her conclusions on feminity. I wanted to know when she started seeing people as possessing a whole mixed bag of traits and not merely the expressions of societally given ones. Debby replied:

> I learned really early that masculine and feminine didn't apply to people. They were just words. People were different. When I was really young I knew that I wasn't dainty or teeny tiny like a ballerina. I also wasn't muscular or strong like a weight-lifter. I wasn't either one of these. I wasn't dainty, never have been. But I wasn't muscular either. Never have been. But I am a person. I am me, so I knew that the categories were wrong.

"But Deb, these are just words," I responded. "When did you really start feeling that the differences were false?"

> I noticed the behavioral difference for the first time in fifth grade. I was told that I shouldn't sit cross legged 'cause I was a girl. Then when I was around eleven or twelve my mother made me stop riding our motorcycle. My foster brother was allowed to continue but I had to stop. We had one of those really little Honda 50s. It was such a thrill! I must have fallen down hundreds of times but I always got up wanting more. I loved riding. Loved it! Then my mother stopped me from riding when I was around fourteen, and let my brother continue. We were the same age. This was first time, besides

the cross-legged incident, that I was confronted with one of those girl/boy things. In most other respects my mother told me that I could do anything. But not with riding. My mother said I could not ride. I left home a month after my sixteenth birthday.

Linda's view of feminine is considerably different from both Jayne's and Debby's. She's a Bikers' Ole Lady and a mother and a nurse who has been riding the rear for years.

Feminine is a good word. But it's not just something that women do. It's not just something that women are. Everyone has a feminine side. It's the nurturing, loving, feeling, social part. Some people have it developed more than others. Some people have it developed less than others but everyone has it. It's like yin/yang. Masculine and feminine each form a part of a total person. Women usually have more feminine parts and men more masculine ones but we all share both parts.

I feel very feminine when I'm on a bike. It's when I get in touch with my feelings. For me, being on a bike is about expressing feelings, it's letting those feelings out and being comfortable with myself. It's when I get the chance to be in touch with feeling free and wonderful and alive.

"Linda," I asked with real curiosity, "what about the men and their feelings?"

I know that this is totally the opposite of the stereotypes but I think that men are at their most feminine when they are riding.

"Linda, are you out of your fucking mind?"

I know that the stereotype of a biker is supposed to be this super macho, anti-feminine man, but all the men I like most, who I've ridden with, get most in touch with their feminine side when they are riding. When they are on the bike they are experiencing their feelings. They are part of the world around them. They are in touch with themselves and its wonderful. It's the best part of them. It's what makes them so much more attractive to me.

Kim VandeWalker had a very different response from Linda's. They are good friends with different views. Kim owns her own computer company. She is casually lesbian, a strong rider, and the only biker I have ever known to have ridden *alone* to the North Pole. She is in her middle thirties.

The most attractive thing about femininity is its strength. I don't find weakness attractive. I see myself as feminine. That means more sensual, refined, and sensitive. It's a very good trait. I see masculine as more crass, sexual rather than sensual, and definitely less refined. But I'm just me. I don't usually define myself as masculine or feminine. Everything is relative. But when I slip out of something silky at night, I feel very feminine.

Pat Thompkins is very clear about her ideas on femininity. At forty she runs her own business, fixes her own motorcycles, and runs her own life.

Femininity is a hard thing to define and even harder to deal with. Society defines feminine as having qualities of weakness and gentleness. It's also seen as being delicate. By those standards I am not feminine. But I believe that society has an antiquated definition of the term. I believe that that definition applied over a generation ago and does not apply now. Women in our generation, especially riding women, have redefined what we are and what we are supposed to do.

We are moving away from set roles and labels. We can define ourselves as we wish. The genders have moved closer. We can all be aggressive and straightforward about our sports, our riding, and about ourselves.

Twenty years ago women like me were automatically assumed to be dykes. In fact, a few of my girlfriends and I used to joke about it. Whenever we went into a bike shop, we knew the guys were all taking bets on whether or not we were lesbians. Guys see a strong independent woman, who is also a good biker, and they don't know what to think. Most of them jump to the conclusion that we must be dykes. I have a lot of friends who are gay. So what! Who you sleep with has nothing to do with riding a bike. Again, old antiquated labels. No basis in reality.

It shouldn't matter if I was or wasn't a dyke. That has nothing to do with how I ride. The statement you make in a bedroom has nothing to do with the statement you make on a bike. But the guys all assume I must be a dyke because I don't fit the stereotype of how they think a heterosexual woman should act. But who cares! I am not delicate, weak, or modest. By that definition I am not feminine. But screw that definition. By my own definition I am. Feminine is just being yourself, not playing any role. If you respect people, you won't turn them off. If you turn out to be competent and aggressive it's OK. Both genders carry characteristics of both masculine and feminine traits.

In the past women weren't allowed to show their masculine side. Men weren't allowed to show their feminine side. But now both men and women can show both sides of their personalities. To do anything less is to compromise yourself. All of us are people who have many, many facets.

Susan Duckstein, like Debby, had to get back to me with her views. Like Debby, she felt it was too big a topic to talk about instantly. She needed to think about it first. Later that day, she called back. Still in her early forties, Susan takes great pride in her profession as a clinical social worker, her marriage, and her accomplishments.

To begin with, femininity is the gentle side of your spirit. It's the softer side of your spirit. It doesn't have anything to do with looks or gender. It's doesn't have anything to do with how I relate to being a passenger on the back of the bike, or a potential rider. It's a self-definition. I could be doing anything and could still feel my feminine side. It's me having the experience of femininity. Now, as a passenger, in Harley culture, some of the time I feel like a nonentity. Like I'm Bradley's appendage. Or like some baggage to be packed. But I always carry my sense of femininity with me no matter what the outside world sees. I have no doubt about who I am as a woman. I have no doubt about who I am as a person. Femininity is one part of it. It's spiritual. I know who I am. Bradley is a man who is in touch with his feminine side. And I love him for it. It's his spiritual side too.

When I'm riding my bicycle, I get in touch with my power. It's not a motorcycle but it's important to me. Riding my bicycle makes me feel like the eagle on the wind. It's not masculine or feminine it's just a wonderful experience. You get all your senses heightened. It's like—"Oh My God, why didn't God give us wings?" We keep wanting to grow them. We keep wanting to fly. In my generation, we see masculine and feminine in everything.

Susan's generation, like all the previous women, came of age in the 1970s. Married to Bradley Brown, she passengers with him and wants, one day, to ride her own. Bernie, on the other hand, came of age in the 1950s. She passengers with her husband, Dick McKay, and has no intention of ever moving to the front seat of the bike. Bernie's definition of femininity is as reflective of her generation as Susan's is of hers. Bernie, alone of all the women, described herself as a housewife.

You can be feminine and still ride on a motorcycle. Being feminine is someone who is very ladylike. This is the opposite of being a rough person. It is a good term. You can be brave but not tough. You can be feminine no matter what you look like. You don't have to be petite. You can be fat and still be very feminine. It means nice tempered.

While Bernie was giving her definition, Dick called in his: "Women who wear dresses, have neat hair, and don't chew tobacco." We both laughed at this, but it highlights an important point. Bernie did not see the clothes as making someone ladylike. To her, it was temperament and manners.

Women who ride are seen by the general public as *gender traitors* while those who passenger are seen as *sexual outlaws*. None of the women interviewed hold anything even remotely resembling these views about themselves. What they have all done, however, is redefine the concept of gender to fit their biking behaviors. All the women expressed feelings of femininity; but their definitions varied considerably from

Debby's behavioral androgyny to Linda's yin/yang interpretations. They varied from Pat and Susan's ideas of both masculinity and femininity existing in varying parts in all of us to Kim's view of femininity as sensitivity and strength.

For "General American Society," stereotypic femininity pivots around two poles: feelings and behaviors. What all the women have in common was taking the concept of femininity out of the behavioral pole while placing it squarely on feelings pole. Femininity became defined by how women felt, not how they behaved. Even Bernie's description of what is ladylike comes closer to how a lady feels, not how she acts. *By divorcing femininity from behavior, biking becomes just another activity.* It neither promotes nor rejects the feminine. If femininity is seen as an internal feeling rather than a particular set of behaviors, then a strong, competent woman, pushing 650 pounds of steel and chrome around, would not be seen as a contradiction. And while Jayne focuses on baking cookies for her kid, it is the underlying feelings of the act, not the act itself that is important. Soft and gentle become positive feelings, not behavioral weaknesses. In fact, soft and gentle, along with caring and sensitive, become strengths. Thus, the concept of the feminine is not a tight shoe to be forced upon women's feet but a loose-fitting robe, large and light enough to allow all kinds of interesting possibilities. It is also a leather jacket, boots, and chaps worn to keep out the wind.

In the women's biking community, the concept of gender has been transformed. Femininity has been seen as a positive force allowing the best in feelings to emerge. It has eliminated the behavioral component completely. It is not what a woman does that makes her feminine; it is how she feels. Femininity has lost one restrictive and dependent component. Thus femininity can be seen as absolutely consistent with biking.

None of these women credited the "women's movement" for either improving women's lives or for helping them to enter into the biking world. They took their entrance into the male motorcycle world as acts of individual bravery. And they are! Yet, there is a hidden element here. The early feminists, whom so many women bikers wish to distance themselves from, helped pave the way for today's riders. Those old-time, serious, relatively rigid, fighting women, now in their 50s and 60s, identified the gender problems, rallied for women's rights, won the freedoms that are now taken for granted, and cleared the path for a redefinition of femininity. All the women interviewed, however, saw feminists as having made femininity a dirty word, and they object to this. All women interviewed clearly distanced themselves from feminism. They felt that feminism had no place in their lives and no part in their histories. They never accepted the historically important cultural fact that feminism set the intellectual stage for the reinterpretation of femininity.

There is a wonderful song by Holly Near that best sums up this historical blank that many younger women draw when contemplating feminism. It's about an "Old Time Woman." She sits on her porch rocking while the younger troubled woman confides in her. The old time woman takes the young woman's face in her hands and says: "If I had not suffered, you wouldn't be wearing those jeans. Being an old time woman ain't as bad as it seems." When I hear that song, I think that if my entire generation of feminists hadn't been such hard-nosed, hard-assed, hard-working, civil-rights pushing, abortion-rights gaining, humorless bitches, there would be damn fewer women in the wind today.

All biking women are extraordinary. Whether they ride or passenger, are hetero or lesbian, are members of motorcycle organizations or ride alone, they share a critical and compelling reality. They share their love of the road. These are ordinary lives made extraordinary. In our society that leaches out most components of primal excitement, biking is one of the few activities open to us common folk that retains its mix of adventure, immediacy, and bravery. Every biker knows this. Biking measures the biker with every ride. Biking women add a dimension of courage to the sport unexperienced by males because they must endure the wrath of public outrage directed against women who dare to be radically different from almost all versions of *stereotypic* femininity. Both groups of women, whether they be viewed as *sexual outlaws* or *gender traitors,* risk public approbation and contempt. Whether they ride or passenger, each woman must forge her own definition of femininity and her own definition of herself. Biking women risk much, but much is gained. The price of admittance to the road is steep because the price is nothing less than your life. That is what is risked. There are safer rides and less safe rides, but ultimately everyone who rides knows that most of the risks are beyond the rider's ability to modify. Much of the risk lies in the weather, the road, the motorists, the animals, and the unknowable. Unpredictability rides with the rider on every trip.

The road, the community of bikers, the sense of adventure, the identity, the courage, and the bravado appear to compensate for the problems. This community of bikers, male and female, lesbian and hetero, passenger and rider, exists as a primal tribute to humanity's lust for freedom.

Put in the words of many bikers:

> We live to ride. There is freedom out there on the road that you can get nowhere else. When you are riding you are *right there.* You are absolutely in the moment. Nothing else can focus you like being on a bike. You never take it for granted. It is a real passion and a real sport. It's something that hits you hard. The bike is like a living thing. It is real, an entity in its own right. It is part of the family. When you are riding, everything else slips away. There is nothing but you and the bike and the road. The whole rest of the world can slip away.

When I started researching bikers as a culture, I never dreamed of participating in the fullness of that life. I started the research with the idea of studying different groups. I thought that it would take me about three years to complete the study. Five years later, I show no signs of finishing the work. I continue to research bikers. That is, I tell myself that I am continuing to do the research. Actually, what I am doing is riding. When I am on a bike, even anthropology can just slip away.

REFERENCES

Baker, Amy Brooke. 1988. "Bugs in Her Teeth." *Christian Science Monitor* 80, 154 (July).

Bolin, Anne. 1988. *In Search of Eve*. Westport, CT: Bergin and Garvey Press.

Fox, Kathryn Joan. 1987. "Real Punks and Pretender: The Social Organization of a Counterculture." *Journal of Contemporary Ethnography* 16, 3:344–70.

Hamblin, Ken. 1996. *Pick a Better Country*. New York, NY: Simon and Schuster.

Hazleton, Lesley. 1990. "Working on the Mechanics." *New York Times* 139 (January 14).

Harris, Maz. 1985. *Bikers: Birth of a Modern-Day Outlaw*. London, England: Faber and Faber.

Hopper, Columbus B., and Johnny Moore. 1983. "Hell on Wheels: The Outlaw Motorcycle Gangs." *Journal of American Culture* 6 (Summer):58–64.

———. 1990. "Women in Outlaw Motorcycle Gangs." *Journal of Contemporary Ethnography* 18 (January):363–87.

Hochswender, Woody. 1991. "Born to be Wild but Feminine." *New York Times* 140 (July 16).

Joans, Barbara. 1992. "Problems in Pocatello: A Study of Linguistic Misunderstanding." In *Applying Anthropology,* ed. Podolefsky and Brown, 160–63. Mountain View, CA: Mayfield Publishing Co.

———. 1995. "Dykes on Bikes Meets Ladies of Harley." In *Beyond the Lavender Lexicon,* ed. William Leap, 87–106. New York, NY: Gordon and Breach.

———. 1994–2002. "BikeRest with BJ." *Thunder Press*. Scotts Valley, CA.

———. 2001. *Bike Lust: Harleys, Women, and American Culture*. Chicago, IL: University of Wisconsin Press.

Lawrence, Elizabeth Artwood. 1982. *Rodeo, An Anthropologist Looks at the Wild and the Tame*. Chicago, IL: University of Chicago Press.

McQuire, Phillip. 1986. "Outlaw Motorcycle Gangs, Part 1." *The National Sheriff* (April–May):68–75.

McCoy, John. 1981. *Concrete Mama, Prison Profiles from Walla Walla.* Columbia, MO: University of Missouri Press.

Quinn, James Francis. 1983. *Outlaw Motorcycle Clubs: A Sociological Analysis.* Master's Thesis, University of Miami, Coral Gables, FL.

Schouten, John W., and James H. McAlexander. 1992. "Hog Heaven: The Structure, Ethos, and Market Impact of a Consumption Subculture." Presented at the Annual Conference of the Association for Consumer Research, Chicago, Illinois.

Thompson, Hunter S. 1966. *Hell's Angels: A Strange and Terrible Saga.* New York, NY: Random House.

Urseth, Mike. 1990. *Sturgis 50th Anniversary Book.* Minneapolis, MN: Midwest Rider Publications.

Watson, J. Mark. 1980. "Outlaw Motorcyclists: An Outgrowth of Lower Class Cultural Concerns." *Deviant Behavior: An Interdisciplinary Journal* 2:31–48.

Wethern, George, and Vincent Colnett. 1978. *A Wayward Angel.* New York, NY: Richard Marek Publishers.

Williams, Lena. 1988. "Yes, Real Women Do Ride Motorcycles." *New York Times* 137 (May11):

Wise and Wise. 1994. *A Mouthful of Rivets: Women at Work in World War Two,* Jossey-Bass.

Wolf, Daniel R. 1991. *The Rebels: A Brotherhood of Outlaw Bikers.* Toronto, Canada: University of Toronto Press.

CHAPTER EIGHT

"I Was There . . .":
Gendered Limitations, Expectations,
and Strategic Assumptions in the
World of Co-ed Softball

FAYE LINDA WACHS

She's pretty good for a girl.

> —An assessment of Kathy's abilities
> made by a player-spectator

INTRODUCTION

At the start of the new millenium, gender relations are in a state of flux. Traditional discourses of gender difference still exist, but, increasingly, men and women are performing the same roles in public and private life. As noted by third wave feminists, this often leads to the paradoxical simultaneous promotion of discourses of equality of opportunity and natural difference (Heywood and Drake 1997; Scott 1996). What gender means, then, is essentially being debated. While many studies have addressed natural versus biological debates, how gender already informs the context in which the debate is set has only recently been problematized (Butler 1990; Grant 1993). Understanding how ideologies of gender structure opportunity, interpretation of performance, and contexts for resistance is paramount to understanding gendered structures of power and privilege.

Sports are one context in which gender relations are reified and contested. Like many other public environments, sports historically have been associated with masculinity. Until very recently, the majority of sporting practices, pleasures, and privileges have been defined as male only (Kimmel 1990; Crosset 1990). Exploring gender reproductions, challenges, and negotiations, which take place in the coed sports scene, can theoretically illuminate understandings of changing ideologies, practices, and bodies. Since recreational adult co-ed softball leagues are environments in which men and women ostensibly perform the same function, such leagues provided the perfect environment in which to study these gender relations. This chapter is part of a larger body of research that focuses on how gendered ideologies, practices, and bodies are reinforced, challenged, and negotiated through participants' expectations, recommendations, and verbal expressions. These things reveal how assumptions about gender can act as self-fulfilling prophecies structuring beliefs and interpretations of events/performances and negating challenges. Those who value challenges can also limit their view of the scene with expectations of challenge and contestation. Studying gender relations in this context may provide parallels to other spheres in American culture that must cope with similar changes, such as many work environments.

SPORT AND GENDER

At the turn of the twentieth century, changing economics and gender roles threatened to undermine masculine privilege. Hegemonic masculinity continued its processes of redefinition and assertion. Sports and success at particular sports were one means to symbolically reify ideologies of hegemonic masculinity and masculine privilege (Connell 1987; Kimmell 1990; Crosset 1990). As a result, sports, especially collision team sports, were defined as masculine-appropriate and in turn shaped ideologies that undergird masculine privilege.

Despite legislation like Title IX, the continued proliferation of gendered ideologies contributes to women being less involved in sports as a form of leisure activity. There are several factors that limit women's access to sports experience. The first factor involves the quantifiably fewer opportunities for women and girls to participate in sports relative to men and boys. The Women's Sports Foundation (1994) reports that while significantly more women and girls are participating in sports, at the high school level boys still outnumber girls three to two.

Second, males and females tend to be channeled into different types of leisure activities. Young boys are more likely to engage in activities that promote hand-eye coordination necessary for most popular team sports, whereas girls are instead encouraged to pursue activities that involve grace, balance, and cooperation (Dowling 2000; Greendorfer 1993). This gives boys a decided advantage as they grow and participate in hegemonic or the most culturally valued masculine sports. Regarding softball, even men with less experience than other men have most likely had more opportunities to develop the types of skills necessary for the game than women.

Third, public cultural representations of sport tend to focus on women playing "female-appropriate" sports and men playing "male-appropriate" sports (Blinde et al. 1991; Duncan and Hasbrook 1988; Kane 1988). Male-appropriate sports tend to be competitive team sports in which victory is based on overpowering or scoring more than an opponent. Female-appropriate sports are sports that involve individual performance, in which winning involves being ranked highest by a panel of judges. Other sports that contain some elements of both, like tennis, are coded as neutral and are considered appropriate for either gender. All of the above make it seem normal or natural for boys and girls to prefer different types of activities or to adopt "different roles."

Fourth, when girls attempt to join boys in sports, they often find themselves ignored, placed in devalued positions (positions to which the ball is rarely hit), and they do not receive the same instruction and encouragement as the boys. In *Gender Play* Barrie Thorne (1993) describes how, except for the one exceptional athlete, the few girls who tried to join the boys for softball were ignored or demeaned. Landers and Fine (1996), in their ethnographic analysis of T-ball, demonstrate how coaches specifically demeaned girls' abilities to play and spent more time and energy teaching the boys. It is therefore not surprising that many of the girls in their study found T-ball to be a distinctly unpleasant experience.

Fifth, girls and women who participate in male-appropriate or gender-neutral sports are often stigmatized through accusations of mannishness and lesbianism (Cahn 1994; Hult 1994). This points to an unresolved cultural paradox that if sports are supposed to teach the values that make boys into men, it is hardly surprising that women or girls who are successful at sports are deemed "mannish." After all, this merely means that they have learned the bodily comportment and competitiveness necessary for success at Western sports. Accusations of mannishness are the equivalent of women being told to "mind one's place." Ironically, reinforcing ideologies of "natural difference," such accusations imply that if a woman acquires the necessary body comportment for success at sports, she is no longer a "true woman." Hence, to be successful at femininity one must not be successful at male-appropriate sports. Mannishness in women is often equated with lesbianism, a stigmatized social identity. While women's sports have provided a haven and meeting place for some lesbians (Cahn 1994), sports do not "make women into lesbians." And, by the same token, lesbianism is tainted with accusations of mannishness or unsexing of women. This allows for a double stigmatization of both gender and sexuality and provides a means of culturally controlling women's participation in sports and to some extent their sexuality. All of these factors contribute to women generally having had less experience at male-appropriate sports.

Finally, given dominant cultural ideologies of female bodies, a woman's relationship with her own body can affect, limit, and shape female sports and physical activity. Duncan (1994) notes how self-surveillance by women of their bodies inhibits sports participation. When one considers how the body necessary for most of the "respected" sports is inconsistent with emphasized femininity (the most valued form of femininity) (Connell 1987; Lorber 1994; Messner 1988), it is hardly surprising that women have difficulty in being comfortable with a sporting body. For women, size is always problematic (Brownmiller 1984); therefore, the muscles necessary for sport may be abhorred as making one appear "fat." In addition, the way of moving that is necessary for success at men's sports is inconsistent with emphasized femininity. Essentially, women are asked to choose between sports ability and femininity.

GENDERED BODIES ARE MADE AND NOT BORN

Despite the proliferation of ideologies of natural gender difference, fears surrounding women's participation in male-appropriate sports point to an underlying belief in the social construction of gender. Some radical feminist theorists argue that gender is constructed through enactments of gendered norms and practices (Bordo 1993; Butler 1993, 1990). For these feminists, gender and sex are not separate as both are part of understandings and physical enactments. This does not mean that the idea of biology is rejected. Rather, they note that biology is always formed and interpreted through the lense of culture. These theorists focus on how gender oppression can only be conquered when gender as a category is radically altered or destroyed (Grant 1993). Feminist theorists like Judith Butler (1993; 1990) and Susan Bordo (1997; 1993) reintroduce the body and experience as essential elements to the study of power. Employing Foucault's concept of power as constitutive, as well as repressive, these theorists demonstrate how gendered social relations are written on the body through the repeated enactment of gendered norms and practices. Power inequity is embedded in the belief and language systems that shape interpretations of experience. Because of the focus on corporeal experience, changing the terms of existence, practices, and interpretations of practice is crucial to altering inequitable gendered power relations (Heywood 1998). However, gendered expectations often shape the forums in which experiences are constructed and interpreted.

GENDERED EXPECTATIONS

Today, most sports and success at sports are still associated with masculinity (Messner 1992). While success at sports unquestionably raises men's social status, success at sports for women is more ambiguous (Messner 1988). Take, for example, the old adage, "Throw like a girl." If one can't throw, one "throws like a girl." This adage calls a boy's masculinity into question, and fathers hurry to ball fields with sons who fall in this category, while the sons quickly try to adjust their arms so as not to be branded a "sissy" or a "girl" (Messner and Sabo 1994). Note that bodily incompetence at sport is synonymous with femininity. Because the status of the female athlete is more ambiguous (Messner 1988), there is no analogous threat to the femininity of a woman who "throws like a girl." In fact, a successful execution of the throw may call her femininity into question. These expectations are shaped by, and in turn shape, a host of ideologies of binary differences in ability by gender. Women are expected or assumed to be "naturally" at a disadvantage in sports, whereas men are presumed to be advantaged (Bryson 1994; Cahn 1994; Hargreaves 1994; Nelson 1994). Tenacious sex testing by international sporting bodies demonstrates the pervasive belief that men are always already advantaged in sports. Such ideologies are analogous to limits placed on women in work environments and justifications for the "pink-collar ghetto." Increasingly, such ideologies are challenged by performances that undermine and transcend gender ideologies. The sub-world of co-ed softball provides a context in which the interpretations of such performances can be observed and analyzed.

METHODS

In 1959 the American Softball Association league in Cleveland, Ohio, decided to innovate with a "mixed couples" league, and co-ed softball was officially recognized as a distinct variety of the game. From its inception, co-ed softball was defined by equal numbers of men and women taking the field at the same time (Dickson 1994). Today more than 42 million individuals play softball, and almost half of the participants are women (Dickson 1994). In particular, there have been huge influxes of individuals into co-ed softball, as participation tripled between 1990 and 1995 (Miller 1995). Not surprisingly, this increase coincides with the entrance into adulthood of the first Title IX recipients, who also are among the first to participate in co-ed physical education. I am one of these women who grew up in entirely co-ed physical education classes. I began playing adult recreational co-ed softball in 1989 at the University of California, Berkeley. Given that I often played ball with male friends, coed softball seemed a fun recreational activity we could do together. After more than ten years of involvement, the parallels between the sub-world of co-ed softball and other co-ed environments were impossible to ignore. Given my history of involvement, ethnography seemed the logical mode of study.

To study this sub-world, I performed participant-observation in five recreational co-ed softball leagues in the greater Los Angeles area from April 1996 to August 1997. Follow-up observations were conducted throughout 1998, 1999, and 2000. I played and observed in four of the leagues, while only observing in the fifth for the purpose of comparison. During the study period, a variety of levels of competitive recreational softball were observed. I also observed several men's games for comparison. Fieldnotes were taken at games, manager's meetings, league advisory board meetings, and the occasional practice. For all softball games, position by gender was recorded, as well as game summaries. Incidents that occurred before and after games were also included.

DISCUSSION AND ANALYSIS: GENDERED EXPECTATIONS AND ASSUMPTIONS—REPRODUCTIONS, CHALLENGES, AND NEGOTIATIONS

Data revealed that gendered ideologies were reproduced, challenged, and (re)negotiated in myriad ways. Interestingly, while performances were integral, the interpretation of performance, set against a context of expectations and assumptions, reflected and (re)defined gender ideologies. This chapter focuses on how gendered assumptions, expectations, and ideologies limited and shaped contexts for resistance and agency. At the same time, a number of men and women openly critiqued such assumptions, providing a context for direct confrontation, something only possible in mixed sex/gender environments.

Gendered assumptions and expectations often acted to reproduce gendered ideologies through two types of gendered strategies frequently enacted by participants. These are 1) strategies that limit the capacity in which women participate; and 2) strategies that limit how women participate. Often "how" translated to whether or not women were given the opportunity to participate at all.

Strategies that Limit the Capacity in which Women Participate

There are a number of strategies that limit the capacity in which women participate. These strategies shaped the positions held by women, thus shaping the context in which both men and women participate. Clear positional segregation by gender provides a potent example.

Positional segregation. Systematically recording gender by position revealed that assumptions about gender clearly influenced the placement of players into specific field positions. Figures 8.1 and 8.2 show the gendering of field positions. Figure 8.1 depicts the percentage of people of each gender who played each position for all defenses observed during the study period. Figure 8.2 presents the percentage of people in each position by gender for all defenses of teams on which I did not participate (either opponents or both teams of a game I observed). The sexing of field positions tends to place men in key positions regardless of the skills and talents of individuals on the team and what the optimum defensive alignment given these skills would be. Generally, certain positions are more desired than others as manager, Gordon Park, remarked, "If I put everyone where they wanted . . . we'd have four first base men, six shortstops, and a couple of left fielders."

As shown in Figure 8.1, most of the positions on the field are gendered. First and foremost was the rover position, which was a perfect correlation between position and gender. In all of the leagues observed, rules required a female rover, whenever a female bats. Since batting orders alternate male-female, all teams placed a woman at this position. If a team only had nine players, the rover is automatically eliminated. Since the conclusion of the study period, this rule has been amended to allow four male outfielders as long as none of them play in front of a designated line in the outfield when a woman is batting. Tagged as female, and not a part of fast-pitch softball or baseball, it was not considered a prestigious position. During the study period, no male outfielders lamented being excluded from this position and being relegated to left, center, or right field. Because the rover is always female, one less woman was available to play different and more prestigious positions. This also meant that if only one outfielder was female, she was necessarily the rover. This excluded her from more prestigious positions that have more authority in directing the traffic of the ball, like centerfield. In addition to the rover position, women

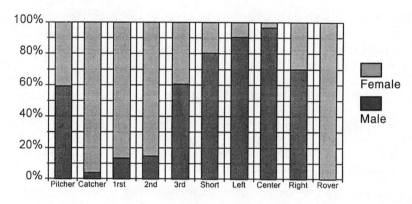

FIGURE 8.1
Position by Sex—All Participants

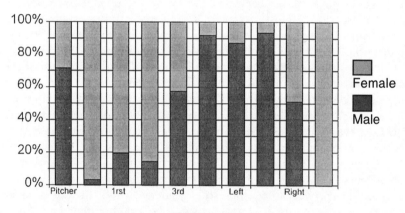

FIGURE 8.2
Position by Sex—Opponents Only

played three other positions in the majority of defenses. Women played catcher more than any other position, with 95.7% of all defenses having women at catcher and 96.5% of defenses in which I was not involved placing women at this position. Because of the speed of the pitches and the fact that other players could often cover plays at the homeplate, novice players were most often placed at catcher. Generally it was assumed that the most novice player on a team would be female and placed at catcher. It was frequently assumed that the catcher was a novice, which was often not the case, making catchers most often subject to position usurpation, which will be discussed in a latter section.

First base (86.3% and 79.8%) and second base (85% and 85.1%) were also female-dominated positions. By contrast, men were most likely to play center field (97.% and 93.9%), left field (91.5% and 88.5%), and shortstop (80.8% and 92.1%). In addition, the pitcher was male about two-thirds of the time (59.4% and 71.9%). The remaining positions of third base and right field were occupied more often by men, but frequently by women. Third base was made 61.1% and 57.9% of the time, making it female-occupied 38.9% and 42.1% of the time. Right field was male-occupied 70.5% and 51.8% of the time and female-occupied 29.5% and 48.2%. There was no consistent predictor of level of ability by field position. This is because a team manager's goal is to maximize the marginal utility of players' abilities in each game. Hence, if a team had an intermediate-level player who could play third or outfield and an expert level player who could do the same, defensive positioning may be based on knowledge of the opposition. Further, an expert-level first base person like Patty will usually get to play his/her position, even if lower level players are placed at other key positions. While there is no consistent predictor of the ability level of individuals placed at field positions, there were some general trends. Usually the shortstop and centerfield were experienced, while the inexperienced players were usually placed at catcher.

While a casual observer might assume that decisions about field positions reflect the relative talents of the individuals involved, observations revealed that men were consistently given priority for the "higher status" positions. Similar to stacking studies that demonstrated how in the past African American athletes have been denied access to particular positions in sports, especially the more prestigious, such as quarterback or pitcher (Loy and McElvogue 1970; Medoff 1977; Phillips 1991), women were denied the more prestigious positions in co-ed softball. While this no longer seems to be the case for race in baseball (Lavoie and Leonard 1994), these patterns are evident by gender in co-ed softball. Moreover, similar to a study on the Dutch co-ed game Korfball (Summerfield and White 1989), women were clustered in "helper" positions. In softball this meant positions more likely to receive a thrown ball than make a play on a batted ball, catcher and first base as the two positions in which this was often true are also the two most female-dominated positions (excluding the rover, who by definition must always be female). Mirroring patterns in the world of work, women were excluded from the more prestigious positions (Kanter 1977; Reskin and Padavic 1994), but retained in positions of support. Just as most women are effectively shut out of management positions, or ghettoized into a few positions deemed appropriate for exceptional women in the workforce (Kanter 1977; McKay 1997; Reskin and Padavic 1994), the gendering of field positions keeps the few talented women consigned to gender-neutral positions, while preserving the most respected positions, the positions that most often involve crucial decision-making (in softball, shortstop and centerfield) for men.

While some may argue that this reflects the skills of the players involved, during the course of my study I estimated that while there were more expert men than women (55% compared to 37%), there was a tremendous amount of overlap. Indeed, 45% of men were intermediate level while 50% of women were. The main difference in ability was at the novice level where less than 1% of the men compared to 14% of the women were novices. Since most of the individuals involved have acquired their skills in single-sex sport, it is likely that both men and women have had experience at positions that they were unlikely to be selected to occupy. The degree of overlap in ability makes the gendering of field positions seem even more inequitable. For example, teammate Kathy and regular rival Tommy (who is a woman) were rarely selected to play the high-status position of shortstop, though both were generally the most experienced infielders available. This exclusion is undergirded by ideologies of both male superiority and entitlement. The view that men are simply more skilled athletes, and therefore belong at the most prestigious positions, and that men are somehow entitled to positions that give them an opportunity to field more plays reflects the history of female exclusion from and facilitation of men's leisure (Cahn 1994; Hargreaves 1994).

The "switch." These tendencies are further exemplified by what I call "the switch." In this case male and female defensive players temporarily switch positions for specific game situations. For example, batters are generally assumed to hit the ball with more skill and force to the same side of the plate at which he/she stands when batting. A right-handed batter "pulls" the ball to the left side of the infield. Since most batters are right-handed, not coincidentally these positions (shortstop, third base, left field) are considered the most prestigious and are male-defined. Teams were observed making defensive adjustments when left-handed batters came up to bat. This was more common in the outfield. The most frequent switch was between left-center and right-center fielders (one usually being the centerfielder, the other generally being the rover). Sometimes a switch was made between the right and right-center fielder as well. With some regularity, usually under the direction of a male man-ager or shortstop, male shortstops and female second base persons switched when a hard-hitting left-handed player batted. For example, during a Center City game, the male shortstop took over second base every time one of our three left handed batters came up. A second exam-ple occurred in one of the two San Gabriel Valley Leagues when both the infielders and the outfielders switched when left-handed players batted. In this case women's capacity to perform is undermined by their exclusion from circumstances in which they may have an opportunity to demonstrate excellence or to acquire experience. This fundamentally demonstrates an assumption that male leisure experience is more central than female experiences. While the heavy valuation of winning in a leisure context requires further study, to a large extent victory was used as an excuse to limit women's leisure experience in relation to men's by reserving the right to attempt more plays. Another series of strategies limits how women participate within their limited capacity.

STRATEGIES THAT STRUCTURE HOW WOMEN PARTICIPATE

In similar ways assumptions and expectations limited and structured how women were able to perform within the position to which they were relegated. Positional usurpation and encouraging women to take walks as often as possible provide two potent examples of these types of limitations.

Positional Usurpation

I use the term "positional usurpation" to refer to incidences in which a fielder covered another's position during a game situation in which this does not regularly occur. Hence, while a shortstop would normally cover second base on a ball hit to the right field side, a pitcher would not normally come home to cover potential plays at the plate with a catcher in position. (However, the pitcher may be expected to come home and back up potential plays at the plate.) Women were often not given an opportunity to play their position when other fielders "covered" for them. For example, the following occurred during a San Gabriel Valley Game:

The ball is a routine fly hit directly at the rover, who is playing back. She calls for the ball with the traditional "I got it." The nearest male outfielder is running across the field. He is coming a long way, but instead of backing up the fielder who just called for the ball, he slows down, looks at her, tells her, "NO, I GOT IT," and steps right in front of her, catching the ball right in front of her glove.

While this occurred frequently in the outfield, the catcher was particularly susceptible to this type of position usurpation. Male pitchers or infielders were observed running home to take a play on more occasions than not. While this was not surprising when the catcher was a novice player, teammates often did this to intermediate and expert-level catchers. Often when this occurred the catcher was in position and ready to attempt the play. This occurred in almost every game in which there was a male pitcher. Unfortunately, this made it impossible for these catchers to gain experience or demonstrate competence. Interestingly, female pitchers were much less likely to do this, however, often electing to back up the play instead of usurping it. In addition, sometimes male third base men would also cover the plate.[1]

When players covered their positions, many catchers acquiesced and didn't bother attempting to cover their positions after the first few potential plays. For example, in the West Los Angeles League, the female catcher was covered on every play by the male pitcher despite the fact she could both catch and throw competently. After having the pitcher cover for her on the first couple of potential plays, she found a new role for herself. While the male pitcher took all of the plays at the plate, she busied herself making sure the bat was not in the way of a potential play. This relegation to what I called "diamond maid" was consistent with literature on women's lower status in the world of work (Kanter 1977; McKay 1997; Reskin and Padavic 1994). In such situations women, already relegated to less prestigious positions, are prevented from fully participating in such positions. This lack of access to experience also creates a lack of access to situations in which one can demonstrate ability, thereby perpetuating ideologies of gender difference by negating contexts in which challenges can occur. Further, such usurpations perpetuate the types of "double binds" to which Frye (1983) refers, as demonstrated in a second example.

It's a balmy Wednesday evening in West Los Angeles. Animal House is facing it's primary rival, Latin Connection (one of several teams encountered during the study had a name that celebrated Latin ancestry though several team members were not Latino/a). They have played in this league for several years and are viewed as strong competitors. In fact, this season, Latin Connection is in first place and has only lost to one team, but it's Animal House, tonight's opponent, in third and rising fast. Latin Connection has men playing pitcher, shortstop, left field, centerfield and right field, while placing their five women at first base, second base, third base, rover, and catcher. When Animal House begins batting, it becomes clear that the women on Latin Connection are expected to defer to the male fielders. In the first inning during Animal House's at bat, Kate hits a hard ground ball to the shortstop. As soon as the ball is hit, the pitcher runs over to first base, knocking the intermediate-level first-base person out of his way with his hand and forearm. He literally elbows her out of her own position. "I'll take those . . . ," he tells her. She gives him an annoyed look and a faint "tch" escapes her clenched teeth. During the course of the game, the pitcher covers for the women at first, third, catcher, and second whenever pos-

sible. This draws the ire of all the women on Animal House. Beating them becomes about proving sexist strategies wrong for Kate, Kathy, and Lori, three of the most vocal team members. In the final inning Animal House is down by one run. The first batter again, Kate, hits a ball to the second-base person. Obviously disappointed, she is enough of a veteran to know that she needs to run the ball out well. Head down, she runs hard. The pitcher breaks first for the ball, but then back for first as he realizes the ball is right at the second-base woman. As he races toward first, he realizes that he won't make it in time to take the throw and stops—about two feet shy of the bag. The first-base person had seen him break, however, and had stopped about four feet shy of the bag. Meanwhile, the second-base woman is cleanly fielding the slow roller, she comes up ready to throw, expecting to see an open glove, tries to hold up, and makes a decent throw right to where the first-base person should be. Kate, watching the play unfolding in front of her, is digging hard. Realizing that she has it, she stretches out. Safe. The ball hits the dugout fence and rolls back onto the field. No chance for extra bases. Kate is safely aboard on what should have been an easy out. Infuriated, the male pitcher picks up the ball and turns to the first-base woman, "You've gotta cover. . . . What are you doing. . . ," he exclaims, exacerbated. The blame for the miscue is placed squarely on her shoulders. For one brief moment protest gleams in her eyes, but then the fire dies and her body slumps and she looks down at her feet. The pitcher glowers angrily at her for the rest of the inning. Animal House goes on to score two to win the game. After the game, when the pitcher ignores her, obviously distressed, the first-base person is comforted by two of her teammates: "It's OK, but you have to cover. . . ." Hearing this, Kathy turns to Animal House and argues, "Well, what do you expect, he pushed her out of the way on every other play. It's his fault. . . . She did what was expected, but now he blames it on her."

In the above example a classic double bind exists. In this case the women are expected to defer to their male teammates. However, when this deference leads to a miscue that ultimately contributes to a loss, the woman is at fault, not the gendered system of inequity in which the miscue occurred. Moments like these contribute to the reproduction of gendered ideologies, expectations, and assumptions. Given ideologies of male physical ability that pervade Western culture (Lacquer 1994; Lorber 1994; Sennett 1993) and that sport is one of the primary institutions that have transmitted and reproduced these ideologies (Cahn 1994; Connell 1995, 1987; Crossett 1990; Kimmell 1990), it is hardly surprising that they are prevalent in co-ed softball. By calling women off of potential plays, men deny women the possibility of gaining, exercising, enjoying, and displaying bodily competence. This ultimately minimizes the accumulation and enjoyment of athletic capital (Wacquant 1995) and shaped and limited their lived experiences. Similar tendencies were revealed in offensive strategies.

Taking Walks

Women's offensive participation was similarly limited by the prevailing assumption that women should always do everything in their power to walk. Take the following example from my fieldnotes from West Los Angeles: *Late in the game it is close. The manager of Busload tells all of the women on his team regardless of ability to "take until you get two strikes called. . . ."* The men are not given this exhortation.

One team in West L.A. used all of the oft-repeated phrases used to instruct women on any occasion in which a woman has three balls and less than two strikes. These include *"only take it if it's yours . . ."; "Take a look you've got room now . . ."; "He (or she) has to come back to you two more times . . ."; and "Make him (her) work."* Four balls in an at-bat lead to a walk. Generally if a player has three balls and no strikes, it seems a good strategy to "take" or not swing at the next pitch. This strategy differed by gender. Despite the fact that male participants received a two-base walk if no strikes were thrown, some men were routinely "given a green light" (to swing) by managers with a three ball, no strike count. No woman during the study period was. In fact, any woman who swung at a three ball and no strike pitch was chastised, regardless of outcome, and frequently women who swung at three ball, one strike counts were admonished. Overall, the assumption underlying this was that men were "better" hitters. Certainly some men were better hitters than some women, but there were also many women who were better hitters than most men. Of course, the issue of what defines "better" must be analyzed in more depth. For example, during the summer of 1997 in Center City, Darren sometimes hit homeruns, yet he also popped up frequently. By contrast, two of his female teammates, Kathy and myself, had batting averages over 150 points higher, more RBIs and runs scored, though neither of us had hit any homeruns that season. In other seasons four out of seven women had higher batting averages than four of seven male teammates. In the San Gabriel Valley Leagues most of the women had similar levels of experience with judging balls and strikes, yet categorical gender assumptions consistently overrode individual demonstrations of ability. Women's access to experience and enjoyment in hitting was severely limited by these types of strategies. If female players were more often instructed to try to take walks and to even let hitable pitches pass, women were limited to secondary, less physical and less prestigious roles. By contrast, men who popped up often were not similarly encouraged to try to take walks, giving them free reign, while their line-drive-hitting counterparts may be asked to let good pitches pass simply because of gender. Just as women's entrance into the world of work has often been restricted to the "pink-collar ghetto" or inhibited by a glass ceiling (Reskin and Padavic 1994), women's participation in softball was limited by similar assumptions that women are inferior and are less likely to succeed. This becomes a self-fulfilling prophecy as women are denied opportunities to demonstrate ability or gain valuable experience. However, despite these restrictions, co-ed space provides a context for resistance to gender and ideologies of difference not possible in single-sex environments.

CHALLENGING WOMEN'S ROLES

Women Excelling at Male Positions

Despite the gendering of field positions, women did occasionally play high-status male-defined positions, as women played shortstop 19.2% of the time in all defenses and 7.9% of the time for defenses with which I was not affiliated. Centerfield was played by women 3% and 6.1%, and left field was played by women 8.5% and 12.3%. When women played these positions and excelled, such performances called gendered ideologies into question. Take the following example:

It's the championship game against our old rivals, the Whoppers. Usually reliable Tomàs and Janey have not shown up! (Later we find out that they had the wrong game time). Fortunately, we still have nine players here. Kathy will have to play shortstop today. At first we are a little tense, playing out of position and a player short. But Kathy is on her game today. She is like Ozzie Smith—she can't miss. Cheating deep on one of the woman, she makes a spectacular over-the-shoulder catch. Her defense leads us to the championship and the whole team congratulates her. Even the other team is impressed. Two of their women yell out, "You go girl . . . ," when she makes a great stop on a hard-hit ball and completes the throw for an out.

Hence, in the few cases in which women are given the opportunity to play "male-defined" positions, they are frequently able to challenge the efficacy of positional segregation through performance. However, such performances are often undermined with a series of discursive strategies (Wachs, under review). While such performances challenge the relevance of categorical gender difference, paradoxically, noting such performances also calls up gendered ideologies that to some extent reproduces them despite a context of resistance (Wachs, forthcoming;

Wachs, under review). Women's performance at female-defined positions presented similar paradoxes between ideologies of difference and equality of performance.

Women's Performance at Female-Defined Positions as a Negotiation

Women's performance at female-defined positions can also represent a negotiation between dominant norms that assume women's inability and the reality of women's performance. When women demonstrated competence and excellence at female-defined positions, they were in essence making the most of a limited situation. Like the "pink-collar ghetto" in the world of work, the gendering of positions leaves women with less prestige, fewer opportunities to excel, and fewer rewards (Reskin and Padavic 1994). Yet women were given the opportunity to demonstrate ability in this limited sphere. For example, several female catchers were witnessed making good throws down to first in an attempt to pick off runners. These women were playing their positions at a higher level than expected, thereby demonstrating female ability, even though it was in a female-defined role. These women's performances challenged the idea of feminine weakness or inability; but, because they were in female-defined positions, ideologies of male physical superiority remained viable as notions of separatism that left women in "helper roles" (Summerfield and White 1994). Resisting strategies that pertain to how individuals are asked to play undermines the second series of strategies that limit women's experience.

CHALLENGING HOW WE PLAY

Resistance to Position Usurpation

As previously mentioned, women are often subject to position usurpation, or having male fielders "cover" for them. Opponents, teammates, and the women covered for sometimes resisted verbally when position usurpation occurred. Opponents, especially female opponents on teams that did not engage in these practices, often made loud comments meant to be overheard by the usurpers. Taunts of "let the women play," "she was there . . . ," "if you don't want the girls to play, go play men's . . ." were regularly hurled. In my previous example from a game between Latin Connection and Animal House, my teammates' disgust for position usurpation was obvious. The following examples involve a later contest between Latin Connection and Animal House.

The pitcher for Latin Connection is covering for all the women as often as possible. He does this every time we play them. This practice annoys several women on our team. After he covers for the catcher yet again, Kate, an experienced pitcher, comments loudly. Since the pitcher is only about fifteen feet from our dugout, he cannot help but hear these comments, the whole point of yelling them out. "Let the girls play, come on." Kathy adds, "If he doesn't want to let the women play, why does he play with them? Why doesn't he play men's?" As these comments are made, the three women sitting together are also staring at him with disgust.

Kathy and Kate object not only to his assumptions of superiority, but for his failing to let the women on his team engage fully in the field. That all players should be given an opportunity to play was presented as the issue. This ethic of participation was frequently invoked when players were excluded from participation. Such challenges resist not only gendered assumptions, but ideologies of victory over participation so common in North American sports environments.

Often one's own teammates even censured such practices as the following example from a San Gabriel Valley Placement game illustrates: *We are playing a placement game today. We have seven women and only five men, so for much of the game we play with six women. Later in the game, however, our manager, Guy, becomes concerned that having two women in the outfield is detrimental. Guy decides against putting Monica or me in the outfield, in favor of himself. He gets one ball that inning. It is a fairly routine popup to straightaway right field. Guy positions himself under it, but what should have been an easy out hits his glove and drops out. Watching the play, Tomàs yells out in a joking yet reproving tone, "Yeah, we don't want to put a girl there . . ."*

In this example Tomàs is critical of Guy for assuming that a male player, in this case himself, is necessarily more valuable or talented than a female player. On another occasion, later that season: *Our male short-stop, Jesse, asked me (at second base) to switch with him when a hard-hitting left-handed man came to the plate. Jesse missed the hard hit ground ball the man delivered. Later in the game, Tomàs played short-stop. He told me, "I'm not going to switch. . . . Because I have confidence in your abilities. He didn't make the play. . . . Besides, you should get to play. . . . It's a team sport. . . . If you want to do everything, play tennis."* This verbal chastisement makes it clear that ideologies about gender roles and participation ethics are hotly contested. In this example Tomàs challenged both ideologies of male physical superiority and greater access to leisure experience. His challenge is particularly noteworthy, as he is in the privileged category.

Participants often defended their own territory. During the course of the study, several catchers protested, *"Hey I was here . . ."* or *"I got it covered"* when the pitcher tried to take a play at the plate. The following incident occurred during a West L.A. Game: *The woman playing catcher is a petite brunette; her attire suggests some experience with softball. After the pitcher comes home to cover a potential play at the plate, she tells him angrily, "Hey, I don't mind playing catcher, as long as I get to play my position." The pitcher, looking chagrined, replies, "Well, I'm not used to having a catcher who can play." But he backs her up, as opposed to taking her plays for the rest of the game.* This example demonstrates a challenge to assumptions of inferiority, as well as her exclusion from the recreational experience. Though on this occasion the pitcher yields to the catcher's assertions that she should be allowed to "play," this did not necessarily challenge all male position usurpation of female players, only those in which the female player has a high level of ability or is willing to fight for her right to participate.

Other women often supported such challenges. Frequently, when a woman refused to be covered and then successfully completed a play, spectators and women on the other team would congratulate the player loudly and yell comments such as: *"Look what happens when you let the girls play . . ."* or *"See, you should have let her play all along. . . ."* Janey and Kathy, two players on San Gabriel Valley I & II, were particularly vocal in these situations. Such resistance counters gendered expectations and creates bodies capable of performing (Dowling 2000). Similar acts of resistance were witnessed with regards to encouraging women to take walks.

Should Women Always Try to Take Walks?

As discussed in preceding sections, often managers invoke a different strategy for the male and female players. Frequently this takes the form of encouraging women to "try to take walks" or to "work the count." While no one would dispute the importance of the walk as an offensive strategy, the fact that women were often encouraged and instructed to take walks, while men were not, even though they might receive two bases, irked many female and a few male participants. This was manifest in verbal remarks such as the following from a West L.A. Game:

Late in the game, the home team, Big Truck Load, is down by a few runs. The manager instructs all of the women on his team to take until they get two strikes on them. Making a face at his retreating back to demonstrate her annoyance, the woman batting, Sherri, follows his orders and walks. The next batter is a man, Armen. While he is batting the manager makes sure to reiterate his instructions to the women waiting to bat. He does not give these instructions to any of the men. Armen pops up on a one ball, no strike count. Two women on the team exchange looks. Steph turns to Nadra and shakes her head and says clearly, "Irony, irony. . . ." Nadra nods in agreement. The manager pretends not to hear, but glances over ruefully.

In this example the women realized that the manager should not be treating all women as if they were inferior hitters who therefore need to work the count for a walk. These women did not physically resist this assumption of inferiority and differential treatment by gender, but instead resisted with humor, as Steph's comment was ironic in content as well as tone. Steph was verbally marking the fact that the strategy should not be gendered and that, given Armen's performance, the assumption that only and all women should be subject to trying to work the count was inappropriate.

On another occasion in Center City:

During a close game a man on one team gives excessive instructions to one of the women on his team. "Take, take," he authoritatively declares. She takes the first pitch for a ball. The second pitch is thrown high, her eyes follow it's arc—predator watching prey. My focus (so I can only imagine hers, too) is disturbed by a sudden and insistent, "No, No. . . ." She lets it go, just deep. The next pitch is declared "a good one" and she hits it hard just foul. The next isn't even close for ball three. This is followed by a taken ("No, let it go") ball three. The count is full. As the pitch comes in he tells her confidently, "Deep, let it go. . . ." When it falls for strike three the umpire comments to some of the women standing around the dugout, "Some guys are always trying to tell the women what to do, and they're usually wrong." Then he looks pointedly at her teammate with eyebrows raised. The offender turns away to talk to some teammates.

Such challenges undermine gendered ideologies by pointing to the inaccuracy and the imprudence of such ideologies. More than that, equal participation, so essential to closing performance gaps by gender (Dowling 2000), is advocated. Such challenges demonstrate the contested nature of gender relations today.

CONCLUSION: WHERE DO WE GO FROM HERE?

Co-ed softball provides a microcosm in which gender relations can be explored. Similar observations can apply to other co-ed environments like the world of work. Strategies, such as positional segregation and "the switch," limited the capacity in which women participate. Analogous to women's relegation to limited and feminized managerial positions (Reskin and Padavic 1994; Kantor 1978; Kessler-Harris 1990), such tendencies denied women access to the most prestigious and powerful team roles. These tendencies were resisted, however, by women's performance and verbally by participants. The context for resistance, though, is shaped by ideologies of competition and gender and limited by gendered expectations. Other strategies, positional usurpation, and strategies that encouraged women to always try to take walks limited how women participated. These limitations gave women fewer opportunities to demonstrate and acquire competence and skill and were often critically resisted for these very reasons. The idea that experience and practice are a component of ability tacitly raises a number of other challenges. In the first case binary sex difference in ability is called into question.

The acknowledgment that body forms are the result of practice (Hargreaves 1994) reflects the complexity of lived experience in which there is a great deal of overlap and ambiguity (Kane 1995; Thorne 1993). Feminists demonstrate the inter-relationship between bodies and cultural practices (Bordo 1997, 1993; Butler 1996; Kane 1995). The demonstrations witnessed revealed the self-fulfilling nature of ideologies of binary and relational gender difference. As noted by scholars, the binary and relational ideologies of gender always inform discourse about sex, bodies, and gender (Connell 1987; Grant 1993; Kessler and McKenna 1978). Clearly, an overlapping continuum of bodily ability (Kane 1995) revealed the effects of experience/practice on ability (Bordo 1993; Butler 1996, 1993, 1990).

Further, moments of reproduction provided moments during which ideologies could be directly contested. This meant, paradoxically, that gendered ideologies were most often challenged when they were being most rigorously reproduced. The complexity of situations that can be simultaneously reproductive, resistant, and compromising is characterized by Third Wave theorizing (Heywood and Drake 1997). Developing ways of thinking, which move beyond these binaries, is essential to the project of eradicating gender inequity. I see now the limits of using diametrically opposed concepts like reproduction and resistance to guide understandings, when both are omnipresent and each impacts experience in a way that becomes essential to social theorizing. Moving toward theories that capture the quality of embodied experience and the options available to bodies must become fundamental to understanding and eradicating inequity in the social world.

NOTE

1. This practice was more disputed than pitchers covering home plate because frequently this gave other base runners an additional base, or base runners who would have been sure outs at the plate, were able to get back to third base.

REFERENCES

Blinde, E. M., S. L. Greendorfer, and R. J. Shanker. 1991. "Differential Media Coverage of Men's and Women's Intercollegiate Basketball: Reflections of Gender Ideology." *Journal of Sport and Social Issues* 15(2):98–114.

Bordo, S. 1993. *Unbearable Weight: Feminism, Western Culture, and the Body.* Berkeley, CA: University of California Press.

———. 1997. *Twighlight Zones.* Berkeley, CA: University of California Press.

Brownmiller, S. 1984. *Femininity.* New York, NY: Linden Press/Simon & Schuster.

Bryson, L. 1994. "Sport and the Maintenance of Masculine Hegemony." In *Women, Sport, and Culture,* ed. S. Birrell and C. Cole, 47–64. Champaign, IL: Human Kinetics.

Butler, J. 1990. *Gender Trouble: Feminism and the Subversion of Identity.* New York, NY: Routledge.

———. 1993. *Bodies that Matter: On the Discursive Limits of "Sex."* New York, NY: Routledge.

———. 1996. "Performativity's Social Magic." In *The Social and Political Body,* ed. Theodore R. Schatzki and Wolfgang Natter, 29–48. New York, NY: The Guilford Press.

Cahn, S. 1994. *Coming on Strong: Gender and Sexuality in Twentieth-Century Women's Sport.* New York, NY: Free Press.

Connell, R. W. 1987. *Gender and Power.* Stanford, CA: Stanford University Press.

Connell, R. W. 1995. *Masculinities.* Berkeley: University of California Press.

Crosset, T. 1990. "Masculinity, Sexuality, and the Development of Early Modern Sport." In *Sport, Men, and the Gender Order: Critical Feminist Perspectives,* ed. M. Messner and D. Sabo, 45–54. Champaign, IL: Human Kinetics Books.

Dickson, P. 1994. *The Worth Book of Softball: A Celebration of America's True National Pastime.* New York, NY: Facts on File.

Dowling, C. 2000. *The Frailty Myth.* New York, NY: Random House.

Duncan, M. C. 1994. "The Politics of Women's Body Images and Practices: Foucault, the Panopticon, and *Shape* Magazine." *Journal of Sport and Social Issues* 18(1):40–65.

———, and C. Hasbrook. 1988. "Denial of Power in Televised Women's Sports." *Sociology of Sport Journal* 5:1–21.

Frye, M. 1983. *The Politics of Reality.* Trumansburg, NY: Crossing Press.

Grant, J. 1993. *Fundamental Feminism: Contesting the Core Concepts of Feminist Theory*. New York, NY: Routledge.

Greendorfer, S. 1993. "Gender Role Stereotypes and Early Childhood Socialization. In *Women in Sport: Issues and Controversies,* ed. G. Cohen, 3–14. Newbury Park, NY: Sage Publications.

Hargreaves, J. 1994. *Sporting Females: Critical Issues in the History and Sociology of Women's Sports*. New York, NY: Routledge.

Heywood, L. 1998. *Bodymakers*. New Brunswick, NJ: Rutgers University Press.

Heywood, Leslie, and Jennifer Drake. 1997. *Third Wave Agenda*. Minneapolis, MN: University of Minnesota Press

Hult, J. S. 1994. "The Story of Women's Athletics: Manipulating a Dream, 1890–1985." In *Women and Sport: Interdisciplinary Perspectives,* ed. S. Costa and S. Guthrie, 83–106. Champaign, IL: Human Kinetics.

Kane, M. J. 1988. "Media Coverage of the Female Athlete before, during, and after Title IX: *Sports Illustrated* Revisited." *Journal of Sport Management* 2:87–99.

———. 1995. "Resistance/Transformation of the Oppositional Binary: Exposing Sport as a Continuum. *Journal of Sport and Social Issues* 19:191–218.

Kanter, R. M. 1977. *Men and Women of the Corporation*. New York, NY: Basic Books, Inc.

Kessler, S. J., and W. McKenna. 1974. *Gender: An Ethnomethodological Approach*. New York, NY: John Wiley & Sons.

Kessler-Harris, A. 1990. *A Woman's Wage*. Kentucky: University of Kentucky Press.

Kimmel, M. S. 1990. "Baseball and the Reconstitution of American Masculinity." In *Sport, Men, and the Gender Order: Critical Feminist Perspectives,* ed. M. Messner and D. Sabo, 55–65. Champaign, IL: Human Kinetics Books.

Laqueur, T. 1990. *Making Sex: Body and Gender from the Greeks to Freud*. Cambridge, MA: Harvard University Press.

Landers, M. A., and G. A. Fine. 1996. "Learning Life's Lessons in Tee Ball: The Reinforcement of Gender and Status in Kindergarten Sport." *Sociology of Sport Journal* 13(1):87.

Lavoie, M., and W. M. Leonard II. 1994. "In Search of an Alternative Explanation of Stacking in Baseball: The Uncertainty Hypothesis." *Sociology of Sport Journal* 11(2):140–54.

Lorber, J. 1994. *Paradoxes of Gender*. New Haven, CT: Yale University Press.

Loy, J. W., and J. McElvogue. 1970. "Racial Segregation in American Sport." *International Review of Sport Sociology* 5(1):5–24.

Medoff, M. M. 1977. "Professional Segregation and Professional Baseball." *International Review of Sport Sociology* 12:49–55.

McKay, J. 1997. *Managing Gender: Affirmative Action and Organizational Power in Australian, Canadian, and New Zealand Sport*. Albany, NY: State University of New York Press.

Messner, M. A. 1988. "Sports and Male Domination: The Female Athlete as Contested Ideological Terrain." *Sociology of Sport Journal* 5:197–211.

———. 1992. *Power at Play: Sports and the Problem of Masculinity*. Boston, MA: Beacon Press.

———, and D. Sabo. 1994. *Sex, Violence, and Power in Sports*. Freedom, CA: The Crossing Press.

Miller, S. 1995. "Playing with the Big Boys." *Women's Sports and Fitness*. Pp. 72–79.

Nelson, M. B. 1994. *The Stronger Women Get, the More Men Love Football: Sexism and the American Culture of Sports*. New York, NY: Harcourt Brace & Company.

Phillips, J. 1991. "The Integration of Central Positions in Baseball: The Black Shortstop." *Sociology of Sport Journal* 8:163–67.

Reskin, B., and I. Padavic. 1994. *Women and Men at Work*. Thousand Oaks, CA: Pine Forge Press.

Scott, Joan. 1996. *Only Paradoxes to Offer*. Cambridge, MA: Harvard University Press.

Sennett, R. 1994. *Flesh and Stone: The Body and the City in Western Civilization*. New York, NY: W. W. Norton & Company.

Summerfield, K., and A. White. 1989. "Korfball: A Model of Egalitarianism?" *Sociology of Sport Journal* 6:144–51.

Thorne, B. 1993. *Gender Play: Girls and Boys in School*. New Brunswick, NJ: Rutgers University Press.

Wachs, Faye Linda. Forthcoming. "Leveling the Playing Field: Negotiating Gendered Rules in Coed Softball." *Journal of Sport & Social Issues*.

———. Under Review. "Getting Lucky": Why Women Can't Win for Losing in Coed Environments Such as Softball."

Wacquant, L. J. D. 1995. "Pugs at Work: Bodily Capital and Bodily Labour Among Professional Boxers." *Body & Society* 1:1–15.

Women's Sports Foundation. 1994. "Participation Statistics Packet." New York, NY: Women's Sports Foundation.

CHAPTER NINE

Changing Body Aesthetics: Diet and Excercise Fads in a Newfoundland Outport Community

DONA DAVIS

INTRODUCTION

An anthropological focus on the study of obesity shows that when it comes to health and illness the concept of being overweight is riddled with contradictions. At one time being overweight was a sign of afflu-ence and high status, but it has more recently become a middle- and upper-class "disease" (Ritenbaugh 1982; Stunkard 1975). Yet today this so-called disease has its widest distribution among the lower classes (Maddox et al. 1979; Moore et al. 1962; Stunkard 1975). Exercise and diet are promoted by health-care professionals as a means of improving self-image and attaining or maintaining a healthy, aesthetically appealing body (Badura 1984; Schifter and Ajzen 1985). Yet some feminists (Barron et al. 1984; Millman 1980; Munter 1984) view the popular obsession with being thin as an exam-ple of continuing aspects of the medical oppression of women and as a symbol of the powerlessness of modern women. The final paradox concerns the relationship between obesity and acculturation. As a sign of acculturation, obesity is said to decrease with both decreasing and increasing mobility into the middle class or dominant cultural norms (Garb et al. 1974; Stunkard 1975).

Anthropological studies of obesity have tended to use the anthropometric skills of the physical anthropologist (such as Pollitzer et al. 1970) rather than draw upon the ethnographic skills of the social or cultural anthropologist. However, there is no shortage of fat literature in our sister social sciences, although the sociocultural complexities of obesity remain relatively unexplored. Nevertheless, a rather cursory exploration of the obesity literature identifies several key themes of social science research in this topic area. First is the view that obesity is a product of social class and ethnicity rather than biological heritage (Garn and Clark 1975; Goldblatt et al. 1965; Massara and Stunkard 1979; Stunkard 1975). A second recurrent theme addresses the effect of self-destructive lifestyles on obesity (Bandura 1984). A third topic concerns the exploration of psychosocial factors as they effect obesity, defined as a psychosomatic disease or eating disorder (Halmi et al. 1981; Moore et al. 1962; Schifter and Ajzen 1985; Stunkard 1975). The relative effectiveness of various treatment strategies is also a prominent item of discussion in this literature. Here, the relative merits of individual therapy versus self-help groups or pharmacological therapies as weight-reduction strategies are evaluated (Barron et al. 1984; Terry and Bass 1984; Wing and Jeffrey 1979). Etic versus emic views of obesity and overweight are the focus of research dealing with the measurement of emic body aesthetics (Maddox et al. 1979; Massara and Stunkard 1979) and the nature of obesity as a culture-bound syndrome (Ritenbaugh 1982). Finally, dieting as a practice followed for a time with exaggerated zeal may be viewed as a type of collective behavior defined as fads (Miller 1985; Schwartz 1986; Stunkard 1975).

What follows is an ethnographic analysis of weight loss as a health fad among women in a southwest coast Newfoundland outport fishing community. It covers the time period of 1977 to 1979.[1] At that time, in the village of Grey Rock Harbour,[2] modernization, in the form of the dramatic expansion of health care service over ten years and access to mass media (especially television), had exposed village women to new values regarding ideal body size. An examination of local notions of ethnoanatomy and ethnophysiology shows how weight loss measures were taken largely in terms of achieving a more modern-looking body rather than as a preventive health measure.

Middle-class health care values were introduced into the community by both health professionals and lay outsiders and challenged locals to reevaluate traditional body aesthetics. Through an examination of the sociocultural factors that underlie the rapid emergence and demise of three diet fads—diet pills, jogging, and exercise classes—I intend to demonstrate how collective, traditional community values came to pre-vail over the acculturative strivings of a few villagers and eventually reinforced the more traditional *status quo* for body image or body aes-thetics. As a middle-class, culture-bound syndrome, overweight did not have the appropriate cultural baggage to be adopted as a disease by the Newfoundland women. Instead, local factors negated the urgency for change. An important aspect of all three fads is the way in which people modeled or refused to model their behavior according to body fashion dictates originating from outside the community.

Starting with a review of relevant issues in the social science litera-ture on fat and obesity, this chapter will proceed to introduce the ethno-graphic setting. A description of body image and eating habits of Grey Rock Harbour will be followed by an analysis of the three fads in terms of latent, break-out, peaking, and decline periods. The analytic section will focus on the diet fads as they express two opposing forces in Grey Rock Harbour: the need for individual expression and the need for con-formity. Analysis also will deal with the issue of the relationship between women's perception of their self-worth, status, and body image. The value of self-control versus social control and the negative affect associated with overweight is discussed in relationship to local notions of deviant behavior. "Good" fat women are compared to "bad" fat women. In conclusion, I will reexamine important issues in the rela-tionship among lifestyles, subculture, ethnophysiology, and health care use patterns in Grey Rock Harbour.

THE PROBLEM

Social factors linked to obesity include adult and childhood socioeco-nomic status, acculturation, length of exposure to Western ideals, and ethnic affiliation (Terry and Bass 1984). In this section I will discuss a brief review of the literature on how social class, sex roles, and accul-turation may effect variant rates of obesity.

Studies of weight differentials among members of social classes or different ethnic groups point to the important role that social factors may play in the patterning of obesity. In a Midtown Manhattan study, Emily Massara and Albert Stunkard (1979) found that obesity was seven times more common among lower-class women than those who occupied a higher socioeconomic status. Moreover, among the ethnic groups used in the sample, Italians and Czechs showed more obesity than other ethnic groups regardless of socioeconomic status. Following a study of weight differentials among Midwestern blacks and whites in a ten-state survey, Stanly Garn and Diane Clark (1975) concluded that, with the exception of adolescence, black females are fatter than white females through the ninth decade of life. Other studies have shown obesity to be prevalent among Native American groups (see Terry and Bass 1984:118, for review of the relevant literature). According to Massara and Stunkard (1979:149), "social factors are the strongest determinants of obesity known today." Stunkard (1975:207) states that: "Obesity is to an unusual degree under social environmental control." Phillip Goldblatt et al. (1964:1039) also conclude that "social factors play an important role in human obesity." However willing they are to concede that social factors influence obesity rates, these obesity experts are in less agreement as to how they do so. Stunkard (1975) asserts that social factors operate in an unplanned and uncontrolled manner. Garn and Clark (1975:314) conclude that differences in post-adolescent fat development among blacks and whites are due to "socioeconomic and subcultural manifestations of differential expectancies of fatness, differences in body image, and differential access to calories." However, Garn and Clark fail to identify more specifically these factors or how they actually operate to shape relevant behaviors in the black and white communities.

Not all obesity researchers are as vague in identifying the specific cultural correlates or components to be investigated in obesity research. However, more exacting research specifications are largely limited to suggestions for future study. According to Goldblatt et al. (1964:1044), "obesity may always be unhealthy but it is not always abnormal." Pointing to the prevalence of obesity in the lower classes, Goldblatt et al. (1964) urge that weight reduction treatments be adapted to poor as well as rich populations. Goldblatt et al. propose to extend consideration of the following variables as important in future research: 1) how does slimness come to be valued; 2) why do some subgroups value it more than others; 3) how is its belief inculcated; and 4) what are the different implications for overweight among the different social classes? Similarly, although they are concerned with the weight loss attitudes of individuals, Deborah Schifter and Icek Ajzen (1985) discuss factors with important, more collective sociocultural implications, such as: 1) the degree to which the person has a favorable or unfavorable evaluation of the behavioral goal; 2) the perceived social pressure to lose (or not to lose) weight; and 3) the degree of perceived control over one's body weight.

Sex, as well as social class, raises important issues for the anthropological analysis of the social contexts of obesity. Obesity is more characteristic of women than of men, and feminist studies of obesity provide some relevant cultural insights into the interrelationship among body-image, self-esteem, and women's status. According to Nancy Barron et al. (1984), because obesity is particularly severe and prevalent among women, women moreso than men are subject to the public harassment, media ridicule, and ostracism that accompany obesity in our society. Fat women tend to internalize these norms and develop very self-critical orientations. Similarly, Carol Munter (1984) notes that being fat for women in U.S. society is viewed as a vehicle for transition and perfection ("if I'm fat I can keep imagining that if and when I lose weight my whole life will change"). Barron et al. (1984) agree that self-acceptance and social acceptance in many diet and exercise programs usually comes only after weight loss. According to Barron et al. (1984), the first step in a group treatment program for women should be self-acceptance and the development of a more positive view of the body and one's self regardless of weight.

An important anthropological perspective on obesity has been developed by Cheryl Ritenbaugh in her argument that obesity is a culture-bound syndrome. Ritenbaugh (1982), who is less willing than Garn and Clark (1975) to concede that overweight actually is unhealthy, does address the fact that it is considered to be an abnormal condition among the Western middle classes. According to Ritenbaugh, fat/obesity is described neutrally in bio-medicine as a positive imbalance between energy ingested and energy expended. However, as a culture-bound syndrome, fat is perceived to be problematic, a metaphor for the moral failings of gluttony and sloth. Important themes in American society are individual control and the fear of noncontrol, and obesity is a visual representation of noncontrol. The aesthetic of thinness, especially in women, according to Ritenbaugh, also reflects the emphasis our society places on youth. Although Ritenbaugh's major concern is with how actuarial charts have created "an epidemic of obesity" (1982:356), she also refers to the popularity but ineffectiveness of spas, diet foods, and multiple forms of weight loss therapy among American health consumers as part of obesity as a culture-bound syndrome. Hillel Schwartz (1986), similarly but from a historical perspective, relates diet fads and fat phobias from the mid-eighteenth century onwards to moral issues. Schwartz analyzes diet fads in Western cultural history to argue that dieting is associated with the creation of surpluses. Lack of confidence in the ability to manage a surplus leads the public to believe that they can have everything by consuming nothing. Thus dieting becomes a moral issue and gluttony becomes a deadly sin.

Culture, culture change, and acculturation are also seen as affecters of obesity rates. Stunkard (1975) demonstrates how, with the exception of certain ethnic groups, social class is a more important predictor of weight than is ethnicity in Midtown Manhattan. The longer a group resides in America, the more it adapts to American body values. Rhona Terry and Mary Ann Bass (1984) in their study of the Cherokee recognize social factors associated with obesity to include acculturation and length of exposure to Western ideals as well as ethnic affiliation and socioeconomic status. Although obesity is a prevalent problem among the North Carolina Cherokee, these women did participate in weight reduction activities such as low-calorie diets, drugs, and exercise classes, which were initiated with the assistance of a local public health nutritionist. Stunkard (1975:207) refers to Navaho patterns of obesity (see Garb et al. 1974) and proposes a qualitative model hypothesizing that with decreasing affluence, the constraint on the development of obesity is a lack of food. With increasing affluence, "fads and fashions exert control." Despite the promise of insightful analysis, Stunkard (1975) does not elaborate on his statement. Terry and Bass (1984) also fail to elaborate on diet and exercise programs among the Cherokee.

Ritenbaugh (1982) refers to the role of Western medicine in the geographic dispersal of the negative association between weight, morbidity, and morality to more marginal groups in United State's society. This is especially true among populations where plumpness is considered desirable: for example, Mexican-Americans have coined a new word for fatness—gondura mala or "bad fatness." Maddox et al. (1979) also point to the important role that insurance companies and the "Protestant Ethic" have played in introducing a negative connotation to be responsible for their disability. According to George Maddox et al. (1979), the notion of fat as unsightly and the strong emphasis on impulse control as a moral issue have even trickled down to effect the attitudes toward fat persons among subgroups like the poor black in North Carolina who, despite high incidence of overweight among them, tend to share more middle-class negative attitudes towards fat.

The following is an analysis of the sociocultural complexities underlying changing body aesthetics and women's weight-loss fads in Grey Rock Harbour and is designed to incorporate and expand upon several of the qualitative themes just reviewed. I did not set out to study obesity. Nevertheless, as the following describes, I inadvertently became an intrinsic element in the development of weight-loss fads. The study originally was designed to be a study of menopause (Davis 1983). However, it soon became apparent that body image and ethnophysiology were an important and complex phenomena among village women. The ethnographic section of the chapter introduces three themes. First, the relationships between the history of chronic food shortage, traditional diet, current eating patterns, and the use of food as a sign of conspicuous consumption will be described. Second, the relationship between culture change, collective movements, and acculturation will be investigated. The third section will focus attention on female body image as it reflects female status and health concerns in Grey Rock Harbour.

THE SETTING

Located on the southwest coast of Newfoundland, Grey Rock Harbour, population 766, is a homogeneous community. All villagers are of English descent and Anglican faith with similar lifestyles, socioeconomic, and occupational status. A year-round inshore fishery dominates both the occupational and emotional life of the community. The history of Grey Rock Harbour is a chronicle of poverty, isolation, and the struggle for survival in a harsh environment. However, since confederation with Canada in 1949, material conditions have dramatically although sporadically improved. In the mid 1960s, a dirt road was built connecting the village to larger population centers where service facilities and consumer products are more readily available. The road was soon followed by the introduction of telephones and televisions to the local community, thus dramatically expanding the previously isolated villagers' connection with the outside world (Davis 1983).

Locals take a great deal of pride in the tradition of the fishery. Their stoic endurance of the hard times in the past and preservation of valued traditions are seen as elements intrinsic to the Newfoundland character. The daily life of Harbour folk is continually shaped by their long heritage of common experience and a shared belief that survival of the community rests on everyone remaining the same or equal (Davis 1983).

Food, or more accurately the lack of it, is a popular theme of how difficult life was before the road (which has become a symbol for recent modernization) came to the village (Davis 1983). The terrain surrounding Grey Rock Harbour is not suitable for food production. Although in other parts of Newfoundland dietary staples such as potatoes, turnips, cabbage, onion, and carrots can be grown and stored through the winter, the folk of Grey Rock Harbour have to buy and import all of their food. Vegetables plus lard, molasses, tea, and flour, along with salt beef and pork, are purchased on credit from the local merchant. Fish, game, and berries supplement the purchased diet. Bad years of fishing mean little credit and limited food supplies. Although the people of Grey Rock Harbour have always been comparatively well off, Gerald Sider (1985) has described how merchants would allow entire villages to starve if the fisherman and their families were not considered to be productive workers. An alternative was to provide some families with food and deprive others. Running out of food and running out of fuel (coal) are common symbols of "the hard times past." One woman in her early twenties told me that one of her most vivid childhood memories is of sitting on the day bed with her brothers and sisters, all of whom had severe hunger pains and "stomachs sunk in like the inside of a bowl," watching her mother scrape the last flour from the bin to make bread. When the last of the flour was gone, the children simply went to "visit" the homes of friends at supper time where they could depend on being served a bowl of stew. Families in distress are at the mercy of their fellow villagers. Food sharing continues to play a key role in village reciprocity patterns. Over and over again, I was told about the poverty of the past with "The Christmas Story" ("We were all so poor, us eight kids got to split an apple [substitute orange, cake, candy, pudding, etc.] at Christmas. That was all we had. We knew we had to share. And we knew better than to ask for more").

Just as a lack of food is a symbol of the past, soda pop, chips, and candy bars are symbols of present affluence. Many mothers turn their baby bonus checks[3] over to their children to spend as they wish. Some enterprising women have changed their living rooms into shops that are nothing more than candy stores for children. One mother admits it is not good for the child to have all those sweets, but since she has gone without she just could not bring herself to deprive her own child. Force-feeding babies is common, even if the child is too young to appreciate the food. I watched one mother entice her eight-month-old child to a between-meals snack of cheesies, soda pop, cookies, oranges, marshmallows, and Gerber's baby pudding. The child was not as impressed with the "treat" as her mother was. On Easter, the ten-month-old baby in the family where I resided was given a huge, expensive, eighteen-inch-tall chocolate rabbit. Whenever he would whine for it, his mother would take the rabbit out of the refrigerator and his proud parents would beam as, with the aid of his circled walker, the baby managed to spread a chocolate mess throughout the otherwise immaculate house.

Food is also an important part of social gatherings. A hearty eater compliments the cook. The Newfoundland diet is high in fat, sugar, starch, and salt. The average family eats two large and three small meals a day, which includes breakfast (jam and bread), dinner (a meat and vegetable meal), tea, (an assortment of sweets, breads, cheese, sandwiches), supper (meat and vegetable), and mug-up (warmed-over meats from supper or bread, cheese, and sweets), which is served before bed. The low-calorie value of fish is negated by the fact that it is usually fried in pork fat and served with the drippings as a sauce. Men tend to work off all the excess calories. Women do not. Eating patterns reflect the new affluence. Foods, particularly homemade breads, pastries, and sweets, are highly valued by village women as is their skill in making them. Meals are important family occasions, and elaborate afternoon teas are important social events for women who visit each other every weekday afternoon to view "The Story" (soap operas) on television (Davis 1983).

CHANGING BODY IMAGE

The lack of rigidity concerning norms of physical attractiveness makes it misleading to talk about an ideal body shape among Harbour women. The pervasive ethos is that you are born with the body you have and you just learn to live with it. Body fat, like height, hair color, and temperment, are hereditary givens. Just as slimness per se is not valued, neither is obesity per se valued or devalued. Despite the poverty of the past and although fat babies are viewed as a sign of affluence and well-being, fat adults are not. Women's sense of style and personal attractiveness tend to come from what they put on their body rather than the body itself. In old times women possessed two sets of clothes, work clothes and Sunday clothes. They improve on Mother Nature by changing hair and clothing styles, by staying neat and clean, and fighting to control innate personality flaws such as a hot temper or susceptibility to worry.

This does not preclude the fact that there are local notions of what constitutes an attractive woman. However, local aesthetics differ from the uncompromised standards of slimness that are inflicted on women in Western middle-class society. Village women who would meet our more urbane standards of physical attractiveness would be considered anemic ("She's all skin and bone, she's got no blood") and skinny ("A man could hurt himself on a woman like that") to the traditional Harbour male and female. The pleasurable plumpness described by Ritenbaugh (1982) appears to be the ideal norm. Even with their high-calorie diet, the large majority of Harbour women fall into the local acceptable norms of body attractiveness. Moreover, an obese woman may not be considered unattractive if she dresses nicely, takes care of her hair, and gets along well with other village women.

In our society standards of slimness are closely tied to its equation with youth and sexuality. It is the adolescent body that is considered worthy of emulation. Contrary to these middle-class standards, Harbour women are not expected to maintain a "girlish figure" (my phrase). For example, village women had never heard of the aesthetic ideal of a flat stomach and did not realize that women could have anything but a rounded belly. A woman with large hips is expected to attract a man who likes large hips. When I came to the village at 5'5" and 135 pounds, I was considered to be peaked and scrawny.[4] A considerable number of pounds and one extra chin later, I was told that I was much better looking than when I had arrived. Once married with a family of her own, a woman is expected to bear children, spread out, and take on the shape of a "real woman." A healthy woman has fat cheeks, two chins, and fat you can grab (or "love rolls") around her middle. Nor is a woman's sexual self-esteem tied to her weight. Premarital sex among teens is commonplace. But once married, there is very little adultery. Traditionally, long periods of male absence while fishing enhance the sexual excitement of reunion. The wife, whatever her shape or size, is considered to be the desirable, legitimate, and only sex partner of the married male. Through their constant worry over the real and imagined dangers of their husband's occupation, women romanticize their own roles as fishermen's wives as well as their marriages. The relief a woman feels every time her husband survives a week or day of the dangers of fishing intensifies that affective bond. As one very large woman whose husband was on a five-day boat told me: "My dear, a rest is as good as a change." The very recent availability of contraceptives has also made women more comfortable with sexual relations. Many women look forward to sexual relations with their husbands after menopause and women are known for their sexual ferocity at middle age. The privacy a couple experiences often for the first time in their lives after their children have left home also heightens sexual excitement and helps to negate the association of sexuality with youth and physical fitness. A large postmenopausal informant proudly told me that now that her children had left home, she could not wear a skirt around the house as her husband would be constantly hauling her upstairs to bed. The personalities of marriage partners rather than their physical attributes keeps marriages satisfactory.

The weight norms just described are impartable from the strong egalitarian and collective traditions that characterize Harbour life. Harbour women are not strangers to weight-loss goals. Cutting down on food intake is usually associated with frugality (to avoid the expense of buying new clothes, for example). The view that one's weight is God-given or inherited is an important aspect of a more general body of beliefs concerning ethnophysiology. In Harbour life social roles can be very constraining. Individuality is suppressed. Every woman is expected to be a hard worker and stoically endure life's lot with no complaint. No one is supposed to act superior or too different from other villagers. It is one's responsibility, one's moral duty, to conform to exacting local standards of behavior. However, one cannot help the state and character of one's body. Women, through a complex system of nerves and blood, use their local notions of ethnophysiology to circumvent meeting these exacting standards for proper behavior ("she can't help it, she's got the Taylor temper in her blood"). Thus, the complex and highly developed notions of ethnophysiology have traditionally served to legitimate deviancy or improper behavior rather that to serve as a symbol of self-control or morality (Davis 1988).

With exposure to television, greater opportunities for travel, and the introduction of medical services in the community, however, new weight values are being superimposed on more traditional ones. Harbour women have begun to realize that they are larger than their country's more middle-class norms would tolerate. Weight loss was never a burning community issue until a short time before I started my fieldwork. Three activity fads—diet pills, jogging, and an exercise group—all emerged during the year and a half I spent in the village. The latter two fads were probably inadvertently related to me. The diet pill fad was in its period of decline on my arrival. Each of these weight-loss fads will be described in terms of the general patterns of development and decline sociologists have attributed to fads as a form of collective behavior. The first period is known as the latent period when the object of the fad is known only to a limited or small group. During the breakout period, the first group introduces other groups to the fad. The peaking period occurs when people readily adopt the fad and innovations on the theme occur. At the decline of the period, the fad rapidly fades and may totally disappear or be restricted to a small group (Miller 1985). All three fads were introduced from outside the community. The collective behavior fad model is used to describe the rise and fall of each type of behavior and zeal or enthusiasm with which each fad was adopted. However, the eventual decline of each activity is best understood in terms of local social structure and ethos rather than in terms of fad cycles per se.

Diet Pills

Diet pills were introduced to Grey Rock Harbour by two outsiders, a doctor serving the local population at the "Wednesday clinic"[5] and his first pill patient, the minister's wife. Dr. Moore[6] was an extremely outgoing, amiable, and attractive individual. Other physicians who came to the clinic were far less friendly with local folk, and Dr. Moore immediately became the most popular physician on the clinic rotation. Many villagers would wait for Dr. Moore's turn at the clinic to present their complaints. Hearing about diet pills from friends and family in St. John's, the minister's wife, Vivian, inquired about them on a clinic visit and was readily supplied with a prescription by Dr. Moore. Vivian, who thought that the pills would burn or melt off fat, accepted them as a license for unrestrained eating and failed to loose weight. Meanwhile, her friend Mary also got a prescription from Dr. Moore. Mary lost nineteen pounds in three weeks. However, she had to stop using the pills because she was unable to sleep at night and came down with a bad case of nerves. Mary did, however, pass her remaining pills to her sister Lizzie, who also experienced a sudden and dramatic weight loss.

Encouraged by the successes and easy weight loss of their friends, village women of all ages presented themselves to Dr. Moore or began buying cheaper, over-the-counter diet pills at a drugstore in a nearby town. According to my informants, Dr. Moore freely supplied the prescriptions for the asking. His patients were given no physical nor were they provided with any education on nutrition or dieting. The promise of easy weight loss and the initial dramatic success of the pill users, plus the fact that they had a physician's *and* the minister's wife approval, legitimized their use. Some women would take the pills to lose weight, gain it back, and then lose it again. Initially, the pills were heralded as a miracle. However, in time, the women began to realize the pills had marked side effects. Women attempted to control the jitters or bad nerves attributed to the pills by taking fewer pills, trying different over-the-counter brands or other prescriptions, or by combining the diet pills with sleeping pills or tranquilizers. At this point the women began to reassess the advantages and the liabilities of the pills. The minister's wife, a primary nexus of communication in the community, was sent a newspaper article about diet pill abuse. Somewhere along the line information about birth control pills and diet pills became confused. The rumor began to circulate that you should have regular pap smears (here the birth control pill is confused with the diet pill) if you were taking diet pills. This spurred a new fear: diet pills became associated with womb cancer (Davis 1992). Worried that Dr. Moore may eventually get around to looking at their privates (ob-gyn pelvic exam) and fearing that they were being poisoned, women started to abandon their diet pills.

Eventually Dr. Moore was relieved of his practice (locals said it was because he was selling illegal drugs). The sins of Dr. Moore became a popular topic. Not only was he accused of drug pushing, he was damned for a multitude of other sins including unnecessary surgery—tying too many tubes (see Davis 1983a) and circumcising male babies. A few women continued to use the pills. One particular woman is used as an example of someone "who just never learns." Shirley is a big woman, but by no means obese. She has a number of pills all prescribed by the same doctor. At 10:30 a.m. she takes a diet pill, one-half hour later she takes a nerve pill. At noon she takes another pill but she cannot remember what this one is for. Before bed she takes a birth control pill. Every morning she throws up, but the physician (according to Shirley) tells her to keep taking all of the pills.

Obese women, nonobese teens, and young mothers rapidly began using prescription and nonprescription weight-control drugs. Initially, trust in doctors and modern technology led the women to believe that the pills would melt their fat away and they could simply use them to achieve a desire weight. Once the general public realized that the pills did not work miracles (weight was easily gained back) and had a multitude of unpleasant side-effects, an anti-medical sentiment emerged (Davis 1992), and the departure of Dr. Moore led to a dramatic decline in their use. This lack of an easy and dramatic solution to what was emerging as a recognized disparity between local weight norms and those of the outside began to undermine women's complacency about their size. Despite the high rates of hypertension in the community, which locals recognized as the new blood disease, Dr. Moore had never advised the woman about the effects of obesity on health nor did he take the blood pressure of his patients who asked for diet pills. As the women saw it, weight control was purely a cosmetic and not a health-related issue.

Jogging

During my fieldwork in the 1970s, some local women would order exercise devices advertised on television or in catalogues. Exercise, as opposed to pills, was beginning to emerge as an alternative way to lose weight for those few who still felt the necessity of doing so. I am the one who inadvertently started the jogging fad. When I initially came to the village, I wanted to continue to get the vigorous exercise I had accustomed myself to as a graduate student in North Carolina. Not wishing me to make a spectacle of myself, my landlady (who had heard about jogging on television) suggested a stretch of dead-end highway I could use where no one would see me. I would drive to the strip and jog up and down a short piece of road. Sometimes the minister's wife went with me, but she soon became bored with the activity and gave it up. After a winter of hearty eating and a need for some private time, I once again began my own jogging program in May. This time I selected a fairly level section of public highway above the village and gradually worked up to a four-mile run.

For about three weeks my jog was interrupted only by the occasional carload of travelers to and from neighboring villages. I received a good deal of good-natured teasing about such a "waste of energy." No one ever asked to jog with me, but there was a great deal of local interest in the activity. I scheduled my jogging at the same time every day between tea and supper. I began to notice men collecting on the route. They would jog a couple of hundred feet behind me and then quit. I thought they were "racing" with me. They were very good-humored about it, but out of condition and easy to beat.[7] I did not realize why the men were there until a woman friend teased me about being so "horny" that I had to tear up and down the highway like some kind of idiot. After getting through a long winter without a boyfriend, the villagers concluded that I must be working off stored sexual energy. The men were simply seeing who could keep up with me.

Eventually small groups of women my age (twenty-five to thirty-five) began to jog. They gathered at my place and walked or walk-jogged the entire route I used. They only did this when they knew I had engagements elsewhere. They refused my invitation to jog with me. Some told me that the weight I lost had inspired them to take up jogging too. Others began to jog with their husbands, who were also taking up the practice. Some husbands began to tease their wives about being heartier than they were. (One man told his wife, "You keep that up and I'll have to send you in country to get next year's moose"). Some groups of women began to try alternate routes, although they always jogged well away from village thoroughfares. Most of the joggers did lose weight.

I jogged until black fly season arrived. Then I quit. My landlady, a woman who refused to have anything to do with jogging, chided me about wanting to lose weight or keep fit. As long as my clothes still fit, she couldn't see the point of it. As long as I was not sick I was fit enough. Black fly season also halted the activity of most of the other joggers. A small group of women continued to jog in the parish hall. However, by summer, the jogging rites of spring had ceased. Although it soon became inconvenient, exercise had become established as a demanding but effective way to lose weight.

Exercise Club

The final fad arose in the fall of 1978. The wife of a schoolteacher, Marion, had taken an exercise course in St. John's while her husband was attending the university. She decided to start doing the exercises at home and eventually brought in a few friends to exercise with her in her living room. Eventually she succumbed to a plea to make the classes available to a larger number of women and a community Ladies' Exercise Group was formed in November. The Group met from seven to eight o'clock Wednesday evenings in the church community center. Initially, seventy women, aged twenty to fifty and of all different weights, signed up to participate in the exercise group. Membership fees were collected (to pay rent on the church hall) and a spring banquet was scheduled, thus making the group a formal association.

After a few weeks, attendance dwindled to twenty or thirty. Many women only attended sporadically or when they felt "up to it." Many wore special exercise apparel (leotards from the Simpson-Sears catalogue) that they had purchased especially for the classes. Even the extremely obese women bought leotards and made no attempt to cover their bodies. The element of shame was not in the obesity but in the failure to perform the exercises. The routine was extremely demanding. The group leader stood in the center of a circle of women and led them in their exercises. Most women complained of being lame or sore for several days afterward and began to complain that the group had degenerated to a contest of who could endure the most exercise or work the hardest. The group lasted until mid-February. Two circumstances led to the final demise of the group. First, a pregnant woman participant had a miscarriage. According to village gossip, the doctor *said* exercising had nothing to do with it; but some women were quite sure the exercise had caused the miscarriage. Eventually, rumors began to circulate that the group leader was making a profit from the classes.[8] Finally, one night no one but the leader came to class. Some women continued to exercise at home, but the group didn't survive long enough to hold its banquet, and the banquet funds were returned to the group members.

Diet pills, jogging, and exercise are "activity" fads (Miller 1985). In Grey Rock Harbour each was short-lived. None of the fads resulted in sustained weight loss or realization of any health risks associated with fatness. Regarded as superficial and somewhat silly by the outporters themselves, each fad followed a pattern of latency, break-out, peaking, and decline.

ANALYSIS

Given the ethnographic description just presented, it is now time to study the issues raised in the earlier sections of this chapter. How do diet fads as collective behavior relate to modernization and acculturation in this Newfoundland community? What is the significance of female body image and how and why are ideals or body aesthetics changing among Harbour women? What perspectives can anthropologists bring to the issue that others have ignored? And finally, of what relevance is all of this for health-planning personnel?

"New wealth" fads are common among the women of Grey Rock Harbour. Almost every woman has a (relatively expensive) Labrador coat, Avon cosmetics are widely adopted, and hairstyle changes swept through the village twice while I was there. Previously, telephones, electrical appliances, and new house forms had spread like wildfire through the community. Weight control was only one of many new ideas introduced to the community.

Fads and fashions are noted in the collective behavior literature as accommodating two competing impulses: 1) the imitation impulse or need to belong to or be accepted in the group, and 2) the differentiation impulse or desire for a sense of self-identity and autonomy. Fads among marginal groups in complex societies have been related to the process of acculturation. Through fads, people can experience a sense of identity with the groups to which they aspire to belong (Miller 1985; Simmel 1904).

This dual emphasis on adapting to change (modernization, entrance into Canadian mainstream society) and on maintaining tradition (geographical, cultural, and occupational identity) are present in Grey Rock Harbour society. As geographical and social isolation decrease and access to material wealth increase, Harbour folk are subject to the pull between unity and differentiation. Within the last fifteen years, Grey Rock Harbour folk have become more aware of the differences between themselves and other members of Canadian society. A strong commitment to maintaining the traditions and values of outport life are balanced by a desire to combine the best of the old with the best of the new. Yet there is a lack of certainty over how to go about doing it. The rise and fall of the diet fads represents this process of sorting through the new and the old. Although women were superficially ready to jump on any bandwagon that offered easy solutions to their problems, they never internalized the morality or self-loathing that is part of the culture-bound syndrome of obesity in our own culture. Nor did they equate obesity with disease. Weight remained a personal, cosmetic, or aesthetic issue. In the case of weight control, the more traditional values came to prevail. In order to understand this, attention must be directed to the process of leveling that has maintained Grey Rock Harbour as an egalitarian community for over 150 years.

The Grey Rock Harbour attitude toward modernization can be summed up in the often-repeated phrase: "We all come up together or we don't come up at all." The growth of the fads represents a positive form of leveling: "We all come up together." The decline of the fads represents a negative form of leveling: ". . . or we don't come up at all." Personal involvement in a fad such as the informal jogging groups and the formal Exercise Group communicates a sense of unity, comradeship, and belonging. Once discovered, the miracle property of the pills is readily shared with everyone else. Yet involvement in self-improvement by some can jeopardize the well-being of others and can also set the individuals who become too ambitious apart from the rest of society. Blame for the failure of the pills is directed outside the community. It is Dr. Moore's fault. However, Marion, the Exercise Group leader, shows how the community can turn against one of its own. Although Marion is initially admired for her attractiveness, she is eventually castigated for making an unfair profit from her leadership activities. It is not Marion's exercise activities alone or the charges that she is doing it for personal gain; Marion's problems are compounded by the fact that she is considered uppity, a character flaw she has successfully hid behind health complaints before the tide of community sentiment turned against her. Marion's Exercise Group is the last collective weight-loss movement to spread through the community (see Afterword). Threatened unity in the community appears to have taken priority over adopting upwardly mobile body styles.

The traditional tendency of women to subvert the dictates of leveling and conformity by expressing their individuality in terms of their bodies is intrinsically related to the heightened awareness of body states and body consciousness that initially attracted women to the fads. Yet at the same time acceptance of the fads is countered by a high degree of body acceptance. Women are secure in their status, their sexuality, and their sense of self-worth. They are not in "transition" to a new self nor are they slaves to a fantasy of perfection (middle-class virtues of health care) (cf. Munter 1984). Faced with the hard realities of poverty and the cyclical process of success and failure in the fisheries, they do not believe that changing their bodies will solve their problems. For the Newfoundland woman's self-esteem comes from mental and emotional strength, self-sacrifice, and hard work. Harbour women play important roles in their families and in village life. Fat, thin, beautiful, and homely women, all alike, are lauded as heroines of the past and future, the emotional bulwark of their community. The cultural baggage of morality, insecurity, and self-loathing that accompanies the syndrome of obesity in our own society fails to take root in Grey Rock Harbour.

Nor was the desire for a new body the guiding force behind exercising and jogging. The local joggers who are most admired are not those who lost the most weight but those who could jog as far as I did. Once they achieved this they could quit. The public display of stoicism is also an important motive for participation in the Exercise Group. Here also the major point is to publicly demonstrate endurance. Women of all age groups enter into the competition. Group pressure then operates on participants to keep up with the instructor even if it just about killed you and then come back for more. The exercise group and jogging become public forums for the display of female strength. No woman would jog with me because I, as an outsider, had previous experience at it; this competition would have been unfair.

Affective social pressure to insure conformity to social roles and proper comportment dominates the social dynamics of daily village life. Body shape and size are not as important as behavior is for defining female status. Yet some fat women are ridiculed for their obesity (always behind their back). Body fat by itself does not lead to aspersion of character or negative affect (cf. Maddox et al. 1979). Fatness does not signal the onset of a deviant lifestyle. However, women who are ridiculed as fat are not ridiculed for insufficient will; they are ridiculed for some other character fault, such as being too assertive (Davis 1988). Fat women who behave appropriately are not ridiculed as fat. A truly obese woman with a fat apron that hangs below her crotch, who takes a more than usual interest in her husband's fishing affairs that causes troubles among his crew members' wives, is commonly referred to as "the woman with two stomachs." Another woman with large hips and thighs who is seen as having pretense to superiority is called the "A&W Root Bear."[9] Other women, equally as large or unusually shaped but who abide by community norms, are never referred to or ridiculed as fat. Unlike middle-class mainstream America (cf. Millman 1980), overweight in Grey Rock Harbour does not dominate a woman's social identity, sexuality, and self-concept.

The anthropological analysis of obesity demonstrates how an understanding of weight-loss behavior in Grey Rock Harbour, which on the surface resembles behaviors familiar to more mainstream American, must take into account local notions of ethnophysiology where cognitions of mind and body are merged with more collective facets of village society and local history.

CONCLUSION

Of what relevance is all of this to the health-care program planners and service providers? How do the findings of this study relate to the provision of health-care services in rural or outport Newfoundland? Health education, combined with social mobility and mass communication, has begun to introduce new body image values. Ethnographic data will be reviewed in light of the theories and perspectives of the obesity experts to demonstrate the importance of sociocultural aspects of obesity and weight control with which the health planner should be aware.

Overeating and lack of exercise are unhealthy or self-destructive lifestyles and, according to Bernhard Bandura (1984), should be viewed as a major cause of modern mass disease. From a more critical perspective I might add that poverty is also a major modern lifestyle disease. The need for conformity, which stifles change in Grey Rock Harbour, is part of a historical adaptation to exploitation and oppression. Local folk are extremely skeptical of the motives of outsiders, especially those who come bearing gifts. Any consideration of intravillage lifestyle must take into account that Harbour folk are struggling for the survival of their community and lifeways in a rapidly changing society. When health-care professionals focus on the issue of modernization, they must understand the sociocultural context of forces that inhibit as well as those forces that encourage change. When an obese woman requests diet pills it does not necessarily mean she is on her way to joining the ranks of the middle class. Expecting the Newfoundlander to behave like a more middle-class health-care consumer will not lead her to do so.

Although it is important to take into account the historical processes through which body images relevant to preventive health care have been created (cf. Schwartz 1986), it is also imperative to understand how each local community has *recently* adapted to the introduction of health-care services. An understanding of the recent emergence of contemporary dieting fads, as events described in Grey Rock Harbour, and the factors that lead to their rise and decline will provide the service provider with an insightful view of how Harbour folk do not passively or always positively respond to the well-intentioned increase in services. The fads demonstrate that there is a concern with diet and exercise. However, this concern is limited to the realm of cosmetic or body aesthetics and has not yet expanded into a health concern. But the existing emic interest in weight control could provide a good starting point for a wide variety of health education and lifestyle change programs, especially those affecting diabetes, hypertension, and other cardiovascular diseases.

Phillip Goldblatt et al. (1964) claim that a solution to adapting weight reduction treatments to the poor requires knowledge as to how slimness comes to be valued, why some subgroups value slimness more than others, and an understanding of the implications of overweight. However, knowledge alone will not solve the problem. The ethnographic analysis shows that, although unhealthy, the traditional diet is cheap, easily storable, and valued as a symbol of historical and ethnic traditions. Moreover, a sole focus on weight control can lead to overlooking other relevant factors that to the outsider may seem irrelevant to weight control issues. For example, a focus on weight alone reveals nothing about anti-medical bias towards medical interventions in dieting behavior that has emerged as a by-product of Dr. Moore's abuse of prescription diet pills. The example of Shirley, who takes four pills a day and is never well, is a powerful image that keeps women from further consultation with physicians concerning weight problems. In small communities situational or idiosyncratic factors can have profound and lasting implications for the delivery and acceptability of various health-care services. According to Mary Moore et al. (1962), the concentration of obesity among the lower classes necessitates a program of social control designed to reproduce certain critical influences to which society has already exposed its middle-class members. Feminists such as Munter (1984) and Barron et al. (1984) would take issue with this strategy to the extent that middle-class notions of obesity dehumanize and ridicule women. Any strategy of weight loss that undermines the strong self-esteem of village women would be inappropriate.

Bandura (1984) states that the prevention of lifestyle diseases should take into account psychological, social, and political contexts of behavior. Diet fads in Grey Rock Harbour are viewed by Harbour folk, men and women alike, as superficial and somewhat silly. These fads occurred alongside many other new health fads as locals experimented with various forms of acculturation. However, the health-care provider should realize that concern with obesity in Grey Rock Harbour lacks the characteristics of obesity as a culture-bound syndrome. Among Harbour women there are no rigid or absolute standards of ideal weight, and overweight is not associated with morbidity. The body serves as a vehicle for breaking rules rather than as a symbol of the rules. Physical attractiveness is valued far less than social self. The ability to live up to community expectations of correct behavior rather than body size determines female status. Nor is sexual desirability associated exclusively with youth and slimness. As Terry and Bass (1984) have done for the Cherokee and Garb et al. (1974) have done for the Navaho, it is erroneous and misleading to associate an adoption of middle-class weight loss and exercise behavior with acculturation to middle-class weight norms.

Weight-loss therapy is often focused on individual or group-guided treatments to bring about the elimination of self-destructive behaviors. Fat people are described as immature, rigid, suspicious (Maddox et al. 1979), immoral, unsexy, disabled, and disgusting to look at. Whatever the biological costs of obesity, they are compounded in our culture by great psychic and social costs. We are a fat-obsessed society. Fat women, moreso than fat men, must adapt to what in many ways can be termed a pariah status. Perhaps we have a lot to learn from the more accepting and tolerant attitudes of Grey Rock Harbour women.

AFTERWORD

Although based on research done in the years 1977 to 1979, this piece was originally written in 1986. By depicting women's resistance to the body aesthetics of the national mass media of the late 1970s, little did I know that I had captured a transcendent moment in time rather than a trend for the future. The article shows an assumption on my behalf that the Newfoundland women I came to know so well in the late 1970s—who appeared to be so secure in their personal self-esteem and in their village-wide, locally self-defined high status—would always be able to

face the future on their own terms. What neither they nor I had antici-
pated was a crisis in the local (and North Atlantic) fishery that started
in Grey Rock Harbour in 1989 and will continue at least until the end
of the twentieth century (see Davis 1993, 1995). Today, there is no
longer a village fishery, and the fishplant has been closed since the
1990s. Those who remain in Grey Rock Harbour depend on combinations of government make-work projects, social security, welfare, and
temporary fisheries compensation packages. When I returned to Grey
Rock Harbour to conduct another year of fieldwork, in 1989, I found a
very different community. I take this opportunity to describe changes in
body image that are relevant to themes brought up in the previous discussion—changes that have undermined the high status and esteem that
I have depicted as characterizing almost all of the local women of Grey
Rock Harbour in the 1970s.

The fishery no longer dominates the occupational or emotional life
of the community. No one can make a living today fishing. The highly
valued roles of women as worriers, as fishers' wives and mothers, and as
emotionally tried and strong and inherently valuable are gone. Middle-
and older-aged women no longer dominate the moral order of the community. Today's equivalent cohorts are regarded as old-fashioned, out-
dated, and artifacts of the past. Because the local forces of judgement
and censure no longer keep people in line, one no longer has to resort to
the body in order to express individuality and break the rules. One can
simply be different and make one's own rules. A new stratification system has emerged to replace the old egalitarian social order. Now instead
of "we all come up together or not at all," the catch phrases are that
"you have to break away to get ahead" and "everyone is out for themselves." Schoolteachers, as the most educated locals, and those few with
year-round dependable jobs now dominate the top of the local status
hierarchy. Those who embody traditional values are no longer looked
up to, and the old and middle-aged are no longer seen as role models for
young people. In the present local view, to make a future for yourself
today you must be smart, educated, young, and able to leave the village
to pursue a livelihood elsewhere. There is no future in fishing.

Body aesthetics more familiar to the middle classes through the mass
media have also entered local life. In an unemployment/welfare economy,
gender relations and notions of sexuality have changed dramatically,
with youth and physical attractiveness, and enhanced competition for
sexual partners, figuring more importantly in a women's sense of sexuality (Davis 1993).[10] Traditional sources of self-esteem such as hard work,
self-sacrifice, and emotional strength have been replaced by an emphasis
on competitive consumerism and educational and occupational achievement. Women flock to the government-sponsored self-improvement

courses that are designed to teach them basic dress and grooming skills so that they may become more competitive in the job market. Physical appearance has become more important among youth and there is more emphasis on finding your own style.

Weight control has emerged as a health issue. Traditional foods are no longer valued, but children continue to consume large amounts of junk food and teen socializing takes place at local restaurants where french fries and sweets have become nightly fare. Teens eat less and less of their meals at home. Because they have been the targets of a generation of intensive hypertension, heart disease and healthcare education campaigns, healthy diets have become a big issue with locals. Today's villagers are far more informed about the dangers of salt and fat in their diet and some locals are turning to nutritionists to help them plan diets.

There are no exercise fads anymore. During the early 1980s a diet group of very heavy women met weekly. Their diet consisted of eating commercial liquid diet formulas, and a kind of competitive dieting began where self-control and standing deprivation, not loss of weight per se, became the major issues. Some of the women lost large amounts of weight, but once the diet was completed, they gained it back in a few months time. An aerobics club opened in a nearby community and attracted some local women who eventually failed to attend because of costs and dangers of commuting in bad weather. Nor did their agendas accord very well with the goals of the health club. Grey Rock Harbour women did not want to develop muscle or to become more fit, they just wanted to lose weight. Exercise, unless in the form of a gossipy walk on a nice evening, is not considered to be fun. Women still do not participate in sports, although, like me, several teachers and temporary strangers who have been enthusiastic cross-country skiers or joggers have shown it is locally possible. A make-work project built a baseball field outside the village, and a women's team played for one season and then lost interest in the sport. During the 1980s, the first local case of anorexia occurred and dieting became a major preoccupation of teenage girls.

Standards of beauty have become more demanding. Slimness and youth are more valued than before. The recent adoption of shorts and revealing summer clothes and accompanying changes in standards for modesty have left more of the body, at least seasonally, exposed to the view of others. Although they remain tolerant of differences in body build, and being overweight does not guarantee social outcast status, young women are less secure in their sexuality, self-worth and physical attractiveness than their mothers were and are.

Although physical attractiveness along conventional lines has become more important and young women are less secure, the social self remains important. Today's young women do not believe that changing your body will change yourself. Given the decline of the fishery, they know that to change their lives for the better they must pursue an education and leave the community. One's personality remains important and being overweight does not dominate one's identity or dehumanize women to the degree that it does in a less personally intimate social setting. In this small community everyone still knows everyone else as whole persons, as products of their own shared life histories. They have known each other too well and for too long to relegate any individual to the status of pariah based on weight alone.

NOTES

1. See Afterword for an update on this study.

2. Fieldwork was conducted from October 1977 to December 1978. Research was supported by the National Institute for Maternal and Child Health. Grey Rock Harbour is a fictitious name.

3. Each woman with a child under seventeen years of age received a monthly check. In 1978 it was $27.00 for each child.

4. Throughout my stay, I was known as "the little girl with the book." "Little" did not refer to my size or my age but to my status as an unmarried woman.

5. Introduced to the village in the 1970s, the Wednesday Clinic was a small building that was staffed by a physician on rotation from a nearby town on every other Wednesday, weather permitting.

6. I cannot verify whether the comments about Dr. Moore (a pseudonym) are true or not. They were certainly believed by villagers.

7. Men and women dancing together will often compete as to who can dance the fastest and longest. Sometimes the band enters into the contest by increasing the tempo of the music.

8. These claims were untrue. All community members who take on leadership positions risk defamation as the inevitable leveling takes place (see Davis 1993, 1988).

9. The A&W fast food restaurant chain advertised frequently on local television. The "A&W Root Bear" has a very large rear end.

10. High divorce rates, extramarital sex, development of a local bar culture and with it an exploitative sexual antagonism between men and women have left all women and men feeling less secure in male-female relationships (Davis 1993).

REFERENCES

Badura, Bernhard. 1984. "Life-Style and Health: Some Remarks on Different View Points." *Social Science and Medicine* 19(4):341–47.

Barron, Nancy, Lucia Igou Eakins, and Richard W. Wollert. 1984. "Fat Group: A SNAP-Launched Self-Help Group for Overweight Women." *Human Organization* 43(1):44–49.

Counts, C. R., and H. E. Adams. 1985. "Body Image in Bulimic, Dieting, and Normal Females." *Journal of Psychopathology and Behavioral Assessment* 7(3):289–300.

Davis, Dona. 1983. *Blood and Nerves: An Ethnographic Focus on Menopause.* St. John's, Canada: Memorial University of Newfoundland Institute of Social and Economic Research.

———. 1988. "'Shore Skippers' and 'Grass Widows': Active and Passive Roles for Women in a Newfoundland Fishery." In *To Work and to Weep,* ed. Jane Nadel and Dona Davis. St. John's, Canada: Memorial University of Newfoundland Institute of Social and Economic Research.

———. 1992. "Gender Issues and Elective Surgery in a Newfoundland Fishing Village." In *Gender Constructs and Social Issues,* ed. Tony Whitehead and Barbara Reid. Urbana, IL: University of Illinois.

———. 1993. "When Men Become 'Women': Gender Antagonism and the Changing Sexual Geography of Work in Newfoundland." *Sex Roles* 29(7/8):1–18.

———. 1995. "The Cultural Constructions of Menstruation, Menopause, and Premenstrual Dysphoric Disorder." In *Gender and Health: An International Perspective,* ed. Carolyn Sargent and Carolyn Brettell. Englewood Cliffs, NJ: Prentice-Hall.

Garb, J. L., J. R. Garb, and A. J. Stunkard. 1974. "The Influence of Social Factors on Obesity and Thinness in Navaho Children." *Abstracts,* First International Congress on Obesity, Royal College of Physicians, London, England, Oct. 9–10.

Garn, Stanley M., and Diane C. Clark. 1975. "Nutrition, Growth, Development, and Maturation: Findings from the Ten-State Nutrition Survey of 1968–1970." *Pediatrics* 56(2):306–19.

Goldblatt, Phillip B., Mary E. Moore, and Albert J. Stunkard. 1964. "Social Factors in Obesity." *Journal of the American Medical Association* 192(12):1039–44.

Halmi, Katherine A., James R. Falk, and Estelle Schwartz. 1981. "Binge-eating and Vomiting: A Survey of College Population." *Psychological Medicine* 11:697–706.

Herman, C. Peter, Marion P. Olmsted, and Janet Polivy. 1983. "Obesity, Externality, and Susceptibility to Social Influence: An Integrated Analysis." *Journal of Personality and Social Psychology* 45(4):926–34.

Larsson, Bo, Per Bjorntorp, and Gota Tibblin. 1981. "The Health Consequences of Moderate Obesity." *International Journal of Obesity* 5:97–116.

Maddox, George L., Kurt W. Back, and Veronica R. Liederman. 1979. "Overweight as Social Deviance and Disability." *Journal of Health and Social Behavior* 9:287–98.

Massara, Emily B., and Albert J. Stunkard. 1979. "A Method of Quantifying Cultural Ideals of Beauty and the Obese." *International Journal of Obesity* 3:149–52.

Miller, David L. 1985. *Introduction to Collective Behavior*. Belmont, CA: Wadsworth Publishing Company.

Millman, Marcia. 1980. *Such a Pretty Face: Being Fat in America*. New York, NY: W. W. Norton.

Moore, Mary E., Albert Stunkard, and Leo Srole. 1962. "Obesity, Social Class, and Mental Illness." *Journal of the American Medical Association* 181:962–66.

Munter, Carol. 1984. "Fat and the Fantasy of Perfection." In *Pleasure and Danger: Exploring Female Sexuality*, ed. Carole S. Vance. Boston, MA: Routledge & Kegan Paul.

Pollitzer, W. S. et al. 1970. "The Seminole Indians of Florida: Morphology and Serology." *American Journal of Physical Anthropology* 32:65–82.

Ritenbaugh, Cheryl. 1982. "Obesity as Culture-Bound Syndrome." *Culture, Medicine and Psychiatry* 6(4):347–61.

Schifter, Deborah E., and Icek Ajzen. 1985. "Intention, Perceived Control, and Weight Loss: An Application of the Theory of Planned Behavior." *Journal of Personality and Social Psychology* 49(3):843–51.

Schwartz, Hillel. 1986. *Never Satisfied: A Cultural History of Diets, Fantasy and Fats*. New York, NY: The Free Press.

Sider, Gerald. 1976. *Culture and Class in Anthropology and History: A Newfoundland Illustration*. New York, NY: Cambridge University Press.

Simmel, George. 1904. "Fashion." *International Quarterly* 10:541–58.

Stunkard, Albert J. 1975. "Presidential Address—1974: From Explanation to Action in Psychosomatic Medicine: The Case of Obesity." *Psychosomatic Medicine* 37(3):195–236.

Terry, Rhonda Dale, and Mary Ann Bass. 1984. "Obesity among Eastern Cherokee Indian Women: Prevalence, Self-Perceptions, and Experiences." *Ecology of Food and Nutrition* 14:117–27.

Wing, Rena, and Robert Jeffery. 1979. "Outpatient Treatments of Obesity: A Comparison of Methodology and Clinical Results." *International Journal of Obesity* 3:261–79.

CHAPTER TEN

Kicking Stereotypes into Touch: An Ethnographic Account of Women's Rugby

P. DAVID HOWE

INTRODUCTION

Confrontational contact within women's sport has long been considered taboo. As women strive for empowerment, sport is one of the arenas that they are using to emancipate themselves through challenging the traditional masculine/feminine dichotomy, which has been associated with sport. The expression "kicking into touch" literally means the act of kicking the ball out of play, and this chapter is attempting to do this with the stereotypes involving women who participate in rugby. This chapter reports on an ethnographic study of women's rugby in South Wales. Due to the nature of sport, this discussion will focus on the importance of the embodied female form since it is through the body that an increased understanding of the social barriers faced by women with a passion to participate in contact sports may be achieved.

A structured interactional approach has been taken, focusing upon the interpretations and meaning within the sporting environment, with data gathered through participant-observation and interviews in a variety of settings. The purpose of this chapter is to question the validity of the social barriers imposed upon women who play rugby as well as high-lighting the specific *habitus* that exists at a particular Welsh club, which plays the game at the highest amateur[1] level. This chapter will begin by highlighting the distinctive cultural context in when this research was based, and then explore the perceptions of the public towards women's rugby. These perceptions will be related to the tension that exists between the professional sporting attitude and the game of rugby as women embody it.

CULTURAL CONTEXT

To the people of Wales, the game of rugby union[2] has been one of the vehicles for the establishment of national identity (Williams 1991; Andrews 1991; Andrews and Howells 1993). Unlike in England, where the game developed at Rugby School in the mid-1800s for the enjoyment of upper-middle-class schoolboys, rugby in Wales is often referred to as "the people's game" since it transcends the bounds of class. The expression "the people's game" has been rather at odds with traditional Welsh society considering that it has only been in the last decade that mass participation by women as players and spectators has become popular. Recently, participation in rugby by women has made the women's game one of the fastest growing sports in Britain (Kew 1997). Increased participation of women in contact sports might suggest a general trend towards their emancipation. However, women who play the game of rugby are seen to embody masculinity. The ridicule that is directed at these women to whom the game is a passion is a firm indicator that emancipation of these women is far from complete.

The rugby club that is the focus of this research is unique. English rugby clubs, which field elite women's teams, have men's teams that are fully professional. In England, in fact, the best women's teams are part of the most successful men's clubs in the country. The Welsh team that is central to this research boasts more than half a dozen women international players while the men's team at the same club is nowhere near this level of participation. Because of this, the women's team takes center stage at the club and the players are well respected.

The social background of the club is largely middle-class, which means that it shares similarities with the clubs in England and is thus different from some of the other clubs in Wales. A majority of the women who play for the club are in higher education (or have graduated from such an institution), and this is in keeping with the background of the male members of the club. Therefore, the club is distinctive, and, as a result, observations on which this chapter is based are to be considered only as a reflection of my experience as a male social anthropologist in such an environment.

Many of the observations presented were developed while I was undertaking the "writing-up" of research as part of my Ph.D. The resulting thesis focused on elite men's rugby in Wales as a distinctive sporting community (Howe 1997; see also Howe 1999, 2001). In the process, material and observations were also gathered about the importance of the game of rugby to the women of Wales. Moving out of the community, which was the site for my fieldwork, I settled in a large urban center in Wales. Living in a shared house with three professional women who all play rugby for the same rugby club, I was able to gain access to the social world that surrounds the game of rugby at their club. These women were ideal "gatekeepers," to borrow from Hammersley and Atkinson (1995), into the distinctive *habitus* that is embodied by the women at this club.

WELSH WOMEN'S BODIES

Bodies are always present and have until recently been overlooked, particularly when investigating consumption as social behavior. Everybody consumes; it is fundamental to our existence. Sporting activities, such as rugby, are an example of this. Consumption, according to Falk, leads to the body being ambiguous insofar as it can be discussed in binary opposites. "The body is both the Same and the Other; a subject and an object, of practices and knowledge; it is both a tool and raw material to be worked upon" (Falk 1994:1). These oppositions, which are of fundamental importance, have led to the lack of investigation of the body as a social space as it often evades the anthropological lens. The body is the fundamental tool with which a participant in sport has to work (Howe 2001). One informant suggested, "I work my body so that it will act as it should under pressure. The reality is that I do not have natural talent and as such must train so that my body will do what I tell it when I don't have time to think" (Notebook 4:39).

While this comment could ring true for both sexes, the pressure for social conformity of the body has a greater impact on women (Jennifer Hargreaves 1994; Hall 1996). In the traditional gender roles in Welsh society many of the players felt trapped by the culture of consumerism that surrounds sport. Many of the women felt pressurized to normalize their bodies in much the same way as Hargreaves has suggested that consumerism as fed by sport has a hegemonic control: "The body is clearly an object of crucial importance in consumer culture and its supply industries: and sports, together with fashion, . . . dieting, keep-fit therapy, . . . advertising imagery, . . . are deployed in a constantly elaborating programme whose objective is the production of the new 'normalized' individual" (John Hargreaves 1986:14).

Normalized individuals, who are the products of consumerism in the age of mass media, can begin to transcend geographical regions that in the past could maintain a unique identity and body image; as a result, a more globally normalized concept of body image is today a universal. In concert with the media, consumer culture has influenced the discourses of sport, leisure, and health by appropriating all the desire to manipulate the body and using it to garnish more productive advertising. Western society is currently dominated by the desire to look young, healthy, and beautiful and to be exciting. The sporting body, for the general public as well as for the elite or high-performance athlete, is firmly articulated in the ideology that has established the body as the major focus for consumerism. As a result, participation has become fundamentally a "system of expansive discipline and surveillance [that] produces normal persons by making each individual as visible as possible to each other, and by meticulous work on person's bodies at the instigation of subjects themselves" (John Hargreaves 1987:151).

In spite of this, people often feel that exercise is something that they can control. Featherstone has commented that physical activity is often undertaken for the simple pleasures that it brings to those who enjoy it and not the utilitarian values that are often associated with it. "The notion of running for running's sake, purposiveness without a purpose, a sensuous experience in harmony with embodied physical nature, is completely submerged amidst the welter of benefits called up by the markets and health experts" (1991 [1982]: 185–6). Yet, when discussion switches to the topic of sports such as women's rugby, focus often switches to the lack of normalcy of the female aesthetic and the question of gender appropriateness. In the process of partaking in physical exercise, the individual unconsciously objectifies the values of society that are appropriate to such activities and thus the individual's mind becomes the caretaker of its socially disciplined body. But where does a female who is interested in contact sports such as rugby fit?

The "Greek god" aesthetic no longer stands alone as the bodily ideal since the individuals behind the forces of commercialism have realized the limits of marketing only one ideal bodily form (Gruneau 1993:98). While the sporting body is more broadly idealized, a variation of the ideal body now exists, although lean body form is the ideal in whatever shape. For example, athletes who perform at basketball, ice hockey, and marathon running at the elite level will have different physiques due to the functional requirements of their chosen sport.[3] However, these sporting bodies are all idealized in the media and thus encourage the public to achieve one of the ideal body types by using the products endorsed by the individuals whose form is desired. Women who participate in contact sports have difficulty in achieving acceptance of their bodies. "Because I am a prop,[4] people outside the club will struggle to see the value of me being as big and strong as I am. My size and the strength that in part is related to it is one of the major reasons that I have played for Wales. On the pitch I am valued for my physique . . . off it I am not" (Notebook 4:13). Sporting bodies and changing attitudes towards them therefore will be one way that women who play rugby will be empowered, and changes in attitude in the men's game of rugby may help pave the way in part towards women's emancipation.

Changes that have occurred to the administration of the game of rugby for men have also had an impact on the women's game.[5] The game of rugby since 1995 has become a professional concern. This professionalization of the game has been shown to be a result of the players' desires to be financially rewarded for the sacrifices that they have made in an effort to enhance sporting performance on the field of play (Howe 2001, 1999). As training regimes intensified so too did players' desires to be financially compensated for their efforts. Professionalism, in terms of payment for performances, has yet to occur in women's rugby, but the levels of commitment to training at the elite level mirror those of their professional male counterparts.

Because women at the elite level of the game embody many of the same ideals that men who play professional rugby strive to achieve, this chapter will now turn to the habitual environment, which fosters the games' ethos.

RUGBY CLUB HABITUS

Rugby has long been rooted in masculinity due to the confrontational nature of the sport. However, as women take up the game, the social space of the sport becomes transformed. To many who feel that women should not be involved in contact sport, resistance to the adoption of the game by women is often expressed through homophobia (Fasting 1997; Krane 1996). Scholars such as Messner and Sabo (1990 1994) have in recent years explored the myths of masculinity in sport, and their research has gone a long way to demystifying the gender order in sport. Others specifically discussing rugby have suggested that more research must be done from a feminist psychoanalytic perspective to expose such sports since they "promulgate sexism and homophobia" (White and Vagi 1990:77).

Females have been traditionally subordinated in all areas of society. Contact sport illustrates the subordination of women because of its association with masculinity. Historically, women have been systematically excluded from sport (Jennifer Hargreaves 1994). Social evolution, however, has occurred slowly; and society has been transformed to the point where women now have access to sports that were traditionally solely part of the male domain. Potter has suggested that this traditionally patriarchal view of women's rugby may be a result of the fact that the game "is diametrically opposed in its style and purpose to everything that traditional society has encouraged a women to be" (1999:84). For many of my informants, it is precisely this contradiction that attracts them to the game. Rugby is one sport that indicates the changing position of Welsh females in society, and the success of the team forces dominant definitions of masculinity and femininity to be brought into question.

Rugby for the longest time remained a "male preserve" (Dunning and Sheard 1973, 1979), exhibiting culturally distinctive behavior and resistance to change. As Mariah Burton-Nelson states: "Nowhere are masculinity and misogyny so entwined as on the rugby field" (1996:88). Over the past several decades, however, the game in Wales (and more generally the British Isles) has been transformed. Scholars have argued that the manner in which sport is organized is in fact a definitive description of masculine power (Birrel and Cole 1994) and that women in the past have adopted sports that are based on a cultural definition of femininity. The socially constructed barriers, which inhibit female participants, form the basis of oppressive gender relations in sport.

Since the 1970s women have attempted to liberate themselves through physical activity (Birrel and Cole 1994). In the United Kingdom activities such as aerobics are now challenged by a growing number of participants in sports such as bodybuilding and rugby that illustrate how female expectations of body image and musculature have changed over time. It is no longer safe to assume that physical characteristics such as strength, stamina, and hand-eye coordination are inherently masculine. One informant suggested: "I can mix it with the best of them on the pitch. The fact that I tackle rigorously does not in my opinion take anything away from my belief that I am all woman. To say that I am strong and fit and as a result must be masculine is a touch silly" (Notebook 4:27).

The preparation that is needed to participate in an elite sport has had an impact on the body, and, as a result, the power of hegemonic masculinity that is associated with rugby can impact the women involved in the game. When discussing the power that influences individuals, Foucault's conceptualization of the socially disciplined body as described in *Discipline and Punish* (1979) is of fundamental importance. This concept has been, in one form or other, perhaps unconsciously, a focus for good coaches' training procedures for generations. Recent discussions of Foucault's work (Andrews 1993; Hargreaves 1987; Turner

1991, 1996) have detailed how influential his thoughts can be for social research into sport. "Sport is also a subject that lends itself to a Foucaultian analysis. The modern sporting system is potentially of singular importance to the understanding of the way power is structured and exerted within contemporary society" (Andrews 1993:149).

While enthusiasts of team sports may observe the functional importance of a disciplined body when "control" is physically evident on the field of play, the influence that such performances have on the wider community is more difficult to discern. For a number of historically significant reasons surrounding England's treatment of colonized regions, there has often been a quasi-revolutionary reaction in the form of nationalism when games were played in the colonies (see Williams 1991). Although the English introduced rugby, it became a symbol of Welshness as it became apparent that the Welsh were just as good at it as their English oppressors. For this reason a success by the disciplined body on the field of play became a focus for Welsh nationalism. One player commented: "When I play for my club or country nothing is better than getting one over on the English. They gave us the game but took a lot from us [the Welsh]. Our victories on the pitch may be symbolic but they are still sweet" (Notebook 4:25).

Nationalism is embedded into the culture of Welsh rugby; and, as such, the work of Bourdieu is also useful in increasing the understanding of women's participation in rugby in this context. Bourdieu observed that a distinct *habitus* is present in the sporting contexts and can be altered by the social actor as well as the environment surrounding a given activity.

> The *habitus* as the feel for the game is the social game embodied and turned into a second nature. Nothing is simultaneously freer and more constrained than the action of a good player. He quite naturally materialises at just the place the ball is about to fall, as if the ball were in command of him—but by that very fact, he is in command of the ball. The habitus, as society written into the body, into the biological individual, enables the infinite number of acts of the game—written into the game as possibilities and objective demands—to be produced. . . . (Bourdieu 1990:63)

According to Bourdieu, the habitual training of the body involved in any sporting activity has an impact on the sporting culture, and the manner in which the body is placed in action is also of importance (1990:157). It is therefore fundamental to see the body as much a product of the self as it is of society.

Bourdieu's concept of *habitus* may be seen as related to Foucault's concept of discipline since "the body is used (walks, carries itself) differently by different social groups, and sport is one of the most important ways that the body's *habitus* is learned" (Blake 1996:23). Clément, commenting on the importance of Bourdieu's work on furthering the understanding of sporting culture, suggests that it "shows that the methods of gymnastics and by extension, those of sports or other codified physical activities, are cultural products shaped by those who practice them. These products embody the fundamental particularities of the group to which they belong" (1995:148).

The body may be seen as disciplined on a personal level through training. One type of training that rugby players undertake is designed to give the player the fitness to perform at club training and on match day. Another type of training with clubmates sees the body disciplined on a level where a specific social code is followed, the rules of the game of rugby union. In these two distinct environments *habitus* of the body is established where exercises and drills are repeated until they become automatic. As a result of this automation, the body becomes disciplined. In a sense, then, the body, in the discipline and *habitus* of training and by its alternate presence and absence (Leder 1990), becomes what could be called an *autobody*.

The training that is involved in elite rugby can be intense and as a result may not be associated with women. "Sport can be used to serve as a social and historical theatre for feminine struggle to challenge traditional forms of gender oppression" (Cohen 1993:16). Therefore it is not surprising that the financial reward that is a result of men's professionalism in the sport has not developed in the women's game. Only after rugby for women is accepted by society will those who participate in the game be rewarded in the same manner as their male counterparts. Professionalism in the men's game has allowed for the standard of play to increase, thereby increasing the observable differences in the level of play between men and women. My informants were clear that this comparison was inappropriate. "People seem to make comparisons between our level of ability and that of the men. This does not do us justice. The rules of the game are the same but women's rugby should be seen as a derivative of men's. That is how the game should be marketed" (Notebook 4:7).

After watching my first game of women's rugby I recorded in my notebook that "the performance of the women in the rugby match today was reminiscent of the games that I have watched Pontypridd Junior school boys play" (Notebook 3:45). This highlights that while I now enjoy women's rugby as a spectacle as much I do the men's game, the tendency to compare the two games is difficult to overcome. It takes time to be enculturated into the distinctive world of women's rugby. Wheatley (1994) has argued that the game of rugby as played by women has taken on its own form distinctive from that of the men's game. Women's rugby distorts the male hegemony of the rugby subculture by exploring female physical capabilities in a typical enclave. While Wheatley's research is of interest, it should be remembered that this research is based on a distinctive subculture at an American university. Continued research on women's sporting subcultures will further our understanding of the various barriers that are faced by women who wish to participate in male-dominated sports. Attention will now be turned to how the distinctive game of women's rugby has been overshadowed by ridicule and sometimes hatred, which can have a negative effect on those who participate.

PERCEPTION OF WOMEN'S RUGBY

Women who play rugby and other confrontational contact sports are a minority but they can be agents in the resistance against hegemonic masculinity and offer an active, female physicality that can challenge the gender order (Jennifer Hargreaves 1994). The social construction of femininity has often meant that sportswomen should mirror female heterosexuality in the community at large. "[The] 'problem' for sportswomen has long been defined as 'masculinisation' through the display of muscle, active physicality, aggression and competition, attributes traditionally associated with both masculinity and sport" (Fasting and Scraton 1997:2).

No other sport can be any more "masculinizing" than women's rugby, and as a result the women who choose to participate in it are often confronted with many of the social stereotypes that accompany much of homophobia. Gender boundaries of sport have recently been contested in the examination of other traditionally masculine sports such as boxing (Halbert 1997) and bodybuilding (Mansfield and McGinn 1993). While the competition involved in women's bodybuilding often attempts to maintain the distinction between genders, sports such as boxing and rugby have not done the same. Where makeup and feminine provocative costumes appear to be the performative norm for the female bodybuilder, women who play rugby wear the same style of clothing as their male counterparts. In fact, it is the adornment of this male attire that many of the women who play rugby believe lead to the public perceptions that rugby was a game for lesbians. "Look at the uniforms that we wear on the pitch. There are some really attractive women out here when we get cleaned up. The use of uniforms cut for men certainly doesn't do the image of the sport any good. We look like a bunch of dykes" (Notebook 4:17).

This opinion was expressed continually throughout my time with the club. What became clear was the identity of the players could not be stereotyped in this manner. The work of Fasting and Scraton (1997) explores similar issues in the less contact-oriented game of soccer. This research clearly shows that there is no direct relation between the sport and sexual orientation. This being the case, why is there a lesbian "identity tag" hung around women rugby players' necks?

Those who have little understanding of the game of rugby as it is played by women may be seen to express what Krane (1996) calls homonegativism. This is simply "describing purposeful, not irrational, negative attitudes and behaviors toward nonheterosexuals" (1996:238). The look of the game of women's rugby then is felt to be as important as the physical nature of matches as one of the reasons that the game is seen as a product of a lesbian sporting community. Therefore, because of the physicality of the game, all women who play it fall foul of this inappropriate labeling. A third of the team that is the focus of this research are "out" lesbians, but the point is that no one should be marginalized for their sexual orientation or the activities that they enjoy. Donnelly and Young (1988) examine the process of sport subcultures as an act of identity construction by deliberately adopting mannerisms, attitudes, styles, dress, speech, and behavior.

As the game of rugby for women continues to grow, many new players joined the club under investigation and I was able to observe the process of identity construction first-hand. As individual identity and club identity become intertwined among new recruits through the broad process of socialization, the recruits often have to struggle with the stereotypes associated with contact sports played by women. Once a woman has joined the club, because of homonegativism, she may have a difficult time being accepted in the broader social world. One informant who was a former gymnast stated, "I have not changed. Who I am, as a person, has not changed—only my body has changed—a little. You know, it is really hard to do gymnastics when you are over twenty, and since my brothers play rugby I thought I would give it a go. Now all my old friends react strangely when I am around. It is very upsetting" (Notebook 4:19).

The world of women's rugby is under threat by homonegativism in part due to the image that the game portrays. Crossett (1995) in his ethnography of women's professional golf refers to a similar situation as the "image problem." Those in charge of the Ladies' Professional Golf Association (LPGA) are concerned with the game's image because it is seen to attract a large following within the lesbian community. The fear is that the corporate world will stay away from the game if the lesbian community is encouraged to celebrate the game of golf. Therefore, the LPGA goes out of its way at charity events to celebrate heterosexuality. Crossett (1995:127–33) shows that the marriages of high-profile players or the relationships the players have with men are fundamental in marketing the LPGA.

A professional organized image overhaul has not taken place in the game of women's rugby. Rugby for women is still very much an amateur concern; however, the "image problem" can be seen to have an impact on recruitment. According to information obtained from one informant, "We have real difficulty attracting high school girls to the team. It would be great if we could because by the time they are in there mid-twenties they could be really accomplished at the game. Most of the current team started playing at university . . . I say the earlier the better but there are many rumors that circulate that suggest this club is just a disguise for a lesbian love-in. We really have to work hard to change the image of the game" (Notebook 4:20).

From my observations it is important to note that the women who lead the recruitment of the team have no difficulty accepting the full continuum of sexual orientation in new players, but they continue to be concerned about the image of the game because society and therefore sponsors are seldom as open-minded as the members of the club. Image management is important not only in attracting more players but also in attracting commercial sponsors to the game. Women's rugby is an amateur concern; but, with the men's game going professional, there has been an impact on the women's game at the elite level. While the women who play for the team are very dedicated to their training regimes, which mirror those of elite male sides, their social behavior is different and not akin to the modern professional expectations of the men's game. This has influenced the image of the women's game because often the attitude off the training field is more aligned to the amateur days of men's rugby. The question remains: What is unique about an elite women rugby player's approach to the game that makes her stand out from professional men?

PROFESSIONAL ATTITUDE

The *Shorter Oxford Dictionary* describes an amateur as an individual who cultivates anything as a pastime, whereas, in direct opposition, "professional" may be seen as applied to one who follows by way of profession what is generally followed as a pastime. While these definitions adequately address commonsense notions of the amateurs and professionals of the contemporary sporting world, it could be suggested that all that separates these individuals is the payment for performing services. Stebbins distinguishes this as modern amateurism that has been developing in connection with some leisure activities in which some participants are now able to make a substantial living from their chosen activity and as a result are able to devote themselves to it as a vocation rather than an avocation (1992:8). The continuum below illustrates how closely related the modern amateur is to his/her contemporary professional relative.

It is important to note that I am not making a judgment as to the value of individuals based on this continuum. Rather, it is an illustration to show how an individual may change the focus of activities in his or her life. As life situations change, so does the level of commitment that can be given to a leisure pursuit. The more serious and thus more work-like the endeavor for the individual concerned, the closer to the right side of the continuum his or her activities will occur. It is my belief that the modern amateur can be subdivided into "devotee" and "dabbler," depending on his or her attitude. Stebbins (1992) suggests five attitudes, which can be used to distinguish between the two types of amateur: confidence, perseverance, continuance commitment, preparedness, and self-conception are the attitudes that are suggested that could be placed on a relative continuum. Overall, a *devoted* amateur will go to greater lengths to duplicate a professional's attitude than will an individual who *dabbles* in the pastime. The strength in degree of these attitudes is what separates the amateur from the professional.

The argument between those who advocate amateurism over professionalism has long been rooted in the principle of equality. An amateur has a job and therefore is left with little time for sport as a pastime. This has had two effects on the game of Rugby Union: as long as the game is played by individuals who are in the same circumstance, with regards to the work/training time ratio, teams and competitions of near-equality will generate "fair" matches that are exciting and entertaining. This principle is at the root of the establishment of leagues and divisions

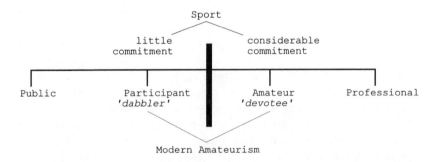

FIGURE 10.1

To move from participant to amateur status an individual must "scale a wall" which incorporates large amounts of commitment.

that typifies British sport today. In this structure, ideally, teams of near equal resources and abilities play together.[6] To have a team that has professionals in its membership in an amateur league is to create inequalities. This has a number of implications: it reduces the excitement that uncertain results can provide as well as upsetting the betting on a given match. As there become clear favorites to win matches, more spectators may take a chance on the "underdog" at the betting shop and thus the nature of an entertaining match may be altered to see whether your side can beat the point spread on which you wagered. Therefore, the shift from amateur to professional, which has led to inequality, may also be seen to play a part in the shift from pastime to spectacle.

As the game of Rugby Union opened to professionalism, some clubs had the financing to contract players services and others did not. The women's game, however, has stayed rooted in the ideals of amateurism; thus the playing field among women remains level. "We do not get the money and seldom do our exploits make the press. The guys get all the headlines and praise. Our game, in spite of being more competitive, is not seen as worthy of attention" (Notebook 4:38).

Many amateur sportsmen and women want to gain advantage over their fellow competitors; therefore, while they are employed to do work other than their sport, they will make sacrifices to achieve better performance. For example, they may limit social outings (parties, nights at the pub, etc.) in order to commit more time to adopting the physical *habitus* required for their sport. This type of sacrifice may lead to increased levels of performance and therefore their approach to the sport may begin to be equal to those of the professionals. Both amateurs and professionals, therefore, may be seen to have created an identity within their sporting activity and club with which they are involved. The complete understanding of club *habitus* may be lacking by some members of an amateur club, since they spend less time developing it than do professionals' clubs and their members; however, for those amateur *devotees* involved, the *habitus* is often just as important.

Since the game of rugby is now professional, talented men are able to make a good living from it. None of my female informants, some of whom were international players, was able to do so because the women's game lacks the media focus of the men's game. Attracting the attention of sponsors to a sport that is often marginalized among women's sport, because of its confrontational nature that traditionally means that it is associated with masculinity, is tremendously difficult. However, the women who play rugby at the club are extremely devoted to their training. In order to represent Wales on the world stage, the international players are training six days a week. The lack of financial support for diligent training regimes has frustrated many. "When I first started playing for Wales eight years ago, I could understand the lack of interest in the game. It was relatively easy to make the Welsh squad. Now with so many younger and stronger girls around, we really have to train our asses off to keep our places. My commitment to the cause is no less than that of the men" (Notebook 4:4).

This attitude was echoed by many of the players who were internationals or had aspirations of that order. Players' commitment to the game was such that the majority of the time spent socializing was with fellow team members. This in itself does not seem out of the ordinary since sports teams of both men and women in Western society are seen to exhibit this behavior. While in the professional world of men's rugby, heavy drinking of alcohol and all the behavior that may be associated with this activity are components of club *habitus* that are in decline. My research suggests that at some elite women's clubs the socializing with alcohol is paramount to the club *habitus*.

THE PARADOX OF ELITE PERFORMANCE

Research that examined rugby football as a male preserve was conducted in the 1970s by Dunning and Sheard (1973, 1979). In this work Dunning and Sheard analyzed post-game party rituals, which played a major role in the rugby subculture of the day. They highlight areas such as enacting clubhouse songs after a match, initiation ceremonies, drinking beer to excess, and singing obscene songs with recurring images of subordinating women and homosexuality. Rugby culture allows "behavior with impunity in a manner which would bring condemnation and punishment were it to occur among other social strata . . . or social settings" (Dunning and Sheard 1973:7). Deviance is a ritual and an integral facet to rugby, which violates social normative behavior in regard to fighting, obscene language, songs, nakedness, drunkenness, and vandalism of property, which outside this distinctive environment is seldom tolerated.

Wheatley's (1994) research on women's rugby illustrates that women can achieve a position of power and control in sport by adopting the same ritualized behavior. She suggests that there is a significant lack of research into how sport produces gender relations and the subordination of females. Masculine hegemony and sport link maleness to highly valued skills and the positively sanctioned use of aggression, force, and violence, which infers females are inferior. Female intrusion into male subcultures such as rugby deconstructs the practices that are considered quintessentially male domains. Indeed, "as marginal and peripheral participants, males are usually surprised and shocked by the profanity, drinking habits, absence of modesty, and apparent approval of homosexuality" (Wheatley 1986; Loy et al. 1987:256).

On many occasions I observed women singing profane drinking songs traditionally associated with men's rugby. The women, who were leading the singing, stripped to the waist as it was their turn for the solo. As alcohol continued to flow, the players' behavior became less and less like that associated with traditional stereotypical images of femininity.

The drinking of alcohol and the associated social games, which have been part of rugby culture for over a century, are recently becoming marginalized in the world of professional rugby in Wales. As the game of men's rugby turned professional, the desire to maintain a lifestyle that was based on physical prowess, rather than more traditional employment, put stress on the "drinking" culture associated with the game. This shift in attitude is emphasized in the fact that it is no longer acceptable to be fit because of rugby—now players must be extremely fit to have a chance to play professionally (Howe 1999, 2001). However, heavy drinking and associated behavior is still very much apparent in elite women's rugby. While professional male players see the abuse of alcohol as detrimental to their training, elite women see it as one of the benefits of playing the game. "We train real hard. We play hard and we drink hard. The men have been doing it for years" (Notebook 4:16).

Another informant commented, "I am really dedicated to my training but as an amateur I realize that life is too short not to live it up! . . . If we were treated as we deserve [as professionals] I think this heavy drinking would be out the window"(Notebook 4:15). If the women who played the game were treated as their full-time professional male counterparts, then the distinctive female rugby *habitus* evident here would be transformed. In light of this, it is important to remember that the entry of women onto the pitch marks a very important change in society.

While Theberge (1995) notes how female athletes face a challenge in constructing a community because society considers their endeavors to be ambivalent in comparison to their male counterparts, I believe this drinking behavior associated with women's rugby has a part to play in the image problem that confronts the sport, simply because such behavior has traditionally been seen as masculine. More importantly, however, it is not the sort of behavior that is considered appropriate for contemporary elite athletes.

CONCLUSIONS

It has been seen throughout this chapter that the disciplined body, emblematic of a specific sporting *habitus,* is of fundamental importance when investigating women's involvement in contact sport. The stereotyping of the women who play rugby may be seen to be a result of homonegativism, which has a significant impact on the outward image of the game. "It is easy to see that the curiosity about the players' sexuality stems from assumptions about the essence of athletic prowess, independence, and ambition" (Crossett 1995:126).

Important progress has been made in realizing that these traits are not gender-specific. Sport should no longer be assumed to be a male domain; and the women, who played for the team that was central to this study, are determined to prove this to be the case.

The barriers of participation, which hinder the women of South Wales from playing the game of rugby, are not physical. In many cases, paradoxically, their lives would be better off if they were. How do you combat social prejudice? At least if barriers for participation are physical, then they can be confronted. My informants were eager to dispel myths about their sporting activities because their perception was that by doing so they can convince the general public that they should be taken seriously as sportswomen and not, as one informant suggested, as "a sexually deviant sideshow pretending they were men" (Notebook 4:6). It will take time to extinguish the traditional dichotomy of masculine/feminine as it relates to sport, but ever-increasing participation levels by women in confrontational contact sports such as rugby will go a long way toward achieving this end.

NOTES

1. At this stage in the development of women's rugby, the game is considered "open," which means that players are eligible to receive payment for playing. At the particular club discussed in this chapter all the players were amateurs to the extent that they were paid for jobs other than rugby and these jobs were key to their livelihood.

2. The sport Rugby Union does not have any particular association to train unions, but rather the term "union" is a reflection of the game's history. When the game was being developed, each rugby club in Wales had an equal say as to the direction the development of the sport would take. For more detail, see Howe 1999.

3. In a rather odd sense the game of rugby can be seen as disembodied. This is possible because the structure of the game of rugby allows for players whose bodies are of various shapes and sizes to play the game at the highest level.

4. This is a rugby position that is central to the physicality and full contact that are part of the game.

5. While it has not been explicitly stated, the changes to an open professional game have focused just on the men's game. For more detail, see Howe 1999, 2001.

6. In North America the league structure is different, with no demotion or promotion into elite professional team sports. What happens as a result is often to the detriment of community ties. The sporting franchise, if it is not making money, will move to a city where it feels it can, with no regard for its supporters.

REFERENCES

Andrews, D. L. 1991. "Welsh Indigenous! and British Imperial?—Welsh Rugby, Culture, and Society 1890–1914." *Journal of Sport History* 18:335–49.

———. 1993. "Desperately Seeking Michel: Foucault's Genealogy, the Body, and Critical Sport Sociology." *Sociology of Sport Journal* 10:148–67.

———, and J. W. Howell. 1993. "Transforming into a Tradition: Rugby and the Making of Imperial Wales, 1890–1914." In *Sport in Social Development: Traditions, Transitions, and Transformations,* ed. A. G. Ingham and J. W. Loy, 77–96. Leeds, England: Human Kinetics Press.

Blake, A. 1996. *The Body Language: The Meaning of Modern Sport.* London, England: Lawrence and Wishart.

Bourdieu, P. 1990. *In Other Words: Essays towards a Reflective Sociology.* London, England: Polity Press.

Birrel, S., and C. Cole. 1994. *Women, Sport, and Culture.* Leeds, England: Human Kinetics.

Blindle, E. M., D. E. Taub, and L. Han. 1994. "Sport as a Site for Women's Group and Societal Empowerment: Perspectives from the College Athlete." *Sociology of Sport Journal* 11:51–59.

Burton-Nelson, M. 1996. *The Stronger Women Get, the More Men Love Football: Sexism and the Culture of Sport.* London, England: Women's Press.

Clement, J. P. 1995. "Contributions of the Sociology of Pierre Bourdieu to the Sociology of Sport." *Sociology of Sport Journal* 12:147–57.

Cohen, G. L. 1993. *Women in Sport: Issues and Controversies.* London, England: Sage.

Cole, C. 1993. "Resisting the Canon: Feminist Cultural Studies, Sport, and Technologies of the Body." *Journal of Sport and Social Issues* 17(2):77–97.

Crossett, T. W. 1995. *Outsiders in the Clubhouse: The World of Women's Professional Golf.* Albany, NY: State University of New York Press.

Donnelly, P., and K. Young. 1988. "The Construction and Confirmation of Identity in Sport Subcultures." *Sociology of Sport Journal* 5:223–40.

Dunning, E. 1986. "Sport as a Male Preserve: Notes on the Social Sources of Masculine Identity and its Transformation." In *Quest for Excitement: Sport and Leisure in the Civilising Process,* ed. N. Elias and E. Dunning, 267–83. Oxford, England: Blackwell.

Dunning, E., and K. Sheard. 1973. "The Rugby Football Club as a Type of Male Preserve: Some Sociological Notes." *International Review of Sport Sociology* 8(3).

———. *Barbarians, Gentlemen and Players: a Sociological Study of the Development of Rugby Football.* Oxford, England: Martin Robinson.

Falk, P. 1994.*The Consuming Body.* London, England: Sage.

Fasting, K. 1997. "Homophobia and Sport: The Experience of Female Top Level Athletes." Paper presented at the Second Annual Congress of the European College of Sport Science, August 20–23, Copenhagen, Denmark.

———, and Scraton, S. 1997. "The Myth of Masculinisation of the Female Athlete: The Experiences of European Sporting Women." Paper presented at NASSS, November 5–8, Toronto, Canada.

Featherstone, M. 1982. "The Body and Consumer Culture." In *The Body: Social Process and Cultural Theory,* ed. M. Featherstone, M. Hepworth, and B. Turner, 170–96. London, England: Sage.

Foucault, M. 1979. *Discipline and Punish: The Birth of the Prison.* London, England: Hammonworth.

Gruneau, R. 1993. "The Critique of Sport in Modernity: Theorising Power, Culture, and the Politics of the Body." In *The Sport Process: A Comparative and Developmental Approach,* ed. E. Dunning, J. A. Maguire, and R. Pearton, 85–109. Leeds, England: Human Kinetics.

Halbert, C. 1997. "Tough Enough and Women Enough." *Journal of Sport and Social Issues* 21:7:36.

Hall, M. 1996. *Feminism and Sporting Bodies: Essays on Theory and Practice.* Leeds, England: Human Kinetics.

Hammersley, M., and P. Atkinson. 1995. *Ethnography: Principles in Practice,* 2nd ed. London, England: Routledge.

Hargreaves, Jennifer. 1994. *Sporting Females: Critical Issues in the History and Sociology of Women's Sport.* London, England: Routledge.

Hargreaves, John. 1986. *Sport, Power, and Culture: A Social and Historical Analysis of Popular Sports in Britain.* Oxford, England: Polity Press.

———. 1987."The Body, Sport, and Power Relation." In *Sports, Leisure, and Social Relations,* ed. J. Horne, D. Jary, and A. Tomlinson, 139–59. London, England: Routledge and Kegan Paul.

Howe, P. D. 1997."Commericialising the Body, Professionalising the Game: The Development of Sports Medicine at Pontypridd Rugby Football Club." Unpublished Ph.D. Thesis. University College, London, England.

———. 1999. "Professionalism, Commercialism, and the Rugby Club: From Embryo to Infant at Pontypridd RFC." In *The Rugby World: Race, Gender, Commerce, and Rugby Union,* ed. T. L. C. Chandler and J. Nauright, 165–81. London, England: Cass.

———. 2001. "An Ethnography of Pain and Injury in Professional Rugby Union: The Case of Pontypridd RFC." *International Review for Sport Sociology* 36(3):289–303.

Kew, F. 1997. *Sport, Social Problems and Issues.* Oxford, England: Butterworth-Heinemann.

Krane, V. 1996. "Lesbians in Sport: Toward Acknowledgment, Understanding and Theory." *Journal of Sport and Exercise Psychology* 18:237–46.

Leder, D. 1990. *The Absent Body.* London, England: University of Chicago Press.

Loy, J. W., B. D. McPherson, and J. E. Curtis. 1989. *The Social Significance of Sport: Introduction to the Sociology of Sport.* Leeds, England: Human Kinetics.

Mansfield, A., and B. McGinn. 1993."Pumping Irony: The Muscular and the Feminine." In *Body Matters,* ed. D. Morgan and S. Scott, 49–69. London, England: Falmer Press.

Marcus, G., and M. Fischer. 1986. *Anthropology as Cultural Critique: An Experimental Moment in the Human Sciences.* London, England: University of Chicago Press.

Messner, M. A., and D. F. Sabo. 1990. *Sport, Men, and the Gender Order: Critical Feminist Perspectives.* Leeds, England: Human Kinetics.

———. 1994. *Sex, Violence, and Power in Sports.* Freedom, CA: Crossing Press.

Potter, J. 1999. "Elegant Violence?" *Inside Rugby.* January.

Stebbins, R. A. 1992. *Amateurs, Professionals and Serious Leisure.* London, England: McGill-Queen's University Press.

Theberge, N. 1995. "Gender, Sport, and the Construction of a Community: A Case Study from Women's Ice Hockey." *Sociology of Sport Journal* 12:389–402.

Thompson, S. M. 1988. "Challenging the Hegemony: New Zealand Women's Opposition to Rugby and the Reproduction of Capitalist Patriarchy." *International Review of Sociology of Sport* 23:205–11.

Turner, B. S. 1991. "Recent Developments in the Theory of the Body." In *The Body: Social Process and Cultural Theory,* ed. M. Featherstone, M. Hepworth, and B. Turner, 1–35. London, England: Sage.

———. 1992. *Regulated Bodies: Essays in Medical Sociology.* London, England: Routledge.

———. 1996. *The Body and Society.* 2nd ed. London, England: Sage.

Wheatley, E. E. 1994. "Subcultural Subversions: Comparing Discourses on Sexuality in Men's and Women's Rugby Songs." In *Women, Sport and Culture,* ed. S. Birrel and C. Cole. Leeds, England: Human Kinetics.

White, P., and A. Vagi. "Rugby in the 19th-Century British Boarding-School System: A Feminist Psychoanalytic Perspective." In *Sport, Men, and the Gender Order: Critical Feminist Perspectives,* ed. M. A. Messner and D. F. Sabo, 67–78. Leeds, England: Human Kinetics.

Williams, G. 1991. *1905 and All That: Essays on Rugby Football and Welsh Society.* Llandysul, Wales: Gomer Press.

Pastimes and Presentimes: Theoretical Issues in Research on Women in Action

ANNE BOLIN AND JANE GRANSKOG

INTRODUCTION: FEMINISM, SPORT, AND BORDERS

Susan J. Birrell (1988:450–502) and M. Ann Hall (1990:223–39; 1993:48–68; 1996), two of the leaders in the history of the study of sport research, present a thorough socio-historical overview of developments in the field. Taken together, their research spans the entire history of sport study, emphasizing four major cultural-historical periods, each of which generated specific foci, questions, methods, and issues related to the cultural context of women's place in sports. The focus of Birrell's "Discourses on the Gender/Sport Relationship: From Women in Sport to the Study of Gender Relations" (1988) is: ". . . on the past twenty-five years, when physical educators formally began to question women's exclusion from sport. Scholarly attention to women in sport developed in three stages that roughly parallel the decades: a slow, tentative start from 1960 to 1971, a period of groping for identity and direction from 1971 to 1980, and the current trend, evident since 1980, toward greater theoretical sophistication and diversity."

Ann Hall's articles, "How Should We Theorize Gender in the Context of Sport?" (1990) and "Gender and Sport in the 1990s: Feminism, Culture, and Politics" (1993), along with her *Feminism and Sporting Bodies: Essays on Theory and Practice* (1996), extend the review of feminist socio-cultural studies of women and sport into the 1990s. The seminal research carried out by Birrell, Hall, and others, coupled with a review of the socio-historical foundations and current research on women in sport, are also brought together in the edited text by D. Margaret Costa and Sharon R Guthrie (1994), *Women and Sport: Interdisciplinary Perspectives*. The focus of this chapter is to use this body of research to present a summary review of the study of women in sport and to situate the role and contributions made by *Athletic Intruders* to further this process.

The paradigms shaping research on women in sports are embedded in the changing cultural matrix in which women approach sports and exercise through their bodies, through models of femininity, and in conjunction with gender inequity in a complex society. We will provide a brief overview of this history, relying on Birrell, Hall, and Costa and Guthrie but will also extend this review to include anthropology and women's physical activity. One cannot approach the history of the study of women in sports from a feminist perspective without addressing categories of research and definitions. These include defining feminism, or more accurately feminisms, and the domain of sport. As we shall discuss, the faces of feminism have changed historically along with the changing character of sport research, and these factors are both cause and consequence of the increasing participation of women in athletic activities. The historical-cultural context for this included broader legal, political, economic, and social change invigorated by the civil rights and feminist movements of the 1960s. However, for introductory purposes, what we are generally referring to by the term "feminism" is research in which women and gender have been made visible and centralized in inquiry into the organization of social life. This perspective relates to the feminist stance that sport is ". . . a site for relations of domination and subordination . . . and as a site of resistance and transformation" (Hall 1996:31). Feminism is *de facto* related to a generalized political and humanist position that will settle for nothing less than socio-cultural equality for women, with sports as a vehicle for achieving these ends. While there is a diversity of extant feminisms, the feminisms of this book are of the cultural constructionist brand that challenge an ideology of biological essentialism. Moreover, as Costa and Guthrie note (1994:231), it is precisely the development of such feminist theories that has helped to transform our understanding of women's sporting experience while providing an important venue for challenging sexist oppression and simultaneously promoting social change.

APPROACHES TO THE GENDERING OF SPORT
AND THE ANTHROPOLOGICAL VOICE

The symbolic realm, where meanings are enacted, reproduces and sustains the material sector that is dominated by a patriarchal political-economy assuring women's subordinate position. However, the personal and experiential, the symbolic and the interpretive are also powerful domains that may be used to challenge the established order as well as maintain it and can ultimately impact the material conditions whereby gender inequity is perpetuated through social systems and structures. Birrell and Hall locate women/sport relations as part of a dynamic, interactive domain whereby women's disparate sports participation raised research questions that subsequently fueled the development of women's sports as part of an academic discipline while it simultaneously affected policy that encouraged women in sports/athletics. A critical component of this approach is the emphasis given to socially constructed notions of gender, race, and class. Male domination, subordination, and resistance may be manifested in a multitude of forms depending on the specific socio-historical and cultural context; the experiences of women from different ethnic, racial, and class backgrounds will not necessarily be the same.

The dominant sociological approaches to the investigation of women in sport, however, have placed primary emphasis upon the institutional framework within which individuals operate rather than on the variable and more subjective qualitative experiences of women themselves. As both Hall and Birrell have noted, sociologists view gender and gender differences as a social construction. An emphasis in recent research, therefore, has been on providing formal structural analyses of quantitative data that focus on the ways in which sport reproduces the ideology of natural differences—male dominance, and correspondingly, the "natural" inferiority of females—and which thereby perpetuates the notion of sport as a male preserve. As Theberge (1994) and others (cf. Cole and Birrell 1994; Costa and Guthrie 1994) have so cogently argued, it is clear that despite the significant increase in female participation in sport since the passage of Title IX in 1972, sport remains a male preserve into which women are unwelcome intruders. The title of our text, *Athletic Intruders,* serves to highlight the pervasiveness of this fact. Theberge delineates three general ways in which male dominance in sport continues to be manifested: 1) much "higher rates of male participation in organized competitive sport" overall and their almost complete dominance of professional sport; 2) dominance in the "administration and organization of sport," including the relative loss of coaching and administrative positions for women in athletic departments after passage of Title IX and their almost total exclusion from leadership positions in professional sport; and 3) "cultural images of women's sporting activity" that often "denigrate and trivialize women's sporting experience" (1994:182) expressed by the media in both print and electronic form. According to Theberge, the relevance of this should not be underestimated because gender inequality in sport has significant ramifications for the continuance of gender inequality in society at large. Exploring the ways in which male dominance in sport is sustained, along with its consequences for women, is one of the central themes addressed in the ethnographic studies in this book.

Along with the emphasis on analysis of the institutional framework within which sporting behavior takes place, much of the sociological research carried out in the past (and to some extent today) also focused on the processes by which individuals are socialized into sport. A dominant approach historically has been to look at the process of socialization into sport as a mechanism by which individuals are molded to fit the dictates of societal mores. Sport participation is a means for learning the appropriate roles as they are defined by society. As Theberge (1984:30–31) notes, however, this approach places too much emphasis upon the capacity of the social system to determine the behavior of compliant, conforming individuals. The ability of individuals to define creatively their own roles in dynamic interaction with others and to construct actively a new gender role identity in the process has not been sufficiently examined. However, although much more attention needs to be given to the subjective experiences of individuals in the construction of their gender role identities as noted above, we must also place this process within the sociohistorical and cultural context of our patriarchal society. As discussed by both Hall and Birrell, herein lies the importance of the cultural studies approach to sport, which focuses on both the structural and ideological dimensions of differential power relations manifested in sport that, in turn, reflect the pattern of gender relations within the larger society. Given the differential rewards, status, and prestige that are allocated within our society based on gender, how do individuals incorporate these differences within their definition of self and how is this reflected in their attitudes toward and participation in sport? Giving voice to the differential perspectives of women as they negotiate this cultural landscape forms the basis of the contributions that the more qualitative approach of anthropological inquiry brings to the study of women in sport. In other words, while an anthropological inquiry takes into account the significance of the institutional framework within which socialization processes take place, it also takes the analysis one step further by placing primary attention upon the ways in which those cultural constraints are manifested in the qualitative experiences of the participants themselves.

HISTORY OF THE FIELD OF WOMEN, SPORTS, EXERCISE, PHYSICAL ACTIVITY, AND THE BODY

A brief overview of the history of the field over the past thirty years locates socio-cultural studies of sport as awaiting development. Although the very beginnings of socio-cultural concepts were applied to the women in sport relationship in the 1970s, these were conceived in primarily psychological, not cultural, terms. Primary attention focused on delimiting the factors surrounding elite athletic performance with an implicit emphasis on male personality traits and behavior in sport as being normative for all individuals. Examination of the participation of women in sport was thus viewed in terms of the extent to which individual women could incorporate the characteristics defined by male participants. Another key assumption underlying this research was the perception of gender as a dichotomous variable—that is, that the differences between males and females were far more significant than intragender differences. It was also assumed that the presumed gender differences in personality traits could be used to explain gendered behavioral differences. As Hall (1993:48–49) notes, this type of categoric research (focusing on differences between categories of individuals based on gender, race, etc., and on explanations based on biology and/or socialization) is still being carried out, primarily by psychologists and social psychologists. By focusing attention at the level of the individual, however, such approaches fail to take into account the critical determining role differential power relations play within society in molding and constraining women's various sporting experiences

The 1980s marked the development and expansion of multiple and varied investigations into the socio-cultural context in which sport takes place. Sociology of sport identified itself as a distinct field and entered an expansion phase, continuing distributive and atheoretical studies dominated by the empirical hypothesis model. The empirical hypothesis model views women's participation as a variable that has relationships to other variables impacting their general participation. As noted above, the focus is on delineating the institutional framework within which behavior takes place from the summary perspective of the investigator. Those aspects of culture that anthropologists routinely encounter as part of our methods and theory, however, were deemed unmeasurable and hence of little interest. A key feature of qualitative research lies in exploring the dynamic interaction between all players in the field, including the relationship between the researcher and researched. It has been this more reflexive approach that seeks to delineate the relation between researcher and those researched that has been ignored.

The 1980s also opened the venue to a feminist study of women in sports from a socio-cultural perspective. With feminism, as we noted in our introductory remarks, the field of women in sport was transformed to that of women and sports as relations. Feminist research in the study of women and sport relations and within the sociology of sport incorporated dynamic paradigms from cultural studies. Cultural studies brought to feminist sports studies high regard for symbolic and interpretive theories and perspectives into the meanings generated by individuals as they live their culture and practice athletics, exercise, and sports. This perspective is a vital one in which the importance of cultural context is emphasized. It moves beyond unidirectional Marxist models to a dynamic view of gender in which subversion and contestation confront co-optation in a variety of cultural channels. Culture is alive and imbued with agency and action. The ways in which both agency and action are made manifest on multiple levels, however, need to be explored. This, in turn, means that we necessarily need to take our theorizing about women/sports relations one step further and investigate ways in which our new understanding of the dynamics of gender can be used to institute change both on the level of the individual and in the larger socio-political realm. It also means that we need to examine the ongoing changing relationship between ourselves as researchers and the research we do. A feminist researcher's own work is personal as well as political. As Hall notes (1996:78–79), the 1990s continued the growth of theoretically thick and diverse feminist perspectives with praxis-oriented (or policy-oriented) research at the cutting edge of the process.

Athletic Intruders is in a feminist socio-cultural tradition. As we have discussed above, cultural studies has provided guiding principles for feminist studies of women/sports relations. We would like to add an absent voice in this discourse of theoretical developments in the field. The editors, as cultural anthropologists, feel the cultural studies critique has had an important and invigorating impact on our own work. We would, however, ask that those working in the cultural studies mode also investigate the theoretical models and methods of cultural anthropology. The core concept of anthropology has been culture since the inception of the field in the mid-nineteenth century, with the development of ethnography as the primary research method by the turn of the century. The holistic approach dominates ethnography, wherein sports, or rather, in more applicable terms for anthropology, play, is regarded as an important component of culture that must be viewed in relationship to other aspects of the culture under study.

Hall's review of "Gender and Sport in the 1990s" eloquently discussed several critical directions offered by cultural studies for furthering the socio-cultural study of the women/sports relations. These include "(a) the importance of historically grounded studies; (b) a sensitivity to difference, specifically race and ethnicity; (c) identifying what is useful to sport and leisure studies in current feminist theorizing and how to apply it; and (d) a reminder that theory, politics, and practice cannot be separated" (Hall 1993:48). The anthropological perspective mandates that ethnographic research be embedded in cultural context and situated historically. By definition, anthropologists are sensitive to cultural difference, and, in the new ethnography, a reflexive stance is taken that recognizes the importance of personally engaged research and the dialogical aspect of participant-observation. Key to this process is recognizing and acknowledging the complex and constantly changing relationship between researcher and researched as co-collaborators in the construction of knowledge and understanding of the subject matter that is being investigated and includes theoretical and methodological components as well as the interpretations reached. Indeed, it is this dynamic interplay between who we are as researcher and researched that lies at the basis of transforming definitions of the subject at hand. Advocacy and activism are, by definition, embedded in the ethnographic experience (Bolin 1992). A unique contribution that *Athletic Intruders* makes to the study of women/sport relations lies in its emphasis upon this feminist, experiential ethnography of sport.

However, the contributions of *Athletic Intruders* lie not only in its emphasis on feminist ethnography but also upon its broad definition of "sport" activity that slides into exercise and other manifestations of physicality. Our primary concern is to delineate the somatic experiences of women, the cultural constraints affecting their somatic experiences, and the corresponding impact of such somatic experiences upon their perception of self in relation to others as well as their perceived role in society. Loy (1968), among others, has defined sport in the sociological tradition as an institutionalized game whose outcome is determined by physical skill, strategy, and chance. This definition not only elevates the formal aspects of the organization of sport, it reinforces the traditional focus upon elite, male-dominated forms of sport that is predominant today. For anthropologists, Loy's definition of sports actually falls under the anthropological rubric of the study of games evident as early as 1879 in Sir Edward Tylor's (a parent of anthropology) article "The History of Games" (in Blanchard 1995:10). However, much of anthropological interest in sports and exercise is more broadly defined and incorporated in the subdiscipline of the anthropology of play. Although there has been a wide variety of approaches to, and discussion of, the importance of play behavior among mammals in general, Huizinga was one of the first to document its underlying importance for all aspects of human life. While Huizinga's (1950) definition of play with its ludic characteristics as a free, nonserious, often spontaneous form is an important work to anthropologists, it does not include the biological basis of play, nor is it an effective definition for cross-cultural comparison because of its limited view of play ". . . as a form of culture rather than having forms in culture " (Blanchard 1995:41). For anthropological purposes, play is defined by Blanchard as a "behavioral form having both biological and cultural dimensions that is difficult to define at the exclusion of all other behavior, yet is distinguishable by a variety of traits. It is pleasurable, voluntary, set apart by temporal parameters, marked by a make-believe quality, but made real by its unreality" (Blanchard 1995:42). It is also precisely these features that mark the intersection of play and sport with ritual. Sport, as well as play in its broader manifestations, can be viewed as ritual: an enactment of myths that serve to validate or justify cultural beliefs and practices; a symbolic validation of group norms by individuals whose very participation in ritual acts may constitute, under some circumstances, a transcendental sacred experience. As ritual, sports activities have magical properties and are endowed with sacred powers in specified settings with spatial and temporal dimensions (Kilmer 1977:44–47). Members of specific sport communities or subcultures thus share a common set of beliefs and practices (ritual activities) that serve to define their boundaries and provide meaning for their members. These activities are, in turn, embedded within a larger cultural framework, and the extent to which societal constraints on what is deemed acceptable behavior are reaffirmed or contested by members of the sport community, which also must be analyzed. When we conduct an analysis on the sport communities or specific subcultures, therefore, these parameters need to be taken into account. It is this non-Western derived expansive definition of sport as somatic experience informed by anthropological studies of games and play and their ritual dimensions that provides the foundation for our selection of the "sports" covered by our contributors.

This broadened definition of sporting activity and exercise also goes hand-in-hand with the emerging dialogue in feminist research concerning the poststructural conceptualization of the women/sports relationship manifested in the research centering on the meaning of body image. As Costa and Guthrie (1994:310) note, there has been considerable and longstanding interdisciplinary theoretical interest in the connections between the mind, body, and self represented in the notion of body image. They identify six major themes concerning body image that have emerged from this substantial body of research. Body images are: 1) "multidimensional and multifaceted"; 2) "personalized and subjective experiences"; 3) "dynamic and changeable"; 4) "socially constructed"; 5) "influence information processing and behavior"; and 6) "intimately related to self-concept" (p. 310–11). Despite the research findings that reflect these themes, however, most conclusions about the significance of body image, particularly as manifested by sport psychologists, rest upon perceptions of the individual body based on normative male standards; or, if they take a more feminist stance based on gendered differences, assume an essentialist position that defines women's experience universally in terms of their reproductive and sexual characteristics (p. 311–14).

Costa and Guthrie argue that what is needed is an approach that takes these themes into account, one that incorporates "diverse social constructions of the female body." The conceptualization of the body reflected in the seminal work by Michael Foucault and Maurice Merleau-Ponty provides the theoretical basis for just such an approach. Foucault's historical analysis of "bodily disciplinary practices" is genderized "to better understand the socialization of female bodies," which they refer to as the "feminine body beauty discourse" and argue that "it is this feminizing body beauty discourse that provides the social component of women's body image" (p. 314). Critical to the assessment of body image in terms of feminine body beauty discourse are the ideological constraints imposed on women wherein, they are presumed to define themselves uniformly in terms of the dominant male-defined reality. No attention is given to individual agency or the degree to which women may resist such dominant discourses to redefine the body and body image in their own terms.

Maurice Merleau-Ponty's concept of "bodies in motion" (that "the defining feature of human existence is the movement of human bodies in the world") goes a step beyond Foucault and is used to reframe the discourse on the body to emphasize the body as subject in dynamic interaction with the world (p. 316). Like Foucault, however, Merleau-Ponty's theoretical approach is one that presumes that the body as a dynamic, changing subject is, by definition, male. To fruitfully make use of his contributions, his work also requires genderizing to fit the particular constraints faced by women in their assessment of the body and body image. As Costa and Guthrie note, however, the critical component that Merleau-Ponty brings to the foreground is his view of individuals ("bodies") as "intersubjective fields" that interact with others in a shared historical context. Primary attention is thus given to the subjective, personal experiences that individuals express and share with likeminded individuals as they engage in physical bodily activities and the effect that these shared embodied experiences have on how they view and interact with the world around them (p. 316–17). This represents a shift in emphasis from the ideological, power-based, societal construction of reality for individuals stressed in the work of Foucault to a focus on the agency of women as they become more aware through bodily experiences to actively reconstruct and resist the dominant ideological images of women presented by society. Key to this process of consciousness-raising is the bonding and sharing of experiences that takes place between women engaging in similar activity coupled with a feminist awareness of the ideological constraints under which women operate. A feminist awareness of ideological constraints also means becoming aware of the different ways in which race, class, ethnic background, and age, along with gender, factor into the construction of reality as defined by the dominant forces in society. According to Costa and Guthrie, only when the transformational possibilities embodied in somatic experiences are combined with a feminist consciousness will we be truly able to effectively challenge male hegemony in sport and in the culture at large (p. 320).

OVERVIEW AND RATIONALE FOR *ATHLETIC INTRUDERS*

In accordance with both the work of Costa and Guthrie (1994), as well as Ann Hall's (1996) review of research trends in the study of women and sport/exercise, we have identified three prominent "ways of knowing" or themes embossed in the works of the contributors to this book. Ann Hall has discussed the value of 1) interpretive research with a nonpositivist thrust, and 2) situated analysis with regards to the "importance of history." Key to these two themes is the recognition of the multiplex ways in which women are constrained and contained by the patriarchal structures within which they operate. As cultural anthropologists and feminists, we offer a third theme that is emergent in sport studies, born of anthropology but adopted by other disciplines and is 3) interpretive analysis based on the qualitative methodology of ethnography, specifically postmodern/reflexive ethnography.

It is this third theme that most clearly articulates the transformational possibilities of somatic experience as discussed by Costa and Guthrie. It also represents an arena of nascent research in which relatively little has been published so far. It is for this reason that we have focused this collection on such ethnographic case studies. In addition, the ethnographic studies contained herein blend the interpretive and situated analysis of the first two themes. We feel that the most important contribution of our book lies in offering nine examples of ethnographic studies of women and sports from feminist perspectives in the anthropology and sociology of sport and exercise.

These nine case studies illustrate the critical importance of situating feminist research within the context of women's bodily experiences as manifested in personal, social, and cultural discourses; this is one of the strengths of this anthology to feminist research. Each of the ethnographic contributions addresses women's somatic experiences and their consequences for the transformation of women's lives as well as the cultural context within which they are located in triathlons, aerobics, basketball, bodybuilding, weightlifting, motorcycle riding, softball, casual exercise, and rugby. Moreover, the majority of the case studies, including those by Granskog, Markula, Bolin, Dworkin, Joans, and Wachs are presented by insiders who are active participants in the sport cultures that they have investigated.

Following the first chapter, "Reflexive Ethnography, Women, and Sporting Activities," the editors provide an overview of reflexive ethnography. Granskog then starts off the ethnographic case studies by analyzing the impact that participation in triathlons and duathlons have upon the identity construction of women at different stages of life and by focusing on the way in which this shared set of somatic experiences is used to redefine and reconstruct their relationships with others and the world at large. In chapter 3 Markula carries out a similar ethnographic analysis of women's participation in an aerobics lifestyle and investigates the ways in which such participation simultaneously supports and subverts the dominant ideological constructions of femininity.

In chapter 4 Stratta takes a slightly different tack and explores the extent to which African American female collegiate athletes are able to express their own African American heritage within the context of a predominantly white collegiate sport culture. Her analysis of the way in which such athletes negotiate the diverse domains that influence the expression of the African American female sport culture provides a unique insight into the influence of race and class upon the meaning of such somatic experiences for these athletes.

Bolin provides a lens in chapter 5 into the world of competitive women bodybuilders and offers insight into the multivocality and contradiction embodied in the ever-so-muscular body. Despite cultural frosting with symbols of traditional "femininity" that pervade the public realm of competitive bodybuilding, Bolin argues that women bodybuilders' muscular physiques are critical, rebellious, and reforming. In this chapter Bolin locates the backstage "beast" in women's competitive bodybuilding in spite of the "beauty" that is present during the frontstage in contests and bodybuilding magazines.

While Bolin's chapter focuses on women at the extreme, Dworkin (chapter 6) addresses the ways in which women use the local gym to maintain an image of toned fitness and reaffirms the more traditional notions of femininity. Her article also addresses the backlash that women who become "too muscular" may face from the dominant male-defined culture, illustrating once again the significance of the ideological constraints that keep women in a subordinate position.

Joans's article (chapter 7) explores an area of potentially strenuous physical activity that is not usually considered a traditional women's sport—the world of motorcycle riding. Traditionally, males have dominated motorcycle riding while females take on the role of "the bitch on the back" and appear submissive to the male in the driver's seat. Only recently have women begun to create a new place for themselves in the motorcycling world. Joans provides a unique insight into the way in which women are contesting and redefining their position in this dangerous and predominantly male world.

In chapter 8 Wachs, like Joans, investigates the way in which individuals "do gender." Instead of the risky, male-dominated world of motorcycling, Wachs looks at the dynamics of gender relations played out in a more traditionally defined sporting arena, the world of co-ed softball. Focusing on how gendered ideologies, bodies, and practices construct experience, she delineates the ways in which gendered ideologies and practices are at once reinforced and yet contested and renegotiated by the somatic capabilities of women expressed in their athletic performance.

As we noted earlier, an important focal point of the studies presented here is to document the somatic experiences of women as well as the variable impact of cultural constraints affecting such somatic experiences manifested in various forms of physicality and perceptions of the body. Davis's ethnohistorical analysis in chapter 9, of the emergence of exercise fads and attendant concerns with body image and weight loss among Newfoundland women provides a novel perspective on these issues. Her critical contribution lies not only in exploring the changing perceptions of body image expressed within a traditional homogeneous community but also in locating such changes within the larger historical context of the impact of modernization.

Like Davis, in chapter 10, Howe incorporates a historical perspective by examining the cultural evolution of Welsh women's rugby within the context of the prior development of men's rugby. In this regard it is fitting that this is the final article because he incorporates all three of the central themes addressed herein. Not only does he focus on interpretive research with a particular "sensitivity to difference" as manifested in his attention to dissecting the cultural barriers faced by women who choose to participate in a high-contact sport, he also situates his study within the broader socio-historical context of rugby players in general. Moreover, his detailed ethnographic analysis of dynamic dialectic between hegemonic Western defined ideals of masculinity and femininity and the lived reality of women rugby players as they negotiate the contradictory meanings such embodied experiences entail clearly illustrates the importance given to the interaction between actor, agency, and culture.

In sum, all of the case studies presented here reflect the wide scope with which we have sought to describe the complex issues that necessarily attend an investigation of the interrelationships manifested in the study of women's participation in sports, exercise, physical activity, and somatic culture in general. Yet as Whitson (1994) so cogently points out in his analysis of the discourses of masculinity and femininity represented in the gendering of sport, play, and physicality in its myriad forms, it is only with such a broad lens that we will be able to capture the significance of the embodiment of gender that informs our lives and sets the parameters for constructing the reality we currently experience. And, as we noted in the outset of this text, it is only by becoming aware of the constraints that circumscribe our expression of ourselves within the world that we have defined will we be able to transcend such perceptions to create a different reality that honors the contributions and roles of all members. It is with this objective in mind that we collaborated to create *Athletic Intruders: Ethnographic Research on Women, Culture and Exercise.*

REFERENCES

Birrell, Susan. 1988. "Discourses on the Gender/Sport Relationship: From Women in Sport to the Study of Gender Relations." *Exercise and Sport Science Reviews* 16:459–502.

Blanchard, Kendall. 1995. *The Anthropology of Sport.* South Hadley, MA: Bergin and Garvey.

Bolin, Anne. 1992. "Vandalized Vanity: Feminine Physiques Betrayed and Portrayed." In *Tattoo, Torture, Adornment and Disfigurement: The Denaturalization of the Body in Culture and Text,* ed. Francis Mascia-Lees and Patricia Sharpe, 79–99. Albany, NY: State University of New York Press.

Cole, Cheryl, and Nancy Birrell, eds. 1994. *Women, Sport, and Culture.* Champaign, IL: Human Kinetics.

Costa, D. Margaret, and Sharon Guthrie, eds. 1994. *Women and Sport, Interdisciplinary Perspectives.* Champaign, IL: Human Kinetics.

Hall, Ann. 1990. "How Should We Theorize Gender in the Context of Sport?" In *Sport, Men, and the Gender Order: Critical Feminist Perspectives,* ed. Michael Messner and Donald Sabo. Champaign, IL: Human Kinetics.

———. 1993. "Gender and Sport in the 1990s: Feminism, Culture and Politics." *Social Science Review* 2(1):48–68.

———. 1996. *Feminism and Sporting Bodies: Essays on Theory and Practice.* Champaign, IL: Human Kinetics.

Huizinga, Johan. 1950. *Homo Ludens: A Study of Play Elements in Culture.* Boston MA: Beacon Press.

Kilmer, Scott. 1977. "Sport as Ritual: A Theoretical Approach." In *The Study of Play: Problems and Prospects,* 44–49. David Lancy and Alan Tindall eds. West Point, NY: Leisure Press.

Loy, John W. 1968. "The Nature of Sport: A Definitional Effort." *Quest* 10:1–5.

Therberge, Nancy. 1984. "On the Need for a More Adequate Theory of Sport Participation." *Sociology of Sport Journal* 1:26–35.

———. 1994. "Toward a Feminist Alternative to Sport as a Male Preserve." In *Women, Sport, and Culture,* ed. Cole and Birrell. Champaign, IL: Human Kinetics.

Whitson, David. 1994. "The Embodiment of Gender: Discipline, Domination, and Empowerment." In *Women, Sport, and Culture,* ed. Cole and Birrell. Champaign, IL: Human Kinetics.

CONTRIBUTORS

Anne Bolin received her Ph.D. in anthropology from the University of Colorado. She is a Professor of Anthropology in the Department of Sociology and Anthropology at Elon University, Elon, North Carolina. She has presented and published extensively in the research areas of sport ethnography and bodybuilding, gender and the body, human sexuality, and gender variance. Her publications include numerous articles and several books. Her book *In Search of Eve: Transsexual Rites of Passage* received a CHOICE Magazine Award for Outstanding Academic Book for 1988–89. She has co-authored an anthropology of human sexuality textbook with Patricia Whelehan, *Perspectives on Human Sexuality*. Her current ethnographic research is with competitive women bodybuilders for a book entitled *Elegant Ironworkers: Beauties and Beasts in Bodybuilding*. She is an active competitor in amateur women's bodybuilding, having competed at the state and national levels.

Dona Davis received her Ph.D. in anthropology from the University of North Carolina at Chapel Hill in 1980. She is currently Professor of Anthropology at the University of South Dakota and Visiting Professor of Social Anthropology at the University of Tromso in Tromso, Norway. Her areas of research and publication include North Atlantic Maritime cultures, Human Sexuality, Gender, Anthropology of the Body, and Women's Health.

Shari L. Dworkin received her Ph.D. in sociology from the University of Southern California (USC) in 2000 and is a Visiting Assistant Professor at Pitzer College in Claremont, California. Her substantive areas of research include gender, bodies/sport, media, and sexuality. Some of her published works include: "'Holding Back:' Negotiating a Glass Ceiling on Women's Muscular Strength" (2001, *Sociological Perspectives*); "Just Do What? Sport Bodies, Gender" (1999, in Judith Lorber, Beth Hess, and Myra Marx Ferree, eds., *Revisinging Gender*); "Discipling the Body: HIV Positive Male Athletes, Media Surveillance and the Policing of Sexuality" (1998, *Sociology of Sport Journal,* coauthored with Faye Linda Wachs). She is currently coauthor on a book with Leslie Heywood, entitled *Built to Win: The Rise of the Female Athele as Cultural Icon.* She teaches courses in the sociology of gender, qualitative methods, social inequality, family, sport and the body, and sexuality and culture.

Jane Granskog received her Ph.D. in anthropology from the University of Texas at Austin. She is a Professor of Anthropology in the Department of Sociology/Anthropology at California State University, Bakersfield. She has been conducting ethnographic research on women in sport for the past sixteen years and has presented and published a number of articles on sport ethnography and the participatory sport of triathlons. Some of her more recent publications in this area include: "Women in Triathlons," in the *International Encyclopedia of Women & Sport* (2000); "In Search of the Ultimate—Ritual Aspects of the Hawaiian Ironman Triathlon," in the *Journal of Ritual Studies* (1993); and "Tri-ing Together: An Exploratory Analysis of the Social Networks of Female and Male Triathletes," in *Play and Culture* (1992). Her research in this area is from an insider's perspective as an elite Master's (over age 40) triathlete. She has completed over 170 triathlons and duathlons (run/bike events) since 1985 and twelve ultradistance ("Ironman") triathlons, including the Hawaiian Ironman World Championship Triathlon in 1987, 1988, 1989, 1990, 1991, and 1995. She is currently working on an ethnography of the triathlon sport culture entitled *The Tri-ing Life: Ethnography of a Triathlon Community.* In addition to her ongoing research on participatory sports in the United States, she has conducted extended ethnographic fieldwork among the Tzeltal Mayan and Zapotec Indians in Mexico and peasants in Honduras. She has recently also expanded her research interests in sport as ritual into other types of ritual activity, specifically shamanic practices as expressed as part of "New Age" activities and an aspect of alternative healing strategies manifested in the West as well as in more traditional non-Western contexts.

P. David Howe is Lecturer in the Anthropology of Sport in the School of Sport and Leisure at the University of Gloucestershire. Trained as a medical anthropologist, he is currently completing a book entitled "Pain, Injury, and the Culture of Risk." His research interests also include the impact of sport on marginalized communities, particularly those involving athletes with impairment.

Barbara Joans holds a Ph.D. from CUNY Graduate School and is an American Anthropologist specializing in urban, legal, and subcultural anthropology. She is Director of the Merritt Museum of Anthropology and Chair of the Anthropology Department at Merritt College. She is author of *Bike Lust: Harleys, Women, and American Society* (2001, University of Wisconsin Press). She rides a Harley Low Rider.

Pirkko Markula is an ethnographer and sport sociologist. She is a native of Finland and has lived and worked in the United States, New Zealand, and the United Kingdom. She received her Ph.D. at the University of Illinois at Urbana-Champaign, where she studied women's experiences in aerobics. Her current research interests include how fitness practices and the media shape our understanding of physically active bodies, how mindful fitness forms such as yoga, Pilates training, and Tai Chi have become popular, and how new ethnographic writing practices such as autoethnography have made research a more self-reflexive process. In addition, she is a contemporary dancer and choreographer.

Terese M. Peretto Stratta is currently an Assistant Professor of Sport Management at the University of Tennessee in Knoxville, where she teaches undergraduate and graduate sport management courses. She also serves as a marketing research consultant with the Tournament Sponsors Association of the Ladies Professional Golf Association and works with businesses throughout the metro Atlanta area. Prior to working at UT, Dr. Stratta served as Assistant Professor of Sports Administration at Georgia State University in Atlanta and Coordinator of the Sport Management program at Anderson College in Anderson, South Carolina. During her stint in South Carolina, she was also president and owner of Education Consulting Services. Dr. Stratta was a scholarship intercollegiate athlete, taught in elementary through college-level Physical Education programs, coached a variety of sports at all educational levels, and administered sport programs at the college level. She has delivered numerous presentations during the past decade at national conferences and published manuscripts on African American women in sport and on sport from socio-cultural and sport management perspectives.

Faye Linda Wachs is currently an Assistant Professor of Sociology in the Behavioral Sciences Department at California Polytechnic University, Pomona. A Los Angeles native, she received her Ph.D. and a Graduate Certificate in Gender Studies from the University of Southern California in 1999. Current research involves gender, bodies, consumption, and the health and fitness movement. An avid runner, she is also investigating performance gaps by gender among recreational runners.

INDEX

265

List of Books in Series

Alan M. Klein, *Little Big Men: Bodybuilding Subculture and Gender Construction.*

Todd W. Crosset, *Outsiders in the Clubhouse: The World of Women's Professional Golf.* Winner North American Society for the Sociology of Sport (NASSS) Book Award.

Wanda Ellen Wakefield, *Playing to Win: Sports and the American Military, 1898–1945.*

Laurel R. Davis, *The Swimsuit Issue and Sport: Hegemonic Masculinity in Sports Illustrated.*

Jim McKay, *Managing Gender: Affirmative Action and Organizational Power in Australian, Canadian, and New Zealand Sport.*

Juan-Miguel Fernandez-Balboa, (ed.), *Critical Postmodernism in Human Movement, Physical Education, and Sport.*

Genevieve Rail, (ed.), *Sport and Postmodern Times.*

Shona M. Tompson, *Mother's Taxi: Sport and Women's Labor.*

Nancy Theberge, *Higher Goals: Women's Ice Hockey and the Politics of Gender.* Winner, North American Society for the Sociology of Sport (NASSS) Book Award.

Helen Jefferson Lenskyj, *Inside the Olympic Industry: Power, Politics, and Activism.*

C. Richard King and Charles Fruehling Springwood, *Beyond the Cheers: Race as Spectacle in College Sport.*

David Andrews (ed.), *Michael Jordan, Inc: Corporate Sport, Media Culture, and Late Modern America.*

Margaret Gatz, Michael A. Messner, and Sandra J. Ball-Rokeach (eds.), *Paradoxes of Youth and Sport.*

Helen Jefferson Lenskyj, *The Best Olympics Ever? Social Impacts of Sydney 2000.*

Ralph C. Wilcox, David L. Andrews, Robert Pitter, and Richard L. Irwin (eds.), *Sporting Dystopias: The Making and Meaning of Urban Sport Cultures.*

Robert E. Rinehart and Synthia Sydnor (eds.), *To the Extreme: Alternative Sports, Inside and Out.*